D1617581

Politics, Philosophy, Terror

Politics, Philosophy, Terror

ESSAYS ON THE THOUGHT OF

HANNAH ARENDT

Dana R. Villa

PRINCETON UNIVERSITY PRESS

PRINCETON, NEW JERSEY

Copyright © 1999 by Princeton University Press
Published by Princeton University Press, 41 William Street,
Princeton, New Jersey 08540
In the United Kingdom: Princeton University Press,
Chichester, West Sussex
All Rights Reserved

Library of Congress Cataloging-in-Publication Data
Villa, Dana Richard.
Politics, philosophy, terror : essays on the
thought of Hannah Arendt / by Dana R. Villa.
p.   cm.
Includes bibliographical references.
ISBN 0-691-00934-1 (cloth : alk. paper). —
ISBN 0-691-00935-X (pbk. : alk. paper)
1. Arendt, Hannah—Contributions in political sicence.   I. Title
JC251.A74V57   1999
320.5′092—dc21   99-21302

This book has been composed in Janson Text

The paper used in this publication meets the minimum requirements
of ANSI/NISO Z39.48-1992 (R1997) (*Permanence of Paper*)

http://pup.princeton.edu

Printed in the United States of America

1   2   3   4   5   6   7   8   9   10

1   2   3   4   5   6   7   8   9   10
(pbk.)

TO SVETLANA

Contents

Acknowledgments

I AM QUITE grateful to two institutions and the people who make them so friendly to scholars. First, I wrote many of these essays at the Center for European Studies at Harvard University, which has been my summer "residence" for a number of years. I would like to thank Charles Maier, Abby Collins, Sandy Selesky, and Anna Popiel for enabling me to spend much fruitful time there. I would also like to thank two friends and colleagues at the Center, Seyla Benhabib and Danny Goldhagen, whose good humor and patience with my critical impulse is much appreciated.

The other institution is the Center for Human Values at Princeton University, where I wrote several chapters and put this book together while a Laurance S. Rockefeller Fellow in 1997–1998. I particularly want to thank George Kateb and Amy Gutmann, whose guidance of the Center made it the perfect place for collegial but eminently serious intellectual exchange. I want to single out two of my fellow Fellows, John Kleinig and Bernard Reginster, from whom I learned much. The presence of Stephen Holmes, Jeremy Waldron, Josh Ober, Alexander Nehamas, John Cooper, and Harry Frankfurt at assorted Center events and political-philosophy colloquia was a delightful bonus.

Several of the chapters in this book began life as conference presentations. Seyla Benhabib organized a major Arendt conference at Harvard in 1996, from which I received much feedback and stimulation. A spring 1997 conference in Potsdam, organized by Gary Smith around Arendt's *Eichmann in Jerusalem*, put me in touch with the work of many German and Israeli scholars, as did an international gathering on Arendt in Jerusalem organized by Steven Aschheim later that year. Finally, a conference on totalitarianism at Yale organized by Michael Halberstam and Michael Holquist in early 1996 helped me gain some comparative perspective on the Nazi and Soviet cases. My thanks to the organizers and participants at all these events.

I would also like to thank Fred Dolan, Peter Digeser, Susan Shell, Jim Schmidt, Mark Lilla, Omer Bartov, Andy Rabinbach, Peter Euben, Tracy Strong, and Josh Dienstag for helpful critical

ix

comment and insight, and Tycho Manson, Cathy Ciepiela, Tom Levin, Elizabeth Cousens, and Giovanna Borradori for equally helpful distraction. I am grateful to Ann Wald at Princeton University Press for her sustained interest in my work. I am also indebted to Michael Walzer, Joan Scott, Clifford Geertz, and the School of Social Science at the Institute for Advanced Study for providing the ideal place to bid this project adieu and embark on another.

Finally, I would like to thank my parents, Virginia Barrett Villa and Alfred Villa, once again. The book is dedicated to Svetlana Boym, who knows why.

Chapter 7 initially appeared in *Political Theory*, vol. 26, no. 2 (1998): 147–72, copyright © Sage Publications, reprinted by permission, Sage Publications.

Politics, Philosophy, Terror

Introduction

IN A 1964 interview with the German journalist Gunter Gaus, Hannah Arendt refused the honorific title of "philosopher." "I do not belong to the circle of philosophers," she stated, adding "My profession, if one can even speak of it at all, is political theory. I neither feel like a philosopher, nor do I believe I have been accepted in the circle of philosophers. . . ."

Thirty-five years later, it is safe to say that this state of affairs has been transformed. Arendt is now accepted as a full-fledged canonical figure in political philosophy (although her reception by Anglo-American analytic philosophers remains cool, on the whole). This marks a significant, and not easily explained, change in her status. From the mid-1950s until her death in 1975, Arendt was best known as a public intellectual, one whose work reached an astonishingly wide audience despite its demanding character. Her major works— *The Origins of Totalitarianism, The Human Condition, On Revolution,* and the posthumously published two-volume *The Life of the Mind*— are all difficult texts, dense with arguments, allusions, and complicated narratives. Yet despite their difficulty they found a wide readership both within and outside the academy, something almost unthinkable today (it boggles the mind to recall that the first volume of *The Life of the Mind* initially appeared in *The New Yorker*).

Arendt's audience is perhaps numerically smaller today than when she was alive, but it is also more serious and more genuinely international in character. Indeed, one could argue that her influence is greater now than it has ever been, as increasing numbers of scholars and students the world over mine her books for insight into the nature of democratic politics and the dynamics of political evil. The truly remarkable thing about the current Hannah Arendt renaissance is that it knows neither partisan nor disciplinary boundaries, despite the fact that academic discussion has become both more narrowly specialized (and ill-temperedly political) in recent years. In part this has to do with the fact that her work always defied categorization, at least in terms of the usual Left/Right or liberal/conservative labels. But it also has to do with the end of the Cold War, with the fading of clear ideological battle lines and the generalized uncertainty this has produced. The greatest evil has, for a time, been removed from the world stage, leaving us to face the elementary problems of politics without the comforting orientation provided by a bipolar world. It is in this context, where the most seemingly solid of political verities have dissolved, that so many have turned to Arendt's work, making her (in Seyla Benhabib's felicitous phrase) "the thinker of the post-totalitarian moment."

The resulting torrent of books and articles on Arendt is, therefore, not entirely surprising. However, readers encountering this literature for the first time are bound to be a bit confused, for in it they will find a dizzying proliferation of Arendts, some familiar (the civic republican Arendt), some novel (the Habermasian Arendt; the postmodern Arendt), some revisionist (the feminist Arendt), and some more than a little ironic (the empathic Arendt). Of course, the writings of any great thinker generate numerous and conflicting interpretations—one need only think of the many versions of Rousseau that have appeared over the last fifty years, from proto-totalitarian to romantic individualist to participatory democrat. But there is clearly something specific to Arendt's writing which invites creative interpretation and (just as often) misinterpretation. The fact that the short essays which make up the sections of her books are often aphoristic in their density has the effect of turning them into a kind of Rorschach test for her interpreters. Unsurprisingly, many tend to find reflections of their own most cherished ideas, commitments, or prejudices in her work—a form of narcissism less harmless than it first appears. A version of this dynamic can also be found in Arendt's harsher critics. Armed with prejudgments about the significance of her work, they approach her texts unburdened of the usual constraints of careful reading. Thus it is all too often the case, for readers both well and ill disposed, that what Arendt actually said takes a distinctly subordinate place to what it is *assumed* she said or must have meant. Although her mode of expression sometimes encourages this tendency to read one's self or prejudices into her work, the fact remains that we, Arendt's readers, are solely responsible for this interpretive violence, and (ultimately) the intellectual laziness it reflects.

The essays collected in this volume make no pretense to correcting this state of affairs by uncovering the "real" Arendt or by providing a comprehensive account of her work.[1] They address subjects—such as the banality of evil, the nature of totalitarian terror, and the Socratic dimension of Arendt's thought—which fell beyond the scope of my study of the relation of Arendt's political theory to Martin Heidegger's philosophical thought.[2] While diverse in topic, the essays are animated by the desire to preserve the uniqueness of Arendt's insights from the distortion introduced by comforting (but false) analogies. Of course, analogies are often helpful in providing a grasp of a complex thinker's thought. When the thinker is as idiosyncratic as Arendt, recourse to them is all but unavoidable. Nevertheless, any approach that tends to domesticate her thought threatens to destroy what is essential to it, what makes it unique in the first place.

In this regard, I find it striking that some of Arendt's most famous and widely discussed ideas—the banality of evil is the obvious example—are among the least well understood by her readers and critics. My effort in these essays is to highlight those places where readers and critics of Arendt have been too quick in their praise or condemnation, too confident in their grasp of what she is up to. Critical judgment is, of course, the prerogative of all readers, and the controversial nature of many of Arendt's ideas certainly invites it. But we would do well to remember what she herself pointed out with respect to the nature of political judgment, namely, that judgment without understanding does not really qualify as judgment at all.

Chapter 1, "Terror and Radical Evil," looks at what Arendt meant when she described terror as the "essence" of totalitarian regimes. As with many of her leading ideas, we *think* we know what she means by this. But Arendt confounds our expectations. She is *not* saying that Hitler or Stalin gave terror a special place in his arsenal of total domination, that it was his preferred (and characteristic) means. In fact, totalitarian terror differed from the more familiar cases of revolutionary or tyrannical terror in that it was not really a means at all, but rather a process without end. Its "goal," according to Arendt, was to reveal the sheer superfluousness of human beings, to show that there are no built-in limits to power's ability to dehumanize individuals or to render them mere specimens of the human species. Once *this* is demonstrated, the all-determining law of Nature or History posited by totalitarian ideology is no longer a ludicrous fiction. To a horrifying degree, such "laws" were confirmed by the concentration and extermination camps, whose job it was to speed up the process of the supposedly fated course of development of the human species. "Dying" classes, doomed by History, received a push, just as "inferior" races were helped on their way to an extinction supposedly predestined by natural selection. It was this drive to reveal the superfluousness of human beings, to strip *all* human individuals of intrinsic dignity by demanding absolute submission to the determining power of the law of Nature or History, which led Arendt to label totalitarian evil *radical* evil. With this term, she was not trying to draw attention to the sheer scale of political evil in the twentieth century (something obvious to all). Rather, she meant to underline the implicit *telos* of totalitarianism, which was to change human nature.

Chapter 2, "Conscience, the Banality of Evil, and the Idea of a Representative Perpetrator," turns from the idea of radical evil to Arendt's more widely known (and controversial) notion of the banality of evil. This concept occurred to her in the course of covering the trial of Adolf Eichmann in Jerusalem for *The New Yorker*. Arendt was struck by the sheer thoughtlessness of the "monster" Eichmann, his depthless "normality." With the "banality of evil" she attempted to convey not only her impression of Eichmann's unmonstrous personality, but the far more discomforting idea that the performance of great political evil does not necessarily depend on the presence of any wicked motive or ideological fervor. This point was lost in the controversy that followed the publication of *Eichmann in Jerusalem*. Many thought (and evidently still think) that Arendt lessened Eichmann's guilt by turning him into a mere "cog" of the Nazi extermination machine (a notion she explicitly and repeatedly refutes in her trial report). Such misunderstandings have been given new life thanks to the debate spurred by Daniel Goldhagen's book, *Hitler's Willing Executioners* (which, as its title indicates, emphasizes the antisemitic fervor of "ordinary Germans" during the Nazi period). I show, *contra* Goldhagen and numerous others, that Arendt was not trying to provide a picture of the "representative perpetrator" (if there is such a thing), and that those who mistake her specific judgment of Eichmann for a thesis about the character of the Nazi extermination of the Jews have grotesquely misread her book.

Chapter 3, "The Anxiety of Influence: On Arendt's Relationship to Heidegger," looks at a more recent controversy that has embroiled Arendt. The revelation of Arendt's youthful romance with Heidegger in Elzbieta Ettinger's book *Hannah Arendt / Martin Heidegger* led many to condemn her for allegedly "whitewashing" Heidegger's unsavory political past, something she was said to have done out of unswerving devotion to her former teacher (their affair took place during the twenties, long before Heidegger, as rector of Freiburg University, affiliated himself with the Nazi regime in 1933). The central question raised by this controversy was whether Arendt could see Heidegger clearly, for what he was (namely, a great philosopher but a political idiot) or whether she allowed herself to be duped by "the Magician from Messkirch" (as Richard Wolin dubbed Heidegger in a review of Ettinger's book). I argue, against Ettinger and Wolin, that Arendt was quite capable of seeing Heidegger clearly, and that her work in political theory constitutes the greatest possible refutation of the political ideas Heidegger enslaved himself to during the period 1933 to 1945.

Chapter 4, "Thinking and Judging," turns to equally tangled but decidedly less controversial matters. In it, I grapple with the relation between thinking and acting in Arendt's political theory, and with her conception of political judgement. Is the latter, sketched but never fully rendered by Arendt, the "bridge" between the activities of thought and political action, as some of her most sensitive commentators have suggested? I argue that it is not. In her ruminations on judgment, Arendt was not looking for a way of overcoming the distinction between thought and action, nor was she searching for the elusive synthesis of theory and practice. I find Arendt's reasons for holding the two activities distinct compelling and largely persuasive, even though they go against the contemporary tendency (in academia, at least) to consider theory a kind of practice. I also address what, precisely, Arendt meant by her idea of a specifically political or "representative" mode of thinking, an idea that has proved enormously suggestive yet which remains surprisingly elusive.

Chapter 5, "Democratizing the Agon: Nietzsche, Arendt, and the Agonistic Tendency in Recent Political Theory," examines the use made of Arendt by advocates of "agonistic democracy." There is little doubt that Arendt emphasized the agonistic dimension of politics (it is central to her picture of her beloved Greeks), and that she viewed this dimension in a largely positive light—a fact which more consensus-oriented theorists find hard to swallow. Contemporary agonists—roughly, those political theorists who emphasize the contestability of key political terms and the incessant, boundless character of contemporary struggles for justice and recognition—applaud her energetic image of politics while decrying its narrowly "elitist" character. I argue that this criticism reflects a Nietzschean, vitalist

7

heritage, one that turns a deaf ear to the most thought-provoking aspect of Arendt's agonism, namely, her insistence upon the impersonal quality of a genuinely agonistic politics. This insistence on impersonality is closely tied to Arendt's emphasis on public-spiritedness as the *sine qua non* of a healthy politics. The latter is viewed with a certain embarrassment by contemporary agonists, who tend to dismiss it as an anachronism born of the civic republican tradition. The idea of a public-spirited, impersonal agonistic politics is one which supposedly cannot survive the Foucault-inspired critique of "exclusionary" republicanism nor the feminist critique of a strong public/ private distinction. I suggest that we approach such critical claims with a certain amount of skepticism, lest we miss one of Arendt's most important lessons about the nature of political action and the public realm.

Chapter 6, "Theatricality and the Public Realm," expands on the Arendtian theme of impersonality by looking at her use of theatrical metaphors to describe the public realm (a "stage" for words and deeds). Some commentators have argued that Arendt's preference for such metaphors reflects her Grecophilia and the desire for a centered, "ocular" public space much like the Athenian Assembly. They go on to point out that this model of the public realm has little purchase on the decentered, discursive public sphere of modern representative democracies. While this criticism has a certain general validity, it neglects the deeper lesson of Arendt's appeal to theatricality. Her primary point is that a vibrant sense of the public tends to be found only in those cultures where a form of social theatricality—and the distinction between a public and a private self—is clearly present, almost second nature. Where such theatricality is absent, and where the distinction between a public and private self is seen as mere hypocrisy or deception, there we are bound to encounter some version of the politics of authenticity. Such a politics focuses on the personality of the political actor, rather than on the content of his words and deeds. The resulting personalization of the political characterizes much of contemporary American politics, and is at the root of the shallow cynicism many citizens retreat to when they discover that their politicians have failed to live up to the personality they projected in public.

Chapter 7, "The Philosopher vs. the Citizen: Arendt, Strauss, and Socrates," looks at the very different appropriations of Plato's Socrates performed by Arendt and by another celebrated German-

Jewish emigré to America, the conservative political philosopher Leo Strauss. Arendt viewed Socratic dialogue as an attempt to contain the intensely competitive spirit of the Athenians, a spirit which (as any reader of Thucydides knows) threatened to spin out of control and tear the *polis* apart. According to Arendt, Socrates was less a philosopher seeking a unitary truth beyond the realm of opinion than a "citizen among citizens" devoted to helping his fellow citizens find the truth inherent in their particular *doxa*. In marked contrast, Strauss presented Socrates as standing for a way of life—the philosophical—which is directly opposed to the energies and claims of political life in general and Athenian democracy in particular. My essay shows how, their intense partisanship for the political life and the philosophical life notwithstanding, Arendt and Strauss point toward the episodic overcoming of the dichotomy between the philosopher and the citizen.

Chapter 8, "Totalitarianism, Modernity, and the Tradition," examines the vexed question of what relationship, if any, Arendt saw between totalitarianism and the "great tradition" of Western political thought. In the 1940s and early 1950s, Arendt was quite dismissive of those who wanted to find some kind of affiliation between this tradition and what she described as the "gutter-born" ideology of Nazism. She was forced to modify her position, however, when she considered in greater depth the role Marxism—a clear product of the tradition—played in making Soviet totalitarianism possible. The result of this reconsideration (most fully worked out in *The Human Condition*) was a qualified indictment of the Western tradition—not for in any way "causing" the totalitarian disaster, but for fostering a conception of political community which all but effaced the basic phenomenon of human plurality. When Arendt connected this devaluation of human plurality with what she considered to be the "world-destroying" forces of the modern age, she came to the conclusion that totalitarianism was something less than the total aberration it initially appeared to be.

Chapter 9, "Arendt and Socrates," returns to the tense relation between philosophy and politics in Arendt's thought, offering a decidedly different perspective from Chapter 7. Here I question whether Arendt's version of Socrates is genuinely Socratic—that is to say, philosophical—at all. My conclusion is that, for Arendt, the philosophical life (and the alienation it presumes) has at best an instrumental importance, one which does not fundamentally trans-

9

form the experience of citizenship, but which merely facilitates it. This conclusion represents my more considered opinion of Arendt's stance in the war between philosophy and politics, as well as her refusal to acknowledge the absolute importance of the alienated mode of citizenship introduced by Socrates. This refusal is all the more painful given that it comes from one of the greatest and most courageous practitioners of *Selbstdenken*—independent thinking for oneself—of this or any other age.

CHAPTER ONE

Terror and Radical Evil

> If it is true that the concentration camps are the
> most consequential institution of totalitarian rule,
> "dwelling on horrors" would seem to be
> indispensable for the understanding of
> totalitarianism. But recollection can no more do
> this than can the uncommunicative eyewitness
> report. In both these genres there is an inherent
> tendency to run away from the experience. . . .
> Only the fearful imagination of those who have
> been aroused by such reports but have not actually
> been smitten in their own flesh . . . can afford to
> keep thinking about horrors.
> (*Hannah Arendt*, The Origins of Totalitarianism)
>
> Today, at this very moment as I sit writing at a
> table, I myself am not convinced that these things
> really happened.
> (*Primo Levi*, Survival in Auschwitz)

INTRODUCTION

As the twentieth century draws to a close, it is difficult to avoid being
overwhelmed by moral nausea. There are the well-known numbers:
ten million dead in the First World War, a war fought over virtually
nothing; roughly forty million in the Second World War, including
the six million Jews killed in the Nazi concentration and extermination camps; twenty million or more in the Soviet gulag; thirty million dead as the result of the debacle of Mao's "Great Leap
Forward"; plus the millions from a host of less spectacular but no less
horrific massacres. Any conception of human dignity that hinges
upon the presumption of the moral progress of the species has been
shattered by these events. Montaigne, the skeptical observer of humanity's persistent moral idiocy, not Kant, has been proven right.
No hidden hand of providence or nature is guiding us forward.

11

The residual hope that we have, finally, put all the nightmares behind us is baseless, as the ethnic, religious, and ideological slaughters of Bosnia, Rwanda, Cambodia, and Algeria make plain.[1] Add to this the social disruptions born of integrating the former "Second World" into a global market economy, plus a burgeoning world population which is estimated to reach ten billion by early in the next century, and one would have to be blithe indeed to maintain that the morality of rights and the concept of human dignity are not under stress. In a world in which millions can be periodically slaughtered for no reason, and in which untold millions will have to suffer the crushing fate of being no use to the world economy, the dignity of the individual often seems a luxury enjoyed only by the lucky or by those who can afford it.

Of course, it would be wrong to underestimate the world-historical significance of the revolutions that swept Eastern Europe in 1989. But the enthusiasm generated by these events was remarkably short-lived. It soon became clear that the morality of rights and Enlightenment secularism faced a powerful array of fiercely illiberal (but previously repressed) forces. Worse, moral individualism—the belief in individual human dignity which grounds the morality of rights—was confused or conflated with the sheer selfishness encouraged by the market, a development that only heightened the appeal of such illiberal forces. Ethnic nationalism, religious intolerance, and new local and global forms of gangsterism combined to exploit the tensions introduced by the utilitarian ethic of global capitalism, a utilitarianism that dissolves the individual's claim to any intrinsic dignity (in this regard at least, Marx's critical radicalization of Kant was not entirely incorrect).

Thus, in a world of "billions and billions" of people, increasing numbers are faced with the desperate fact of their own (apparent) superfluousness. While the twenty-first century will not likely reproduce the situation of the Weimar Republic blown up to world proportions, one can safely say that it will provide countless situations in which political leaders find it easier to mobilize the sentiments of group identity (ethnic, racial, religious) at no matter what cost, than to bear up under the pressure of an unforgiving world economy. The morality of rights—never without its enemies, not even in the West—will be an export of limited appeal, and even more limited efficacy, for the foreseeable future.

In this context it is helpful to return to Hannah Arendt's analysis of the nature of totalitarianism's assault on human dignity or (to use her phrase) the human status. It is helpful not because the future necessarily holds the threat of a renascent totalitarianism (or even a "soft totalitarianism" as some misguided French intellectuals have argued), nor because Arendt helps us to see ways in which the morality of rights can be bolstered in the face of such assaults (she was eminently skeptical of the capacity of rights-based doctrines to effectively counteract the forces that give rise to totalitarianism).[2] Rather, what gives her analysis an urgent contemporary relevance is Arendt's insight into the form of political evil created by totalitarian regimes, an evil that she designated as "radical" in order to distinguish it from the more familiar horrors perpetrated by political regimes throughout the centuries.

For Arendt, the unique horror of totalitarianism was that it created a system in which "all men have become equally superfluous," equally deprived of their individuality and equally suited to the role of executioner or victim.[3] It created a world, most purely instanced in the concentration camps, in which the human capacity for spontaneity was eradicated—in which, in other words, human nature was successfully altered, creating beings who could only react, like Pavlov's dogs, but never initiate. Deprived of this capacity, thrust into a world in which they experienced their own superfluousness as a daily, hourly reality, the victims of totalitarian terror presented Arendt with the most palpable evidence imaginable that human beings could be remade into "perverted animals" through the novel arts of total domination.[4]

In this chapter I want to focus on Arendt's description of the process of literal dehumanization as it occurred in the camps, as well as her analysis of the role terror played in totalitarian regimes. Both aspects underline her fear of a future world in which human dignity no longer exists, in which "masses of people are continuously rendered superfluous," either through totalitarian instruments or social and economic trends.[5] The concentration camps actualized such a world by successfully destroying the basis of human dignity: individuality, understood as the capacity to initiate and thus stand apart from the automatism of nature and mere behavior. The preponderant sense of Arendt's analysis is that this is something radically new in the realm of human affairs, something undreamt of by even the most bloodthirsty of tyrants.

If the horror of totalitarianism, its "radical evil," is the creation and treatment of masses of human beings as superfluous, then it presents us with a new danger to the human status, one which continues to darken our moral horizon. As liberals—that is, as believers in the dignity of the individual—we cannot afford to be overly sanguine about the prospects the future holds. The words Arendt wrote in 1951 as historical description now read as prophecy: "political, social, and economic events everywhere are in a silent conspiracy with totalitarian instruments devised for making men superfluous."[6] The totalitarian instruments may, for the time being, have been mostly destroyed, but the trends that render increasing numbers of people superfluous continue apace.[7] We can only shudder at the thought of what new political configurations might arise in the next century, and how they might feed off of and accelerate these trends. For all we know, the Age of Genocides and industrial killing may be just beginning.

TOTALITARIANISM AND TERROR

The problem confronted by any attempt to analyze a genuinely new danger to the human status is our overwhelming tendency to read the strange back into the familiar. With respect to the horrors of totalitarianism, this human-all-too-human tendency is particularly strong. We assume that the totalitarian assault on human freedom and dignity is of a piece with the tyrannies of the past; that Hitler and Stalin were power-mad, and that the concentration-camp system reflects their lust for power. According to this view, the death of millions of innocents in the camps reveals the depth of the leaders' megalomania. Works of fiction like Arthur Koestler's *Darkness at Noon* encourage us in this tendency. For Koestler, Stalinist totalitarianism was essentially Machiavellianism run amock, the elevation of an "end justifies the means" utilitarianism to the status of the last word in political ethics. A ruthlessness born of political idealism paves the way for the ascension of a tyrant who combines a Machiavellian lack of scruples with limitless paranoia. Cold calculation gives way to lunatic excess as absolute power corrupts absolutely. Totalitarian evil is thus causally reduced to the rejection of traditional moral limits and personal pathology.

Hannah Arendt was convinced that, so long as we approach the totalitarian phenomenon in terms of such "liberal" prejudgments, we systematically distort it. The first step in understanding totalitarianism must be to purge ourselves of the tendency to personalize the

evil of the regime, to reduce it to an emanation of the demonic genius of the leader. We must also lay aside the limited understanding
of political evil we have inherited from the "great tradition," since
this understanding focuses almost exclusively on the immoderate
passions of the ruler or populace. Indeed, one could go so far as to
say that the great tradition of Western political thought is not much
concerned with *political* evil—evil as policy—at all.[8] It is, rather,
concerned with questions of justice and character formation (or de-
formation), and therefore throws little light on the nature of political evil, let alone on the distinctively modern phenomenon of evil
as policy.

Nor are the tools of social science much help in grasping the
peculiar evil of totalitarian regimes, since these almost always presuppose some model of means/end rationality as the basis for explaining the workings of a social system or political regime.[9] Totalitarian evil certainly required highly evolved instrumentalities of
bureaucratic rationality, but it cannot be reduced to these means or
their effects. Evaluated from the standpoint of utilitarian criteria,
the camps were a tremendous waste of scarce resources (the German
escalation of the deportation process in the final stages of World
War II, when transport was desperately needed as defensive fronts
collapsed, testifies to their strategic irrationality).

And yet terror and concentration camps *define* the totalitarian
system, giving it its distinctive shape and its uncanny novelty. For
Arendt, engaging in what she called the "interminable dialogue with
the essence of totalitarianism" meant placing terror and the camps
at the very center of any analysis. Only then could one have some
minimal reassurance that one was not reading the strange back into
the familiar; that one wasn't indulging one's "liberal" prejudices
concerning the nature and causes of political evil.[10] Understanding
the unprecedented meant that the faculty of human judgment, deprived of its usual ground in "common sense," had to rely on a "fearful imagination" prepared to "dwell on horrors."

Focusing on terror and the camps, however, poses its own problems, since neither political terror nor concentration camps were
invented by totalitarianism. The process of understanding and judgment must therefore begin by establishing the uniqueness of totalitarian terror and the Nazi and Soviet camp systems. This is by
no means a simple task, nor one that can be performed by the historical as opposed to the theoretical imagination. The former

TERROR AND RADICAL EVIL

provides us with precedents and, as Arendt reminds us in *The Origins of Totalitarianism*:

> Many things that nowadays have become the specialty of totalitarian government are only too well known from the study of history. There have almost always been wars of aggression; the massacre of hostile populations after a victory went unchecked until the Romans mitigated it by introducing the *parcere subjectis*; through centuries the extermination of native peoples went hand in hand with the colonization of the Americas, Australia, and Africa; slavery is one of the oldest institutions of mankind and all empires of antiquity were based on the labor of state-owned slaves who erected their public buildings. Not even concentration camps are an invention of totalitarian movements. They emerge for the first time during the Boer War, at the beginning of the century. . . .[11]

The fact that terror as "a means of frightening people into submission" has taken an "extraordinary number of forms" throughout history places an additional burden on the analyst of totalitarian evil. Not only does the regime form look familiar (tyranny or dictatorship blown up to immense proportions); its very reliance on terror and the means Arendt mentions reinforces, at first glance, the continuity with the past.

If the powers of human understanding and judgment are not to fail—if the strange is not to be read back into the familiar—then one must elucidate the specificity of totalitarian terror, showing what distinguishes it from all other forms. One must face the unnerving possibility that extermination as such was only a part of totalitarian evil, and by no means the most "radical" part. One of Arendt's basic points it that it is not the killing, nor even the scale of the killing, that distinguishes totalitarian evil from all other politically engineered horrors. Rather, it is the fact that terror was far more than a means for these regimes: it was their very *essence*. It was through terror, systematically and continuously applied, that the novel experiment in total domination was performed and the thesis "everything is possible" given credibility. The worst evil is thus not killing, not even mass killing, but the use of terror to prove that there are no limits to human power, and that there is nothing built-in or permanent about human dignity. Indeed, as the camps proved, it is entirely possible to create a self-enclosed universe where human dignity no longer exists.

Arendt famously characterizes the thought that "everything is possible" as the central, animating conviction of totalitarian regimes. This conviction is not reducible to the more familiar credo of nineteenth-century nihilism and imperialism, namely that "everything is permitted." The latter, Arendt observes, is certainly presupposed by totalitarianism; however, as a radicalization of *raison d'état*, it still assumes some tie to "the utilitarian motives and self-interest of the rulers."[12] The totalitarian principle transcends these constraints; its aim is not power nor enrichment nor even political survival. Rather, what totalitarianism assumes is the possibility of dominating human beings entirely ("total domination"), such that they can no longer resist or interfere with the "law of motion"—of Nature or History—which the totalitarian movement seeks to accelerate. Such laws of motion (the "law of history" or the "law of nature") provide the ideological "supersense" of the totalitarian movements, a metanarrative which they then attempt to bring reality into accord with. The *aim* of totalitarianism is nothing less than the remaking of humanity and the world such that "the facts" reflect the truth of the ideological supersense (the inevitable victory of the proletariat in the class struggle; the superiority of the Aryan race in the Darwinian struggle). The horror is the degree to which totalitarian regimes were successful in this project, that is, in creating a world in which experiments in terror were constantly proving the ideological "supersense" correct.[13]

It is this aspect of the totalitarian experience that Arendt fears we have failed to face up to, thanks in part to our "liberal," commonsense prejudices. We want to believe that the distinguishing characteristic of totalitarian terror was its scale, rather than its new ways of organizing and denaturing human beings. Arendt's analysis of totalitarian terror focuses on precisely these neglected dimensions, the better to show us how a world where "everything is possible" was in fact created. She wants to disabuse us of the comforting (but false) belief that there are built-in limits to what human beings can do to each other and to themselves, that a natural repugnance or moral sense will serve as a brake to evil on a gigantic scale. To continue to believe in such pieties after the experience of totalitarianism is to remain blind to the central lesson of the age.[14]

Arendt's disabusing strategy is much in evidence in a 1953 radio address entitled "Mankind and Terror," which provides a concise summary of the reasons why totalitarian terror is different from all other forms. Arendt begins by discussing the terror of tyrannies and revolutionary terror, which (on the face of it) bear more than a little resemblance to totalitarian terror. Yet the similarities are false, since both forms of terror are "directed at an end and find an end." Tyrannical terror finds an end "once it has paralyzed or even totally dispensed with all public life and made private individuals out of all citizens, stripping them of interest in and a connection with public affairs."[15] Revolutionary terror finds an end when the opposition is destroyed, or when "the revolution has exhausted all reserves of strength." Totalitarian terror, in contrast, comes into its own only *after* the opposition has been destroyed. As the cases of Russia after 1930 and Germany after 1936 bear out, it is only when the political struggle has been definitively won that the concentration-camp system rapidly expands. Totalitarian terror comes into its own when it turns on *absolutely innocent* people for its victims, creating an endless reign of terror, one that deprives society of the "graveyard peace" that accompanies all successful tyrannies.

Totalitarian terror thus begins where other (modern) forms of terror leave off. It sets in motion a "permanent flux" that demands not only an unending supply of innocent victims, but also the thorough dissolution of the relative permanence and stability created and preserved by positive law.[16] In the name of accelerating the "laws of motion" guiding Nature or History, totalitarian terror creates a political world in which everyone knows that positive law is merely a facade. Where law provides no genuinely protective boundaries, absolute power can move without resistance, revising the criteria of enemies of the class or race and expanding the categories of the condemned innocent (Arendt notes how, in a 1943 draft for a comprehensive Reich health law, Hitler suggested that after the war all Germans be X-rayed and that families with a history of lung or heart disease be incarcerated in the camps[17]).

But the characterization of totalitarian terror as expansive, endlessly dynamic, and aimed at the innocent raises an obvious question: what is the *purpose* of this terror? Whose needs or interests does it serve? While Arendt thinks there is an answer to the first question, she thinks the second is wrongheaded. It hinges on the supposition that totalitarian terror, like other forms, is essentially an instrument for scaring people into submission. But this is not the case. Totalitarian terror fails even the most elementary test of strategic rationality:

> If, for example, we apply to the phenomenon of totalitarian terror the category of means and ends, by which terror would be a means to retain power, to intimidate people, to make them afraid, and so in this way to

cause them to behave in certain ways and not others, it becomes clear that totalitarian terror will be less effective than any other form of terror in achieving that end. Fear cannot possibly be a reliable guide if what I am constantly afraid of can happen to me regardless of anything I do. . . . One can of course say . . . that in this case the means have become the ends. But this is not really an explanation. It is only a confession, disguised as a paradox, that the category of means and ends no longer works; that terror is apparently without an end; that millions of people are being senselessly sacrificed; that, as in the case of the mass murders during the war, the measures actually run counter to the perpetrator's real interests.[18]

Confronted with the lack of even a minimal level of strategic rationality, one is tempted to locate the purpose or meaning of totalitarian terror in the sheer craziness born of ideological "true believers" or in a particular people's deeply rooted hatred of various "others." Arendt hardly denies the role played by ideology or antisemitism in the Russian and German cases, respectively, but she refuses to locate the meaning of totalitarian terror in the patent irrationality of ideological fantasy or racial hatred. In order to grasp its meaning, she suggests, we first need to take account of "two noteworthy facts." The first fact is that the concentration camps were "holes of oblivion" deliberately isolated from the outside world. The fate of individual victims is never revealed; it is as if they had never existed. Hence Arendt can observe that "the real horror of the concentration and extermination camps lies in the fact that the inmates are more effectively cut off from the world of the living than if they had died, because terror enforces oblivion."[19] Death in the world leads to remembrance of the distinctive appearance, in words and deeds, of the deceased. To live and die in the camps, however, is to be deprived of one's appearance in the world, to be absolutely erased from the realm of appearances and (thus) memory. Here, one's death is no longer one's own.[20]

The second fact essential for grasping the meaning of totalitarian terror is that "no one except for the leader in power at the moment is immune from terror. . . ."[21] The executioners of today can become the victims of tomorrow. This is not a question of the revolution devouring its own children since, as Arendt notes, these have already been disposed of. Rather, it is a reflection of the need of totalitarian regimes for subjects who have internalized their own potential superfluousness; who realize that, according to the logic of the ideology, they may be next on the list of sacrifices demanded by Nature or History. Thus, "a purge that instantaneously transforms the accuser into the accused, the hangman into the hanged, the executioner into the victim puts people to [the] test"—the test of falling completely into line with the regime "no matter what monstrosities it commits."[22]

What do these two facts tell us about the *meaning* of totalitarian terror? The combination of the helplessness, anonymity, and isolation of the camp inmates, on the one hand, and the ideologically programed submissiveness of the regime's functionaries, on the other, suggests that totalitarian terror aims at denaturing individuals, rendering them interchangeable and incapable of initiative or judgment. And this is, in fact, how Arendt interprets the otherworldly isolation of the camps and the submissiveness of the party and police functionaries to their fates: both "mean to make human beings in their infinite variety and their unique individuality superfluous."[23] For it is only when human beings have internalized their own superfluousness, when they submitted mutely to power, that the totalitarian aspiration to total domination becomes realizable. Thus, concentration camps and ideological indoctrination are "experiments" in domination which aim at a qualitatively new form. They are experiments not in fear per se, but in probing the limits of human plasticity. For people have to be remade, rendered completely interchangeable, if the totalitarian goal of total domination is to be achieved. The whole thrust of Arendt's analysis of totalitarianism, and of the role of the camps within the totalitarian system, is that *total* domination is a new aspiration in the history of human power, an aspiration that could arise only when politics entered the hitherto unthinkable realm of "everything is possible."[24]

So understood, totalitarian terror is "no longer a means to an end; it is the very essence of such a government."[25] It is the form which the (in principle) never-ending experiment in total domination takes. The *ultimate* goal of this experiment, achievable only if totalitarian regimes succeeded in "bringing all of humanity under their sway," is "to form and maintain a society, whether one dominated by a particular race or one in which classes and nations no longer exist, in which every individual would be nothing other than a specimen of the species."[26] In such a world, the human species would, at last, become the transparent embodiment of the "all-pervasive, all-powerful" law of Nature or History. Contingency would be eliminated, replaced by an inescapable historical or natural necessity. The Law of History or the Law of Nature—the "supersense" of the movement—would be redeemed.

TOTAL DOMINATION: THE CAMPS

Of course, the totalitarian aspiration was never achieved, nor could it be achieved without the global elimination of human spontaneity, the making over of *all* human beings into interchangeable "bundles of reactions." Nevertheless, it was substantively achieved in the world of the concentration camps, that is, in the isolated environment in which the experiment in total domination could unfold under "scientifically exacting conditions."

Arendt's pages on the camps—in the 1948 essay entitled "The Concentration Camps" and in the "Total Domination" section of *The Origins of Totalitarianism*—are among the most disturbing in her often unsettling *oeuvre*. They are disturbing not merely because they "dwell on horrors," but because they are so adamant in their refusal to provide any false comfort. The single salient fact which Arendt forces us to face is that the camps were *successful*, not only in exterminating countless human beings, but in their goal of destroying the individuality of the victims. Through terror—in the form of the disciplines and deprivations of the Lager—the inmates were transformed into interchangeable "specimens of the human animal." Anyone looking for evidence of the indestructibility of the human spirit, or of the indomitability of our moral sense under extreme conditions, will not find it in Arendt. She wants us to take in—slowly, painfully, miserably—not merely man's inhumanity to man, but the fact that psyche, character, and the moral life were all largely destroyed by the camps. She wants us to realize that human power can, in fact, transform human beings into animals—indeed, into "perverted animals."

If this is true, then it is (to use a phrase of Arendt's from another context) a "terrible truth." But it is a truth we have to face if we are not to deceive ourselves about the nature of totalitarianism and the shape of political evil in this century.

In *Survival in Auschwitz*, Primo Levi recounts how internment in the camp infirmary (the *Krankenbau* or "Ka-Be") allowed him to escape the hellish physical immediacy of hunger, cold, forced labor,

21

and the war of all against all that constituted life in the Lager. For the first time, he could actually register what was going on around him:

> As the bread is distributed one can hear, far from the windows, in the dark air, the band beginning to play: the healthy comrades are leaving in squads for work. . . .
>
> The tunes are few, a dozen, the same ones every day, morning and evening: marches and popular songs dear to every German. They lie engraven on our minds and will be the last thing in Lager that we shall forget: they are the voice of the Lager, the perceptible expression of its geometrical madness, of the resolution of others to annihilate us first as men in order to kill us more slowly afterwards.
>
> When this music plays we know that our comrades, out in the fog, are marching like automatons; their souls are dead and the music drives them, like the wind drives dead leaves, and takes the place of their wills. There is no longer any will: every beat of the drum becomes a step, a reflected contraction of exhausted muscles. The Germans have succeeded in this. They [the laboring inmates] are ten thousand and they are a single grey machine; they are exactly determined; they do not think and they do not desire, they walk.[27]

But internment in the infirmary enables not only reflection on the ongoing dehumanization of others; it also provides Levi with his first opportunity to register how much of his own personality and humanity had been taken away:

> Ka-Be is the Lager without its physical discomforts. So that, whoever still has some seeds of conscience, feels his conscience reawaken; and in the long days, one speaks of other things than hunger and work and one begins to consider what they have made us become, and how much they have taken away from us, what this life is. In this Ka-Be, an enclosure of relative peace, we have learnt that our personality is fragile, that it is in much more danger than our life; and the old wise ones, instead of warning us 'remember that you must die', would have done much better to remind us of this great danger which threatens us.[28]

The triumph of the Lager is that its inmates are "killed in our spirit long before our anonymous death." It is this fact, in all its ramifications, that Arendt wants to develop in the section on "Total Domination" in *The Origins of Totalitarianism*.

How are souls killed and personalities destroyed? How are human beings turned into the blankly marching automatons Levi describes? Arendt provides no detailed account of the instrumentalities (such as starvation, forced labor, exposure to the elements, innumerable absurd rules and relentlessly brutal punishments), nor of the complex and perverse social structure of the camps, the mechanism by which a distinctly Hobbesian universe was created and the claims of ordinary morality suspended for those who wanted to survive.[29] Rather, she focuses her attention on the "historically and politically intelligible" three-step process through which human beings are gradually deprived of their human status, first outside the camps, then within. The delineation of *this* process—the process through which total domination is achieved—is the service which political theory, driven by "fearful imagination," can provide.

The first step toward the preparation of "living corpses" is the destruction of the juridical person, the murder of the legal persona. This was done by placing entire categories of people outside the protection of law, and using what Arendt calls the "instrument of denationalization" as a way of making the nontotalitarian world recognize lawlessness.[30] With this instrument, totalitarian regimes force others to acknowledge the act of disenfranchisement as a legitimate exercise of sovereign state power, enlisting their complicity in the process of destroying the juridical subject. The other avenue to this end was the creation, in the form of the concentration-camp system itself, of a carceral universe separate and distinct from the normal penal system. Only by creating a separate system are inmates placed, for the first time, "outside the normal juridical procedure in which a definite crime entails a predictable penalty."[31] This is an essential step in creating the possibility of an utterly arbitrary, absolute form of power. For so long as there remains even a conceptual link between the prisoner's actions and the prisoner's incarceration, the legal subject retains some force. Thus, as Arendt puts it, "criminals do not properly belong in the concentration camps, if only because it is harder to kill the juridical person in a man who is guilty of some crime than in a totally innocent person."[32] There is and must be an abyss between the concentration-camp system and the penal system; otherwise, an irreducible remnant of the juridical subject is preserved and the possibility of an unconstrained power foreclosed.

This is not to say that criminals did not constitute an important element of the concentration-camp population in both the German and Soviet cases. They provided the initial *raison d'être* of the camps, an excuse for bringing the system into existence in the first place. While ultimately providing an indispensable intermediate level of domination as the "aristocracy" of the camps, the internment of criminals also camouflaged the experiment in power and disenfranchisement that the concentration camp represented. The presence of criminals blurred the distinction between the camps and the penal system, thus making it appear that the camps were merely punishing, in an acceptable manner, those whose actions warranted punishment.

This blurring was also effected by the presence of political prisoners, who—because they had committed political "crimes"—also retained a "remnant of their juridical person." In the case of political prisoners, we are still dealing with the (limited) arbitrary power characteristic of tyranny. Only when a third group, the absolutely innocent, come to constitute the majority of the prisoners in the camps does the concentration camp become "the true central institution of totalitarian organizational power."[33] The camps, their apparent irrationality aside, have a purpose: they are "laboratories" in which experiments in total domination and the exercise of absolute power can occur. The relevance of these experiments extends far beyond the choice of victims, to the shape of totalitarian society at large. The third group, the "absolutely innocent," are guinea pigs for the ultimate society-wide destruction of the juridical person:

> In Germany, after 1938, this element was represented by masses of Jews, in Russia by any groups which, for any reason having nothing to do with their actions, had incurred the disfavor of the authorities. These groups, innocent in every sense, are the most suitable for the thorough experimentation in disenfranchisement and destruction of the juridical person, and therefore they are both qualitatively and quantitatively the most essential category of the camp population. This principle was most fully realized in the gas chambers which, if only because of their enormous capacity, could not be intended for individual cases but only for people in general.[34]

It is with the last sentence of this paragraph that the stakes of Arendt's analysis of the totalitarian destruction of the juridical person become apparent. She is not concerned with how this destruction smoothed the way to the extermination of a particular group (Jews, Gypsies, or homosexuals, for example) but rather with the fact that only masses of utterly innocent people could enable the regime to test its capacity to destroy the protections of civil rights and the boundaries of law. Disenfranchisement, in other words, was tried out in the camps in its "pure" form, the better to pave the way to a state of total domination in the society at large:

> The aim of an arbitrary system is to destroy the civil rights of the whole population, who ultimately become just as outlawed in their own country as the stateless and the homeless. The destruction of a man's rights, the killing of the juridical person in him, is a prerequisite for dominating him entirely. And this applies not only to special categories such as criminals, political opponents, Jews, homosexuals, on whom the early experiments were made, but to every inhabitant of a totalitarian state. Free consent is as much an obstacle to total domination as free opposition.[35]

Here Arendt's focus on the experiment in disenfranchisement performed in the concentration camps seems, perversely perhaps, to deny the specificity of the victims. She seems to be saying that *any* group would do, so long as they were absolutely innocent. And, as an analyst of the concentration camp as the central institution of an "ideal type" totalitarian regime, that is exactly what she is saying. Of course, she is not denying that German racial attitudes and anti-semitism led to the attempt to destroy European Jewry. Rather, her point is that, insofar as Nazi Germany was a totalitarian society, the camps were not an afterthought, the contingent disaster born of one man's (or one nation's) insane, unthinking prejudice. But the fact remains that her insistence upon the novelty of totalitarian terror and the "experiments" of the camps paradoxically undercuts any strong insistence upon the uniqueness of the Holocaust. Like it or not, Arendt's theoretical concern with the "essence of totalitarianism" leads her to frame the attempted extermination of the Jews as but one step in a broader process aimed at total domination.[36] From *this* perspective, what matters is not the particular groups selected for the experiment in complete disenfranchisement, but the fact that the camps open up the possibility of a world in which the juridical subject has been effaced, in which "the continued total disenfranchisement of man" becomes possible.

The second step in the preparation of "living corpses" is what Arendt calls the murder of the "moral person." The "moral person" is neither the legal subject of rights nor the concrete, unique human individual. Perhaps the closest approximation of what Arendt means is provided by the idea of conscientious or moral agency. Being a conscientious agent demands an environment in which moral action is neither suicidal nor meaningless. But the world of the camps destroys the presuppositions of such an environment. The victims cannot choose martyrdom, cannot conscientiously protest their fate, because the isolation and methods of the camps succeed in making death utterly anonymous. Arendt quotes the camp survivor David Rousset, whose books *Les Jours de Notre Mort* and *Univers Concentrationnaire* provide much of the phenomenological description underlying her analysis:

> How many people here [in the camps] still believe that a protest has even historic importance? This skepticism is the real masterpiece of the SS. Their great accomplishment. They have corrupted all human solidarity. Here the night has fallen on the future. When no witnesses are left, there can be no testimony. To demonstrate when death can no longer be postponed is an attempt to give death a meaning, to act beyond one's own death. In order to be successful, a gesture must have a social meaning. There are hundreds of thousands of us here, all living in absolute solitude. That is why we are subdued no matter what happens.[37]

Of course there were exceptions, and—as in the famous case of Mala Zimetbaum who, recaptured and tortured after escaping Auschwitz, addressed her fellow inmates from the scaffold minutes before slashing her own wrists with a concealed razor blade, infuriating the guards through her usurpation of their power[38]—instances of dramatic protest to rival anything in the history of conscientious disobedience. The point is not that such actions occurred, but rather that they were the exceptions which proved the rule, exceptions whose meaning was redeemed by the unforeseen destruction of the concentration camp system itself. For the most part, the utter isolation of the camps, their virtual lack of contact with the outside world, succeeded in creating a world of anonymous mass death.

The other side of the destruction of the "moral person" is found in totalitarianism's creation of conditions that render conscience itself either inadequate or irrelevant. An economy of choice is established in which all decisions are, strictly speaking, tragic. The decision that it is better to die a victim than to become a bureaucrat of murder loses its clear moral sense when "a man is faced with the alternative of betraying and thus murdering his friends or of sending his wife and children, for whom he is in every sense responsible, to their death. . . ."[39] Such a tragic economy was even more of a reality in the Hobbesian world of the camps, where one clear route to longer survival was complicity with one's captors (hence the enormously complicated hierarchy of the German camps, in which virtually all daily activities were overseen by prisoners—the hated *Kapos*—while the SS rarely made an appearance).[40] Arendt is not denying that *some* choices could still be made, that the imperative of survival could issue in greater and lesser betrayals of one's fellows. The point is that when the choice is between murder, theft, or betrayal, on the one hand, and a suicidal adherence to ordinary morality, on the other, the decisions of conscience become "absolutely questionable and equivocal." The conditions of the camps destroyed free will and moral personality by making conscientious behavior the surest route to self-destruction.[41] As Levi puts it, ". . . here in the Lager there are no criminals nor madmen; no criminals because there is no moral law to contravene, no madman because we are wholly devoid of free will, as our every action is, in time and place, the only conceivable one."[42]

Following the destruction of rights and conscience, the totalitarian experiment in total domination focuses its disciplinary energies on the recalcitrant material of human individuality itself. Human personality or character provides the last bulwark against power for the individual who has been stripped of rights and conscience. But it is precisely this dimension of existence that is targeted by the tortures, physical abuse, and the absurdly numerous disciplines and rules of the camps (infractions of which called forth the most brutal of punishments).[43] From the use of cattle-car transport to head shaving, lack of sufficient clothing, rest, or food, and excruciating physical labor, the camps were gigantic machines for the manipulation of the human body, calling forth its "infinite possibilities of suffering" as a means for demolishing the last reserves of personality and spontaneity. Levi's portrait of the "drowned"—the "Muslims" or *Muselmanner* (Auschwitz slang for the living dead)—confirms the success such methods had in breaking down human personality:

> To sink is the easiest of matters; it is enough to carry out all the orders one receives, to eat only the ration, to observe the discipline of the work

and the camp. Experience showed that only exceptionally could one survive more than three months in this way. All the musselmans who finished in the gas chambers have the same story, or more exactly, no story; they followed the slope down to the bottom, like streams that run down to the sea. On their entry into the camp, through basic incapacity, or by misfortune, or through some banal incident, they are overcome before they can adapt themselves; they are beaten by time, they do not begin to learn German, to disentangle the infernal knot of laws and prohibitions until their body is already in decay, and nothing can save them from selections [for the gas chambers] or death by exhaustion. Their life is short, but their number is endless; they, the *Muselmänner*, the drowned, form the backbone of the camp, an anonymous mass, continually renewed and always identical, of non-men who march and labour in silence, the divine spark dead within them, already too empty to really suffer. One hesitates to call them living: one hesitates to call their death death, in the face of which they have no fear, as they are too tired to understand.[44]

This passage may seem brutal in its detachment, in its presupposition of a gap between those who—through talent, energy, or accident—found a way of minimally manipulating the system and those who were its pure victims. The fact that the presence of a certain animal cunning was what all too often determined whether an individual was one of the "drowned" or one of the "saved"—a longer-surviving inmate—does not undercut Arendt's fundamental point. Camp life was an enormously successful apparatus for producing walking dead or *Muselmänner*, examples of the human species who had been stripped of their capacity for spontaneity, for action: "Nothing then remains but ghastly marionettes with human faces, which all behave like the dog in Pavlov's experiments, which all react with perfect reliability even when going to their own death, and which do nothing but react. This is the real triumph of the system. . . ."[45] And, quoting Rousset: "Nothing is more terrible than these processions of human beings going like dummies to their death. The man who sees this says to himself: 'For them to be thus reduced, what power must be concealed in the hands of the masters,' and he turns away, full of bitterness but defeated."[46] With the creation of the *Muselmänner* in their tens of thousands, the camps bring the totalitarian experiment in total domination to a successful conclusion. Instead of human individuals, we find interchangeable specimens of the human species; instead of persons capable of action there are simply bundles of reactions, "perverted animals" whose free will has been destroyed.[47]

RADICAL EVIL

Reading Arendt's analysis, along with the descriptions of Levi and Rousset, tempts one to charge exaggeration. The camps were undoubtedly terrible, a hell on earth. But surely (one wants to say) they could not have been as successful in their experimental eradication of individuality and spontaneity as Arendt, Levi, and Rousset make out. Surely some human dignity, will, moral sense, and human solidarity survived the infernal machinery into which the victims were placed? Surely not all were stripped of their human status, degraded to the level of "perverted animals" by the relentless tortures and struggle for survival?

Such questions animate Tzvetan Todorov's recent *Facing the Extreme: Moral Life in the Concentration Camps.* Todorov's book questions Levi's contention that the camps were successful in creating a Hobbesian world, and challenges Arendt's assessment of their capacity to change human nature in accordance with the needs of total domination.[48] Todorov's account of life in the camps alerts us to the way an exclusive focus on the "heroic virtues" has distorted our perception of moral life in the camps, making it seem as if—in the absence of dramatic gestures—human will and dignity had effectively disappeared. Drawing on the accounts of numerous survivors (including Levi), Todorov insists that, in the camps, staying human was in fact often more important than staying alive. He tries to show how the "ordinary virtues" of solidarity, care for others, and the life of the mind survived under such extreme conditions, providing vehicles for an assaulted humanity. He wants us to appreciate how individual personality and dignity, far from being systematically and completely destroyed, were preserved in a host of small, undramatic yet utterly essential, ways.

Todorov does not deny that the imperatives of morality and survival came into bitter conflict in the camps. Rather, he wants to show how altruism and the moral sense survived even under the most extreme conditions, revealing far deeper roots than Levi's Hobbesian description allows.[49] Human beings may indeed be prepared to do anything as the result of prolonged torture, distress, or deprivation, but this fact reveals nothing (*contra* Levi and Hobbes) about human nature. The catalogue of altruistic actions culled from camp life prove, according to Todorov, that morality is far more than a "superficial convention" which we supposedly wolfish creatures abandon under even moderate pressure.

The problem with Todorov's thesis is not that Hobbes was right about human nature, but that he is the wrong target. Neither Levi nor Arendt write about the camps as if they confirmed the most disillusioned or deterministic account of human nature. Their invocation of the Hobbesian *bellum omnium contra omnes* (explicit in Levi, mostly implicit in Arendt) underlines the unnaturalness of the camps, at least from the perspective of ordinary life and morality. The "experiment" of the camps (Levi also makes use of this Arendtian characterization[50]) aimed not at revealing a brutish human nature beneath the thin veneer of civilization, but rather at *changing this very nature*. As Arendt puts it:

> What totalitarian ideologies . . . aim at is not the transformation of the outside world or the revolutionizing transmutation of society, but the transformation of human nature itself. The concentration camps are laboratories where changes in human nature are tested, and their shamefulness therefore is not just the business of their inmates and those who run them according to strictly "scientific" standards; it is the concern of all men. Suffering is not the issue, nor is the number of victims. *Human nature as such is at stake*, and even though it seems that these experiments succeed not in changing man but only in destroying him, by creating a society in which the nihilistic banality of *homo hominilupus* is consistently realized, one should bear in mind the necessary limitations to an experiment which requires global control in order to show conclusive results.[51]

From *this* perspective, Todorov's Rousseauistic and somewhat sentimentalizing focus on the "ordinary virtues" manifest in camp life is more than a little problematic. It encourages us to posit a good, relational or caring human nature in the place of egoistic Hobbesian amorality. But the question posed by the camps is not whether humanity is naturally good or naturally selfish, but whether there are set limits on human power, limits that prevent the willful transformation of human nature. The triumph of an ideology based on the assumption that "everything is possible" means that no such limits will be recognized, and that human material will be approached as utterly plastic and expendable. It also means that the persistence of the "ordinary virtues" in the interstices of camp life testify to little more than the unavoidable imperfection of the conditions under which the totalitarian experiment is conducted. Given sufficient time and resources, this experiment might well have achieved more than partial success. The lesson to be drawn from the camps is not that man the moral animal never *really* existed (something Todorov thinks is implied by Levi's Hobbesian description of the camps), but that there is no indelible nature we can fall back on as a guarantee that similar experiments will not succeed in the future.

This issue is underlined by Arendt's exchange with the political philosopher Eric Voegelin. Reviewing *The Origins of Totalitarianism* in 1953, Voegelin had taken exception to Arendt's statement (cited above) that "human nature as such is at stake." Voegelin pedantically reminded Arendt that the nature of something is unchangeable, and that to think otherwise is symptomatic of "the intellectual breakdown of Western civilization." To which Arendt responded, in quasi-existentialist fashion:

> . . . the success of totalitarianism is identical with a much more radical liquidation of freedom as a political and as a human reality than anything we have ever witnessed before. Under these conditions, it will hardly be consoling to cling to an unchangeable nature of man and conclude that either man himself is being destroyed or that freedom does not belong to man's essential capacities. Historically we know of man's nature only insofar as it has existence, and no realm of eternal essences will ever console us if man loses his essential capacities.[52]

The camps were the specter that haunted Arendt, not only because millions died in them, but also because they revealed, in the starkest possible way, the relative fragility of the human capacity for moral freedom.

Since the eighteenth century—since Rousseau's *Discourse on the Origins of Inequality* and Kant's *Critique of Pure Reason*—we have grown accustomed to identifying man's humanity with the capacity for free causality, for spontaneity. Arendt's energizing concern with the way the camps transform "the human personality into a mere thing" and reduce human beings to "mere bundles of reactions" reflects this heritage. But it also reflects the strangely prescient fears of another eighteenth-century thinker, Montesquieu, who was unencumbered by the comforting essentialism of either Rousseau or Kant. In the Preface to *The Spirit of the Laws*, Montesquieu wrote:

"Man, this flexible being, who submits himself in society to the thoughts and impressions of his fellow-men, is equally capable of knowing his own nature when it is shown to him and of losing it to the point where he has no realization that he is robbed of it."[53] If a world is created in which the conditions are lacking for the exercise of our essential capacities, then these capacities will be forgotten. If a world is created in which human beings experience themselves and others as essentially superfluous, then human dignity will be forgotten. As Montesquieu teaches us—and as Arendt reminds us—neither our moral freedom nor our human dignity come with any guarantee. The experience of totalitarianism should, if nothing else, drive this lesson home: "human nature as such is at stake."

Only in this context can we fully appreciate what Arendt means when she uses the phrase "radical evil" to describe the significance of the camps. While it has become *de rigeuer* to use the phrase "radical evil" when discussing the camps, such usage generally misses Arendt's point, which (again) is to underscore the novelty of the phenomenon. For Arendt, "radical evil" denotes not the goal of extermination as such, nor the means ("industrialized" killing among them), nor the undoubted sadism of many of the perpetrators. Rather, she employs this phrase because the totalitarian organization of imprisonment and murder on a mass scale was irreducible to any set of recognizably human motivations. Responding in 1951 to her teacher Karl Jaspers's query concerning *The Origins of Totalitarianism*—"Hasn't Jawhe faded too far out of sight?"—Arendt questioned the ability of our religious and philosophical traditions to illuminate a new form of evil:

Evil has proved to be more radical than expected. In objective terms, modern crimes are not provided for in the Ten Commandments. Or: the Western Tradition is suffering from the preconception that the most evil things human beings can do arise from the vice of selfishness. Yet we know that the greatest evils or radical evil has nothing to do anymore with such humanly understandable motives. What radical evil really is I don't know but it seems to me it somehow has to do with the following phenomenon: making human beings as human beings superfluous (not using them as means to an end, which leaves their essence as humans untouched and impinges only on their human dignity; rather, making them superfluous as human beings). This happens as soon as all unpredictability—which, in human beings, is the equivalent of spontaneity—is eliminated. And all this in turn arises from—or better, goes along with—the delusion of the omnipotence (not simply with the lust for power) of an individual man. If an individual man qua man were omnipotent, then there is in fact no reason why men should exist at all. . . .[54]

Making human beings superfluous as humans beings—which Arendt describes as the intrinsic aim of totalitarianism[55]—flows not from the Augustinian *libido dominandi* (the lust to dominate others), nor from the will to ignore the Moral Law (Kant's definition of "radical evil" in *Religion Within the Limits of Reason Alone*). Nor can it be understood or explained "by the evil motives of self-interest, greed, covetousness, resentment, lust for power, and cowardice. . . ."[56] Such traditional sources for evil deeds all refer us to some variant on a sinful human nature, unable to curb its appetites or self-interest. Yet the goal of rendering human beings superfluous as human beings aims not at mastery nor the unrestricted fulfillment of appetite sought by the tyrannical soul (as depicted by Plato in books XIII and IX of the *Republic*), but at erasing all remaining obstacles to the Laws of Nature or History. An equality of vulnerability must be created if these inhuman forces are to truly rage without restriction through mankind. The goal of total domination is to establish such vulnerability, to universalize the incapacity to resist, to render human beings animallike in their acceptance of an inhuman law of motion which decimates them. What this amounts to is nothing less than the destruction of humanity in the name of preserving (and "bettering") the species. As Arendt put it in an even earlier (1947) letter to Jaspers: "Perhaps what is behind it all is only that individual human beings did not kill other individual human beings for human reasons, but that an organized attempt was made to eradicate the concept of the human being."[57]

Arendt's conception of radical evil thus rests upon a specific (and, for some perhaps, idiosyncratic) set of normative presuppositions. As her response to Voegelin demonstrates, it would be wrong to ascribe to her a robust conception of human nature, one that presumed a gap between immutable essence and contingent existence. Nevertheless, Arendt does presume an existentialist variant of the Rousseauian/Kantian point about freedom and spontaneity. If we eliminate the Kantian domiciling of moral causality and freedom beyond the reach of the "mechanism of nature" in the transcendental ego, we are left with something like the Heideggerian insistence upon *Dasein's* capacity to wrench itself free of the determining force of social codes, a capacity which is not metaphysically grounded in any "true" self and which is (as a result) always at risk. The open, relational self of *Being and Time* resonates with Montesquieu's conception of man as a "flexible being," capable of recognizing his nature and equally capable of forgetting it. For Arendt, a human being who has forgotten or been stripped of the capacity for spontaneity is no longer a recognizably *human* being. The camps present us with the most gruesome evidence of totalitarian success in this regard.[58]

But doesn't the aim of the "experiment" of the camps—changing human nature—testify to a remarkable hubris, to Prometheanism run amock, to humanity's blasphemous desire to take the place of God? From the standpoint of Voegelin, it was this aspect that made totalitarianism unquestionably modern, symptomatic of the post-Enlightenment decline in faith. Arendt acknowledges that such a decline played at least a negative role in making totalitarianism possible, but she disputes the idea that the sin of "pride" (in the traditional Augustinian sense) stands behind the totalitarian experiment. What is crucial is not simply the hubris and aspiration to omnipotence manifest in the idea of changing human nature, but the equal role played by submissiveness, of totalitarian leaders as well as the followers. Totalitarianism destroys rights, positive laws, and human individuality in order that The Law (of Nature or History) reign supreme. In this regard, Margaret Canovan has rightly drawn our attention to the "self-abandonment to inhuman forces" that marks the totalitarian mentality.[59] Totalitarian evil is radical or absolute, not because it is a prideful denial of God, but because it seeks to assimilate man to the law of nature (or nature temporalized as History), expunging his contingent freedom in the name of a determinist ideology.

But here one must ask: how novel is *this*? Isn't history full of examples of massacres and genocides carried out as a result of "self-abandonment to inhuman forces"? The Crusaders marching up the hill of Calvary in 1099, "contrite and knee deep in blood" (to use Amos Elon's phrase) come to mind, as does the Spanish conquest of America, whose unparalleled slaughter of the native inhabitants was also undertaken "for the greater glory of God."[60] Throughout history, we see the willingness to deny the other's right to life in the name of something bigger than ourselves, some greater than human "inhuman force" (more often than not, God, unfortunately). If Arendt is making the radical evil of the camps depend, in the last instance, upon such "self-abandonment," then she seems to have discovered not something radically novel, or even authentically modern.

These examples, however, lead us astray. They are based on a binary logic of "us" and "them," of Christians and heathens, of "civilized" and "barbaric." Such logics of group identity undoubtedly played a large role in totalitarian regimes, the Nazi regime in particular (the ordinary German's belief in his racial superiority did not *cause* the Holocaust, but it certainly helped make widespread complicity with political evil possible). But, according to Arendt, they are not really characteristic of such regimes. What totalitarianism introduces to the world stage is a terror that excludes no one, that is rigorously consistent in the application of its animating principles. Hence, the hallmark of a totalitarian regime is that no one is safe. The elimination of various groups of "subhumans" is only the prelude to the larger process of bringing the world into conformity with the dictates of the laws of motion which the regime worships. The most difficult thing Arendt asks of us in posing the idea of a "radical" evil is precisely this: imagining a political universe in which an event like the Holocaust is not the culmination of horrors, but the beginning of a process, an indication of things to come. For the aim of totalitarianism is not, as the Nazi example seems to show, the elimination of the "subhuman." It is, rather, the transformation of the human—not, it should be noted, into a "superman" who makes his own laws, oblivious to the dictates of traditional morality, but into an animal species whose members, mercilessly schooled in their own superfluousness, passively obey the dictates of the (supposed) laws of Nature or History. *This* is the unique and unprecedented evil of totalitarianism—a system "in which *all men have become equally superfluous*"—and why Arendt feels it must be labeled "absolute" or "radical."

CONCLUSION: DWELLING ON HORRORS

Arendt's analysis of terror as the essence of totalitarian regimes and her description of the camps as the "laboratories" in which the experiment to change human nature was most advanced force us to reassess our conception of twentieth-century political evil. They also force us to revise our notions of the chief threats to the concept of human dignity in the modern world. The most shocking implication of Arendt's "dwelling on horrors" is that the camps provided a "logical" solution to the fact that there were more and more people in the world that nobody wanted. The (apparent) total superfluousness of the camp populations could be created only on the basis of the interwar experience of enormous numbers of rightless, homeless refugees, people who had been stripped of their membership in political communities, and thereby deprived of their "right to have rights." "Not the loss of specific rights," Arendt writes, "but the loss of a community willing and able to guarantee any rights whatsoever has been the calamity which has befallen ever-increasing numbers of people. Man, it turns out, can lose all the so-called Rights of Man without losing his essential quality as man, his human dignity. Only the loss of a polity itself expels him from humanity."[61] The three-step totalitarian process for the "preparation of living corpses" builds on the complete rightlessness of the refugees, creating through state action ever new categories of rightless individuals who have been legislatively stripped of their political membership and (thus) their membership in humanity itself. The destruction of the moral subject, and ultimately, of individuality, are the "logical" consequences of a process of expropriation which begins with the right to have rights, with the right to a political "home."

Seen from this perspective, the totalitarian "solution" remains both unprecedented and an ever-present danger. Summing up her account of total domination in *The Origins of Totalitarianism*, Arendt offers a grim view of the future:

> The danger of the corpse factories and holes of oblivion is that today, with populations and homelessness everywhere on the increase, masses of people are continuously rendered superfluous if we continue to think of our world in utilitarian terms. Political, social, and economic events everywhere are in conspiracy with totalitarian instruments devised for making men superfluous. The implied temptation is well understood by the utilitarian common sense of the masses, who in most countries are too desperate to retain much fear of death. The Nazis and the Bolsheviks can be sure that their factories of annihilation which demonstrate the swiftest solution to the problem of overpopulation, of economically superfluous and socially rootless human masses, are as much of an attraction as a warning. Totalitarian solutions may well survive the fall of totalitarian regimes in the form of strong temptations which will come

up whenever it seems impossible to alleviate political, social, or economic misery in a manner worthy of man.[62]

The validity of this remark has been demonstrated by recent events.
Again and again, the unthinkable—genocide, concentration
camps—have reappeared in connection with the dissolution of states
or the need to shore up political power. Indeed, if Arendt's prophecy
is to be faulted, it is for overestimating the level of duress necessary
for such "solutions" to become temptations. In Rwanda and the former Yugoslavia, we have been witness to the cynical manipulation of
mass fears, which has resulted in the unthinkable—not as the last
straw, but as one of the very first. The rallying cry of "never again"
rings hollow against the backdrop of continuing mass slaughter.

This brings us to one of the central paradoxes of the post-totalitarian experience. On the one hand, contemporary human rights
culture is very much a creature of the traumatic experience of the
concentration camps, and of the West's horror that civilized nations
could produce such things. The encounter with radical evil has permanently altered our conception of the importance of human rights,
which can no longer be seen as inevitably flowing from the forward
march of Civilization. As Michael Ignatieff has pointed out, today it
is fear, not hope, which makes us believe in human rights.[63] On the
other hand, however, the trauma of this encounter seems to have
permanently disabled our capacity to appreciate what made the evil
of the camps "radical." Arendt's theoretical labor seems to have been
for naught, as every new horror is reflexively read back to the paradigm of the Holocaust.

There is, I think, an explanation for this, one which does not
simply reduce to the tendency to read the strange back into the familiar.[64] Arendt's prophetic remarks, cited above, help us understand the dialectic of recognition and misrecognition that constitutes our contemporary experience as witnesses to political evil.
There is, at present, nothing like the "organized attempt . . . to eradicate the concept of the human being" performed by totalitarian
regimes, nor do any of the contemporary criminal or authoritarian
regimes we know aim at achieving "total domination." We seem to
have moved back from the precipice of "everything is possible" to
the more recognizable Hell of "everything is permitted"—to preserve the state, the ethnic identity of a people, or the purity of a
religious morality. Yet this "return to normalcy" is deceptive. It is

not merely that some of the techniques of evil are new, but that so many of them are instruments of mass death, next to which Hitler's gas chambers indeed look like "the fumbling toys of an evil child." This technological advance goes hand in hand with a new willingness to think and to do the unthinkable, a kind of moral corruption which affects not only thugs in the Balkans, but also (historically) the leaders of superpowers. The sad truth of the matter is that the legacy of totalitarianism is twofold. There is the new (fear-based) human rights community, but there is also a new "common sense" of the superfluousness of human beings, a "common sense" that enables the thought of ethnic cleansing and of a "limited nuclear exchange" in which tens of millions would die. The post-totalitarian insistence upon human dignity is shadowed by our awareness that all too many political leaders think, at some level at least, of their citizens or subjects as "interchangeable examples of the animal species mankind," to be used and destroyed as the political situation demands. Totalitarianism, itself by no means reducible to the usual motives of *raison d'état*, has permanently altered the range of possibilities states everywhere are willing to contemplate.

In this context—the context of anonymous mass death as an ever-present threat—Arendt's "dwelling on horrors" remains essential. For what she shows in her reflections on radical evil, and in *The Origins of Totalitarianism* as a whole, are the specifically modern tendencies of thought and life which make the systematic assault on the idea of human dignity possible. To repeat, these tendencies have little to do with the traditional conception of evil motives as a perverted form of self-interest. They have everything to do with a world in which millions of people are unwanted by any political community, and in which sheer numbers help promote the kind of abstract thinking necessary to consider the unthinkable. In such a world, radical evil has not exactly become banal. It has, however, become a permanent possibility of modern political life. In the words of Primo Levi, "it happened, therefore it can happen again."

CHAPTER TWO

Conscience, the Banality of Evil, and the Idea of a Representative Perpetrator

IN *Hitler's Willing Executioners* Daniel Goldhagen sets out to debunk several "conventional explanations" of the motives behind the actions of those he calls the "foot soldiers" of the Holocaust. Goldhagen writes that "the notions that the perpetrators contributed to genocide because they were coerced, because they were unthinking, obedient executioners of state orders, because of social psychological pressure, because of prospects of personal advancement, or because they did not comprehend or feel responsible for what they were doing" are "untenable."[1] His lengthy analysis of the individuals involved in killing Jews in the Police Battalions, the work camps, and the death marches isolates a virulent, racial antisemitism as the necessary and sufficient condition for the willful and enthusiastic participation of these "ordinary Germans" in the Nazis' genocidal project.

For the nonspecialist American reader, this catalog of "conventional explanations" is perplexing. Conventional for whom?, one is tempted to ask. Certainly the predominant American image of the perpetrators over the last fifty years has not been one of coerced or reluctant participants. Goldhagen's thesis that German culture was characterized by a deeply rooted, "eliminationist" form of antisemitism, one easily channeled into the exterminationist project of the Nazis, represents the "commonsense" American view of Germans of this period, a view expressed in countless books, movies, and television shows. That virtually all Germans were, in effect, Nazis; that they were enthusiastic supporters of the most irrational and hateful aspects of the Third Reich; that the vast majority harbored a tremendous "latent" hatred of the Jews activated by Hitler and the regime: these have been commonplaces for generations of Americans.

The fact that Goldhagen's central thesis resonates strongly with the clichés of American popular culture has absolutely no bearing on whether or not it is true. But it does raise the question of who, precisely, he thinks he is arguing against. Who is responsible for perpetuating the counter-images of the perpetrators he cites, images that might seem to exculpate the murderous conduct of countless "ordinary Germans"?

There are some obvious opponents, among them German historians anxious to minimize the extent of popular complicity with the Nazis and positivistically inclined social scientists who seek to reduce all phenomena, no matter how complex or unprecedented, to a fixed set of "economically rational" motivations. However, such authors have had next to no influence on the American image of the perpetrators. Yet Goldhagen clearly believes he is combating something bigger than chauvinist apologetics or forgotten social science. His *bête noire* is the idea that the perpetrators were "one-dimensional men," "thoughtless beings performing their tasks reluctantly."[2] It is *this* image of the perpetrators that Goldhagen believes has gained wide currency among American intellectuals, and it is one he wants to demolish. No doubt is left as to who the culprit is: "the person most responsible for this image," Goldhagen writes, "is, of course, Hannah Arendt."[3]

Hitler's Willing Executioners is, then, at least partly intended as a refutation of Arendt's *Eichmann in Jerusalem*. It can be seen, without too much violence, as the latest installment in the controversy surrounding the Eichmann book. Like many contributions to this controversy, it is premised on a substantial misunderstanding of what Arendt has to say in her "trial report." Goldhagen assumes that, like himself, Arendt was trying to provide a global account of the perpetrators' motivations; that she was engaged in the project of historical and sociological explanation of the motives driving the typical (or what I will call "representative") perpetrator.

Arendt was engaged in no such endeavor. As she explained in her 1971 essay, "Thinking and Moral Considerations," her notion of the "banality of evil" was no pithy attempt at characterizing either the Holocaust or the actions and motivations of the perpetrators in general. It was, rather, a descriptive concept she was "put into possession of" when confronted by Eichmann in the flesh at his 1961 trial in Jerusalem. It was, in other words, the product of her *judgment of a particular*—Eichmann. From this reflective judgment (to use Kant's terminology) she drew the following conclusion: extreme wickedness, pathology, or ideological conviction are not necessary for an individual to aid the performance of *infinite* evil.[4] It was Eich-

mann's "extraordinary shallowness," his one distinguishing characteristic, which led Arendt to name an evil that required neither exceptional wickedness nor depravity, but only a profound lack of
thought and judgment. "The banality of evil" named *Eichmann's*
evil, not the evil of the perpetrators or the Holocaust in general.[5]

Yet Goldhagen's indictment cannot be dismissed so easily, if only
because the phrase "banality of evil" lends itself to generalization
and misunderstanding. However Arendt initially intended it, many
of her readers—particularly young Americans confronted by an immoral Vietnam war set in motion by liberal technocrats—found it
all too easy to expand her concept, to the point where it became
reflexive to identify moral horror with the actions of faceless bureaucrats.[6] From this generalization it was but a small step to retrospective projection onto the Nazi machinery of death, a machinery
increasingly viewed as an instance of instrumental rationality run
amock. Modernity, it seemed, not German culture, lay behind both
the bureaucracies of murder and the death factories.[7] It must be
acknowledged that Arendt gave impetus to this tendency by referring to "administrative massacres" and "a new type of criminal" in
the Eichmann book, as well as by extending her characterization of
Eichmann's evil to evil as such in her famous 1963 exchange of letters with Gershom Scholem.[8]

Any adequate account of the dynamics of the Nazi extermination
of European Jewry obviously needs to take account of the dimensions of both culture and modernization. To isolate the latter is to
turn Auschwitz into a metaphor for the underside of modernity; to
focus strictly on the former (as Goldhagen does) is to reduce something unprecedented both in scale and execution to the cultural peculiarities of a particularly irrational tribe, the Germans.[9]

For better or worse, the debate about the Holocaust has been
defined by these two poles, which are viewed by scholars as antithet-
ical. Studies of the perpetrators are invariably seen as lending support to one or the other thesis. Because Arendt was interested in
totalitarianism as a novel (and distinctively modern) political phenomenon, and because she was skeptical of "national character" as
an explanatory category, she appeared to be wedded to what social
scientists and historians call a "structural" account of the extermination, one that radically downplayed the role of culture as a causal
factor.[10]

This point has recently been underlined by Richard Wolin, who draws a straight line from Arendt's "functionalist," quasi-Tocquevillian account of the "disaggregated masses" in *The Origins of Totalitarianism* to her portrait of the "thoughtless," "banal" Adolf Eichmann.[11] According to Wolin, the logical conclusion of such an approach is that "the Holocaust could have happened anywhere."[12] Similarly, we might say the implication of Arendt's focus on Eichmann's banality was that he could have been anyone. And this, indeed, is how "the banality of evil" is often interpreted.[13] While mistaken, this interpretation seems a permissible extension of Arendt's thesis that the "great criminal of the twentieth century" was no group of political extremists, but rather the ordinary man who was willing to adapt his conduct to the most murderous extremes, if only in order to provide for his family.[14]

Considerations such as these, combined with the bitter aftertaste of the *Eichmann* controversy itself, have understandably led some to argue that the "banality of evil" thesis is not the heart of the book, that its moral core lies elsewhere.[15] Seyla Benhabib, for example, would prefer to focus our attention on Arendt's use of the category of "crimes against humanity" and the way she attempts to do justice to both the universal claims of human dignity and the particularity of the people the Nazis attempted to exterminate.[16]

Should we follow Benhabib and try to locate a new and different center for *Eichmann in Jerusalem?* I think to do so would be a mistake. The "banality of evil" is an admittedly difficult idea, one open to gross misinterpretation. It is, however, Arendt's central idea. And, as the *Eichmann* controversy proved beyond any doubt, the responsibility for much of the misunderstanding lay with Arendt's audience rather than with her condensed mode of expression.

This chapter sets aside popular and scholarly misconceptions in order to focus on Arendt's central theme: the problem of Eichmann's *conscience*. I unpack the idea of the "banality of evil" in light of this theme. Specifically, I address the dimension of its particularity as a judgment of Eichmann and the related but distinct use Arendt makes of it in reflecting on the nature of evil. It is the failure to distinguish between these two dimensions—the dimension of *judgment* and the dimension of *philosophical reflection* on the nature of evil—which accounts for much of the confusion surrounding the "banality of evil." I then turn, briefly, to the question of what it means to delineate a "representative" perpetrator, an ideal type of the exterminators. What is at stake in offering such portraits, and why does Arendt explicitly demur from this task? What can we learn from the lack of communication between *Eichmann in Jerusalem* and *Hitler's Willing Executioners*?

. . . . .

If there is one thing which unites both defenders and detractors of *Eichmann in Jerusalem*, it is the view that Arendt's tone leaves much to be desired. From Scholem and Walter Laqueur to Benhabib and Elisabeth Young-Bruehl, critics both hostile and sympathetic have zeroed in on the harsh, imperious, and ironic voice she adopts.[17] Twenty years ago Laqueur suggested that Arendt "was attacked [in the controversy] not so much for what she said, but for how she said it." More recently, Benhabib has drawn our attention to what she calls Arendt's "astonishing lack of perspective, balance of judgment and judicious expression."[18]

Given this critical unanimity, it is important to remember what drove Arendt to write as she did. The harshly critical opening pages of *Eichmann* flow from Arendt's strong disapproval of the Israeli government's use of the Eichmann trial as an pedagogical opportunity, one designed to teach young Israelis (in the words of Prime Minister David Ben-Gurion) "the most tragic facts in world history," and to do so in such a way that they would imbibe the lesson that "Jews are not sheep to be slaughtered but a people who can hit back. . . ."[19] For Arendt, Ben-Gurion's educational agenda converted the Eichmann case into a "show trial" in which the primary focus was not on the dispensation of justice for deeds performed by an individual, but rather on the sufferings of Jews at the hands of the Nazis and, indeed, throughout history.[20] However imperative this educational mission, the courtroom was, in Arendt's eyes, the wrong place to pursue it; yet the view of the trial as a pedagogical opportunity too good to miss shaped the prosecution's presentation from start to finish.[21]

Arendt's tone reflected this clash of the claims of justice with those of political education. Her criticism of Ben-Gurion and the lead prosecutor, Gideon Hausner, arose from her sense of what justice demands in a criminal proceeding, namely, a strict and unvarying focus on the *deeds of the perpetrator*.[22] As Arendt wrote, "On trial

43

[were] his deeds, not the sufferings of the Jews, not the German people or mankind, not even anti-Semitism and racism."[23] Her "Epilogue" emphasizes this point: "The purpose of a trial is to render justice, and nothing else; even the noblest of ulterior purposes . . . can only detract from the law's main business: to weigh the charges brought against the accused, to render judgment, and to mete out due punishment."[24]

From the beginning, then, Arendt's focus in *Eichmann in Jerusalem* was on the particular: Adolf Eichmann and *his* deeds. Such a strict focus was made even more urgent thanks to the prosecution's dubious claim that Eichmann was in charge of virtually all aspects of the deportation and extermination process, in both Western and Eastern Europe. While Arendt fully endorsed the judges' guilty verdict, she felt that Eichmann should hang *for what he had done* (which was bad enough), and not for an imagined comprehensive authority for every aspect of the Final Solution, from planning to execution.[25] Her tone strikes the reader as imperious because she identified herself so completely with the demands of justice in a case where justice seemed, to many, either transindividual or a matter of secondary importance (at least when compared to the need to educate Israeli and world opinion on the nature and extent of the Holocaust). As Arendt repeatedly emphasized, *Eichmann in Jerusalem* was a "trial report" devoted to the motives and deeds of an individual, and not (as so many have assumed) an abbreviated history of the Holocaust or an account of the motivations of the perpetrators en masse.[26]

It is in this context that the central moral, legal, and philosophical questions of the trial arose. For once the cliché of a demon or psychopath was shattered by the sheer unmonstrous presence of the defendant, the whole question of Eichmann's motives in carrying out his murderous duties became complicated indeed. The criminal indictment against Eichmann implied that "not only had he acted on purpose" in transporting so many Jews to their deaths, but that he had done so "out of base motives and in full knowledge of the criminal nature of his deeds."[27] Yet Eichmann, whose "normality" had been attested to by more than a few psychiatrists, insisted that what he had done was no crime at the time. Moreover, he was certain that he was no "dirty bastard" in the depths of his heart, nor did he think that he harbored a fanatical hatred of the Jews. Even more perplexing was how he remembered "perfectly well that he would have had a bad conscience only if he had not done what he had been ordered to do—to ship millions of men, women, and children to their death with great zeal and the most meticulous care. ”[28]

Nobody at the trial, including the judges, chose to believe Eichmann's self-presentation as a law-abiding citizen, free of fanatical hatred, one who was simply unaware of the criminal nature of his actions. As Arendt put it:

> The prosecutor did not believe him, because that was not his job. . . . And the judges did not believe him, because they were too good, and perhaps also too conscious of the very foundations of their profession, to admit that an average, "normal" person, neither feeble-minded nor indoctrinated nor cynical, could be *perfectly incapable of telling right from wrong*. They preferred to conclude from occasional lies that he was a liar—and missed the greatest moral and even legal challenge of the whole case. Their case rested on the assumption that the defendant, like all "normal persons," must have been aware of the criminal nature of his acts, and Eichmann was indeed normal insofar as he was "no exception within the Nazi regime." However, under the conditions of the Third Reich only "exceptions" could be expected to act "normally." This simple truth of the matter created a dilemma for the judges which they could neither resolve nor escape.[29]

The "dilemma" Arendt refers to was not the *absence* of conscience; rather, it was the fact that Eichmann's conscience did not function in the expected manner since it was based on a conflation of *morality* with *legality*. As a result, he was troubled only by the temptation to *do good*, that is, to disregard his *duty* under the laws of a criminal regime and "be soft."

The moral and legal dilemma, then, was how to rethink and preserve the concept of criminal responsibility in instances where conscience fails—not because of a stronger will to wickedness or a kind of moral "insanity," but because its content has become identified with "the duties of a law-abiding citizen." All the controversy surrounding the Eichmann book has served to obscure what it is, in fact, about: the fate of conscience as a moral faculty in the midst of a generalized "moral collapse" such as the one brought about by the Nazi regime. Eichmann's case demonstrated how conscience, in such a context, is perverted: it no longer tells individuals what is right and what is wrong. But neither is it totally silenced, for it continues to tell people like Eichmann what their "duty" is.

Elisabeth Young-Bruehl is, then, only half right when she states that "inability to judge and refusal to judge were [Arendt's] themes in *Eichmann in Jerusalem*."[30] In fact, Arendt's primary theme is the inadequacy of conscience as it has been traditionally (and popularly) conceived, at least when it comes to understanding the "new type of criminal" represented by Eichmann. This theme makes *Eichmann in Jerusalem* a work of moral philosophy, at least implicitly.[31] It is by no means a merely theoretical concern, since it bears directly on the issue of how to preserve responsibility for actions in those circumstances where the struggle of conscience with "base motives" can no longer be honestly (or accurately) invoked. And, as the nature of political evil in the twentieth century demonstrates, such circumstances have become less and less exceptional.

. . . . .

Why was Eichmann "unable to tell right from wrong"? It is certainly not the case that Arendt viewed him as a thoughtless automaton, a robotlike cog in a bureaucratic machine prepared to supply the means to any end whatsoever.[32] Nor did she think that he lacked a conscience and was, therefore, if not a robot, a beast beyond the pale of a common humanity.[33] Rather, Arendt insisted upon Eichmann's humanity and his possession of a conscience, albeit one that failed to operate in the "normal" fashion expected by the judges and assumed by the law.[34] Only when we grasp the peculiar functioning of this conscience can we understand why Eichmann could not tell right from wrong, and why in Jerusalem he felt guilty in God's eyes, but not in humanity's.[35]

The central chapters of *Eichmann in Jerusalem* constitute what Arendt calls her "report on Eichmann's conscience."[36] Since Eichmann knew what he was doing (namely, delivering millions "to the butcher") and was in a position to judge the enormity of his deeds (since he had seen where the deportations terminated at Treblinka, Chelmno, and Minsk, and "was shocked out of his wits"), the only question remaining was whether the killing of Jews had gone against his conscience.[37] From a legal standpoint, the first two factors were sufficient to warrant capital punishment. But it was the moral question, the question of Eichmann's conscience, which attracted Arendt's most intense interest and led her to the idea of the banality of evil.

Arendt recounts how, in September 1941, Eichmann directed his first shipment of twenty thousand Jews from the Rhineland and five thousand Gypsies not to Russian territory (where they would have been immediately shot by the *Einsatzgruppen*, the special mobile killing squads), but rather to the Lodz ghetto where, despite appalling conditions, they would not be summarily executed. This decision displayed an unusual degree of initiative for Eichmann, and wound up causing him a fair amount of grief. Three weeks later, at a meeting in Prague called by Reinhard Heydrich (the real "architect of the Final Solution"), Eichmann proposed using the camps in which Russian Communists were detained for extermination of the Jews also. Arendt sees these two episodes as indicating just "how long it takes an *average* person to overcome his innate repugnance to crime."[38] She concludes her brief account: "we are [now] perhaps in a position to answer Judge Landau's question—the question uppermost in the minds of nearly everyone who followed the trial—of whether the accused had a conscience: yes, he had a conscience, and his conscience functioned in the expected way for about four weeks, whereupon it began to function the other way round."[39]

Admittedly, during the brief phase where Eichmann's conscience functioned in the expected way, it functioned "within rather odd limits." Untroubled by the idea that the *Einsatzgruppen* were exterminating Polish Jews, his conscience rebelled "at the idea that German Jews were being murdered."[40] It was one thing to butcher the "animalized hordes" of "the East," quite another to murder people "from our own cultural milieu."[41] However repellent we find such an attitude, the September 1941 incident nevertheless provided important evidence of a conscience and an "innate repugnance to crime."

How was Eichmann able to overcome this repugnance so quickly, and how was his conscience quieted? Bracketing the supposition of a fanatical antisemitism, the normative legitimation of murder was, for an individual like Eichmann, a function of what "respectable society" endorses or allows. Thus, in Eichmann's mind, the decisive turning point was the Wansee Conference (January 1942), Heydrich's convocation of representatives from various ministries and the Civil Service, whose active cooperation was essential to carrying out the Final Solution. According to Eichmann (who served as secretary at the meeting), Heydrich had expected the greatest difficulties in persuading those assembled of the need for a "radical" solution to the "Jewish question." However, the proposed program of extermination was greeted with "extraordinary enthusiasm" by all in attendance. For Eichmann, it was "an unforgettable day." Arendt writes:

> Although he had been doing his best right along to help with the Final Solution, he had still harbored some doubts about "such a bloody solution through violence," and these doubts had now been dispelled. "Here now, during this conference, the most prominent people had spoken, the Popes of the Third Reich." Now he could see with his own eyes and hear with his own ears that not only Hitler, not only Heydrich . . . not just the S.S. or the Party, but the elite of the good old Civil Service were vying and fighting with each other for the honor of taking the lead in these "bloody" matters. "At that moment, I sensed a kind of Pontius Pilate feeling, for I felt free of all guilt." *Who was he to judge?* Who was he "to have [his] own thoughts in this matter"?[42]

Confronted with the enthusiastic response of the "best" people, the remnants of Eichmann's "crisis of conscience" quickly disappeared: "As Eichmann told it, the most potent factor in the soothing of his own conscience was the simple fact that he could see no one, no one at all, who was actually against the Final Solution."[43] This is not to say, as Goldhagen implies, that German society was so uniformly and deeply antisemitic that no one was opposed on principled, moral grounds. But those who were opposed were few and, for the most part, silent. Even when Eichmann came into contact with Pastor Heinrich Gruber, a man of principle who represented the "other Germany," he encountered no vocal opposition to the general policy of deportation. As Eichmann recalled, "He [Gruber] came to me and sought the alleviation of suffering, but did not actually object to the performance of my duties as such."[44] As Arendt points out, pleaders of special cases like Gruber, who spoke on behalf of Jewish war veterans, had the effect of giving legitimacy to the rule under which Eichmann operated.

Thus it was that Eichmann could honestly claim, despite the incredulity of the prosecution, that "there were no voices from the outside to arouse his conscience" once it had been set at ease by the unanimous agreement of his social betters. Eichmann, according to Arendt, "did not need to 'close his ears to the voice of conscience,' as the judgment has it, not because he had none, but because his conscience spoke with a 'respectable voice,' with the voice of respectable society around him."[45]

. . . . .

This fact takes us to the heart of Arendt's analysis of the problem posed by Eichmann's conscience, as well as underlining important points of agreement with Goldhagen's very different explanatory project. Contrary to what Goldhagen implies when he attacks the thesis that the perpetrators were "one-dimensional men, performing their tasks reluctantly," Arendt emphasizes the zeal with which Eichmann carried out his duties, as well as the fact that German society as a whole tended to overwhelmingly support Hitler.[46] But where Goldhagen turns to a deeply ingrained cultural antisemitism in his search for an adequate causal explanation, Arendt focuses on "the moral debacle of a whole nation" that readily accepted the new set of values propounded by the Nazis.[47] The ease with which Eichmann's conscience was assuaged can be understood only in the context of the "totality of the moral collapse the Nazis caused"—not only in Germany, but in "respectable society" across Europe.[48]

Understanding and judging an individual like Eichmann, then, required resisting the temptation to view his deeds as the expression of a demonic or fanatically antisemitic essence, while taking seriously his acknowledgment of what he had done *and* his insistence that his deeds were not criminal at the time. It also required openness to the possibility that motivation played a far lesser role in this case than either criminal law or Goldhagen's version of *Verstehen* social science can comfortably acknowledge. For both the law and social science assume that the soldier who obeys an obviously criminal order must be driven by motivational forces that overrule his ordinary experience of lawfulness (and the morality inherent in it). The prosecutors in Jerusalem and Goldhagen would agree that only a fanatical antisemitism could possibly account for Eichmann's failure to recognize the "black flag" flying over *his* orders.

For Arendt, on the other hand, it was precisely Eichmann's experience of lawfulness and his deep internalization of "the duties of a law-abiding citizen" which accounted for his conscientious performance of his duties as well as his odd contention that he was not guilty "in the sense of the indictment."[49] As far as Eichmann was concerned—and this point is absolutely crucial if we are to understand Arendt's "report"—he had not simply followed orders, he had also obeyed *the law*.[50]

Grasping this point fully demands that we follow Arendt in attending to one of the more bizarre moments in the trial, namely Eichmann's sudden and emphatic declaration that he had "lived his whole life according to Kant's moral precepts, and especially according to a Kantian definition of duty."[51] This assertion, so patently ludicrous on the surface, becomes more plausible when we understand the foreshortened version of Kant Eichmann had in mind, and it goes a long way to illuminating the peculiar functioning of his conscience.

As Arendt relates, Eichmann surprised everyone at the trial by coming up with a relatively correct formulation of Kant's Categorical Imperative: "I meant by my remark about Kant that the principle of my will must always be such that it can become the principle of general laws."[52] He added that he had read Kant's *Critique of Practical Reason* and explained that he had known that "from the moment he was charged with carrying out the Final Solution he had ceased to live according to Kantian principles. . . ."[53] Distressed at this, he had consoled himself with the thought that he was no longer "master of his own deeds."

This awareness, not only of Kantian moral principles but of his own lapse from them, is strange enough. But Arendt points out how, in fact, Eichmann had remained consistent and "acted from duty" during the implementation of the Final Solution:

> What he [Eichmann] had failed to point out in court was that in this "period of crimes legalized by the state," as he himself now called it, he had not simply dismissed the Kantian formula as no longer applicable, he had distorted it to read: Act as if the principle of your actions were the same as that of the legislator or of the law of the land. . . .[54]

To be sure, such a distortion goes against the spirit of Kant, who had emphasized how every man, as the possessor of "practical reason," is a moral legislator, rather than a mere subject of pregiven duties. Yet Eichmann's distortion *did* agree with what "he himself had called the version of Kant 'for the household use of the little man:'" "In this household use, all that is left of Kant's spirit is the demand that a man do more than obey the law, that he go beyond the mere call of obedience and identify his own will with the principle behind the law—the source from which the law sprang. In Kant's philosophy, that source was practical reason; in Eichmann's household use of him, it was the will of the Führer."[55]

In a regime where the will of the Führer was indeed, both theoretically and practically, the source of law, this "Kantian" reification of duty and law-abidingness was morally fatal. Eichmann was a law-abiding citizen of a regime which had made murder into a law, a legal (and thus "moral") obligation. It is this conflation of moral duty with law-abidingness which accounts for the "peculiar functioning" of his conscience before and after the Wansee Conference. It also accounts for "the uncompromising attitude toward the performance of his duties" in the last year of the war, when he did his best to undercut what he viewed as Himmler's "criminal orders" to halt the Final Solution.[56]

It was Eichmann's very strictness in cleaving to the law of the land that the judges in Jerusalem took as definitive proof of his anti-semitic fanaticism. As a result, "they never came to understand him," since "the very uncomfortable truth of the matter probably was that it was not his fanaticism but *his very conscience* that prompted him to adopt his uncompromising attitude during the last year of the war."[57] Arendt goes on to point out how Eichmann's behavior during this period bears an uncomfortable resemblance to the soldier who, acting in a normal legal order, "refuses to carry out orders that run counter to his ordinary experience of lawfulness. . . ."[58] For Eichmann, the law-abiding citizen par excellence, the "ordinary experience" of lawfulness demanded that he do everything in his power to subvert Himmler's "criminal" orders, so that the law—the order for the Final Solution—would be followed till the very end.

. . . . .

When Arendt writes of "a new type of criminal," then, she does not have in mind cogs in a bureaucratic machine, but individuals who, like Eichmann, willingly participate in crimes legalized by the state.[59] Like Goldhagen, she vehemently repudiates the "cog theory" when it comes to judging the extent of any perpetrator's responsibility for his actions.[60] But at the same time she draws our attention to the morally most puzzling aspect of the case, the fact that Eichmann "had no motives at all," that "he *merely*, to put the matter colloquially, *never realized what he was doing*."[61]

This striking formulation must be clarified. Arendt leaves no doubt that Eichmann knew what he was doing in *factual terms*, namely, transporting Jews "to the butcher."[62] Yet he was unable to view these actions as criminal and (hence) as wrong. This was possible because his conscience and moral sensibility were bounded entirely by law and the opinions of "respectable society." In the context of the Third Reich, neither law nor "respectable" opinion could compensate for the lack of moral imagination and the capacity to think and judge for oneself. "To fall back on the unequivocal voice of conscience" in such a situation "not only begs the question, it signals a deliberate refusal to take notice of the central moral, legal and political phenomena of our century."[63]

The "new type of criminal" represented by Eichmann is neither a party fanatic nor an indoctrinated robot. Rather, he is the individual who participates willingly in the activities of a criminal regime, while viewing himself as insulated from any and all responsibility for his actions by both organizational structure and the law. Through such self-deception (and the "remoteness from reality" it promotes), an individual can successfully avoid ever confronting the question of the morality of his actions. As the case of Eichmann amply demonstrates, where "a law is a law"—where, in other words, thoughtlessness reigns—the faculties of judgment and moral imagination atrophy and then disappear.[64]

The "banality of evil" refers to *this* thoughtlessness, *this* remoteness, *this* lack of motive and "will to prove a villain." Eichmann's deeds show how such self-deception and lack of judgment "can wreak more havoc than all the evil instincts taken together which, perhaps, are inherent in man. . . ." This, according to Arendt, "was in fact the lesson one could learn in Jerusalem."[65] Where the regime is criminal, motives are superfluous and a demonic character unnecessary: only mendacity and conformity to the law are required. Hence the "paradox" of a banal agent whose deeds manifested extreme evil.

. . . . .

Arendt's points about Eichmann's "remoteness from reality" and his "thoughtlessness" flow from her observation of him at the trial, but obviously have a wider province. She sees the former as characteristic not only of Eichmann, but of German society at large.[66] On the other hand, thoughtlessness—the inability to judge—can be found anywhere. It reflects the broader "crisis in judgment" Arendt sees affecting modern Western culture. The "moral collapse of respectable society"—not only in Germany, but in Europe as a whole—pointed to the sad fact that morality had decayed to a mere set of customs.[67] This set of habits proved eminently exchangeable when the Nazis came along with their "new values." Eichmann's thoughtlessness, his adaptability to new rules and new values, was therefore hardly an isolated phenomenon. It is in this sense—and only in this sense—that Arendt views him as typical or representative:

> The trouble with Eichmann was precisely that so many were like him, and that the many were neither perverted or sadistic, that they were, and still are, terribly and terrifyingly normal. From the standpoint of our legal institutions and our moral standards of judgment, this normality was much more terrifying than all the atrocities put together . . . for it implied . . . that this new type of criminal . . . commits his crimes under circumstances that make it well-nigh impossible for him to know or feel that he is doing wrong.[68]

In this passage Arendt confronts the "central legal, moral, and political phenomena of our century," along with their greatest philosophical puzzle. *Contra* Goldhagen's and Wolin's assumptions, her point is not that average individuals have become "disaggregated" from their place in the class structure, transformed into "mass men" and made susceptible to the hateful lies of totalitarian ideology.[69] Rather, she underlines the fact that criminal regimes like Nazi Germany arise; that they are able to exploit people's fears and mobilize their energies and support, without resorting to brainwashing; that such regimes are thereby able to confer upon their laws and policies an *apparent* legitimacy, one which seems real enough in the eyes of their subjects.

In such situations, it is self-deluding to expect either the voice of conscience or traditional moral yardsticks to pick up the slack or present a genuine obstacle to the momentum of the regime. The Holocaust could not have happened "anywhere"; but neither could it have happened unless the vast majority of "ordinary" Germans—nonsadists and nonfanatics—felt that, on balance, the regime's direction and basic policies were morally justifiable. In such circumstances, it may well be impossible for the "new type of criminal" to "know or feel that he is doing wrong."[70] The supposition of a God-given moral compass or "practical reason" that can compensate for the lack of a developed faculty of moral judgment is clearly not tenable. It was this possibility which Arendt insisted we face squarely,

53

without the false comfort of an "inner voice" that operates the same way in all people.

The Holocaust was a unique historical event. But if recent events in Bosnia, Rwanda, and the Congo prove anything, it is the ease with which governments can manipulate the language of ethnic and cultural survival to the point where genocide is perceived by the perpetrators as a necessary act of self-defense. And this, as Goldhagen shows, is how ordinary Germans involved in the extermination tended to view their activities. The presence of sadists and fanatics should not blind us to the fact that the "new type of criminal"—one who is without base motives, but is unable to tell right from wrong—is a thriving species, unlikely to depart the stage of history anytime soon.

The political evil of the twentieth century could not have been performed without the enlistment of thousands, indeed millions, of normal individuals. Nor could it have occurred without a degree of institutional cooperation, which spread complicity throughout society. These basic facts seem to threaten the very idea of moral responsibility for political evil, despite the various tribunals for "war crimes." Eichmann's normality is "terrifying" not only because it confronts us with the fact that monsters are not necessary for extreme evil, but also because it highlights the "human, all too human" tendency to perform one's function and pass the buck—even in the most extreme of circumstances.

It is obviously mistaken to maintain that Eichmann, the transporter of millions of Jews to the butcher, "could have been anyone," or that there is a little "Eichmann in us all." As Arendt emphasizes, Eichmann's cultural context was unique, and the level of his self-deception and thoughtlessness exceptional, even by German standards. He is representative insofar as he stands for the contribution "normal" men have made to political evil and moral horror in the twentieth century. But he is hardly "typical" of the perpetrators, since these included (as Arendt notes repeatedly) fanatics, sadists, thugs and brutes, as well as "desk murderers."[71]

. . . . .

It was Eichmann's thoughtless "normality" that led Arendt to reflect on broader philosophical issues, such as the nature of evil and the role thinking plays in preventing moral catastrophes for the individual. The reader familiar only with her updated brand of civic republicanism will no doubt be astonished by Arendt's appreciation of the moral courage manifest in simple nonparticipation. In "Personal Responsibility Under Dictatorship" (1964) and "Thinking and Moral Considerations" (1971), she stressed the importance of *withdrawal* from public life where continued participation—even if it meant only doing one's job—entailed complicity with evil. There are certain conditions where only the *refusal* of political responsibility saves one from moral and legal responsibility for crime, conditions like the Nazi regime where "every moral act was illegal and every legal act was a crime."[72] Such refusal rests upon a clear recognition of the moral stakes, a perception Arendt thought far more likely to occur among those who followed their own thought and judgment in moral matters rather than rules or traditional values. [73]

This kind of thoughtfulness—the ability to make moral judgments without a banister or preconceived categories—is, unfortunately, all too rare, even if it does not depend upon superlative gifts of intelligence or character. It depends upon a kind of courage or, as Arendt puts it, a kind of arrogance: the arrogance of judging for oneself, of refusing *authority* in matters of judgment.[74] To be a "law-abiding citizen" under all circumstances, to reify duty as a moral category, is to reject *a priori* the arrogance necessary for independent judgment and (ultimately) morality itself.

This brings us to the issue of how her observation of Eichmann led Arendt to revise her conception of evil. As I have noted, her philosophical reflections on the nature of evil flowed from, but were not part of, Arendt's trial report. Thus, when she wrote in *Eichmann in Jerusalem* of "the fearsome, word-and-thought-defying *banality of evil*," she was speaking of something "strictly factual . . . a phenomenon which stared one in the face at the trial."[75] It was in response to Scholem's criticism that the "banality of evil" was a mere "slogan" or "catchword," inferior to the concept of "radical evil" she deployed in *The Origins of Totalitarianism*, that Arendt jumped to the philosophical level, defending "the banality of evil" as a concept relevant to "moral philosophy or political ethics" (Scholem) and not just to the description of Eichmann.[76] What she says is this:

> You are quite right: I changed my mind and do no longer speak of "radical evil". . . . It is indeed my opinion now that evil is never "radical," that it is only extreme, and that it possesses neither depth nor any

demonic dimension. It can overgrow and lay waste the world precisely because it spreads like a fungus on the surface. It is "thought-defying," as I said, because thought tries to reach some depth, to go to the roots, and the moment it concerns itself with evil, it is frustrated because there is nothing. That is its "banality." Only the good has depth and can be radical.[77]

Several recent commentators have tried to diminish the force of this "change of mind," arguing, for example, that the notion of "radical evil" is compatible with that of the "banality of evil," or that, under totalitarianism, radical evil becomes banal, a routine happening.[78] It is certainly possible to reconcile the two notions, particularly if one retains "radical evil" as the *philosophical* conceptualization of the evil of totalitarianism or the Holocaust, supplementing it with the "banality of evil" as a *descriptive* conceptualization of "human, all too human" perpetrators like Eichmann.[79] But such a strategy becomes far less plausible if we remain, with Arendt, at the level of philosophical reflection on the nature of evil. Then there *really is* a contradiction—or at least a tension—between the notions of "radical" and "banal" evil. It is the nature of this tension, and Arendt's reasons for abandoning her previous (and powerful) conceptualization of evil, that I now want to consider.

Why did Arendt respond to Scholem as she did? What motivated her to abandon the description of totalitarian evil as "radical" for the far more elusive view that evil *as such is never radical*, but "banal"? What, in short, drove her to court even more violent misunderstanding by elevating her descriptive judgment of Eichmann to the level of a philosophical generalization?

There are no simple answers to these questions. It doesn't help that Arendt never wrote the philosophical consideration of evil she gestured at in her reply to Scholem.[80] We can, however, begin to outline an answer from remarks scattered throughout her work and correspondence, remarks which show a clear trajectory away from the idea that an abysslike evil requires an author (human or trans-human) of similar depth and proportion.

One aspect of Arendt's "sea-change" on the question of evil had to do with her desire to bring the deeds of the perpetrators within the horizon of human judgment and human law. As she wrote when explaining her turnabout: "There exists a widespread theory, to which I also contributed, that these crimes defy the possibility of human judgment and explode the frame of our legal institutions."[81] Another was tied to the *cura posterior* that the Eichmann trial represented for her, a way of escaping the unbearable thought that behind the death factories there stood an evil so outsized, so monstrous, that *this* attempt to destroy the Jewish people would surely be followed by another, perhaps even grander, manifestation of the same diabolical forces.[82] Confronted by the banality of Eichmann, Arendt was released, after twenty years, from the nightmare of such an evil.

These aspects, however, do not reach the philosophical heart of the matter, which Arendt articulated clearly only in a 1969 letter to Kenneth Thompson of the Rockefeller Foundation. What was at stake, she wrote, is "How can we approach the problem of evil in an entirely secular setting?"[83] She had broached the same theme much earlier in a 1945 review of Denis de Rougemont's *The Devil's Share*, which took him to task for raising the problem of evil in recent European history and then "fleeing reality" by writing about the Devil.[84] De Rougemont had, in Arendt's judgment, failed to face "the music of man's genuine capacity for evil," a capacity that cannot be reduced to an original sinfulness or resolved into a teleology of good and evil, one in which the ultimate triumph of the good is divinely guaranteed.

I believe that Arendt's change of mind on the nature of evil reflected her own awareness that the concept of "radical evil" (at least as she had deployed it in *The Origins of Totalitarianism*) was irreducibly theological. Evil can be radical, can have metaphysical depth and reality, only within a theological framework that posits transhuman forces working for good or evil. In describing the evil represented by the concentration camps as "radical" rather than extreme, Arendt succumbed to the idea that totalitarianism expressed the inner nihilistic currents of the modern age, currents that had been destroying human dignity for some time before they reached their logical *telos* in a system of total domination, one that treats millions of human beings as superfluous, as waste to be eliminated. Arendt's reading of the camps as the "essence" of the totalitarian system in *The Origins of Totalitarianism*, while enormously suggestive, hinges on a dubious (and quasi-Heideggerian) linearity, one in which nihilistic evil surpasses itself and comes to threaten the human status as such.[85] Thus, Arendt repeatedly speaks of the *aim* of totalitarianism as made manifest in the camps, as if there were an explicit *totalitarian project* designed to destroy both the concept and reality of humanity. This may, in fact, be the ultimate *significance* of this novel form of regime. Nevertheless, it is highly misleading to ascribe such metaphysical ambitions to the regimes themselves.[86]

We cannot understand Arendt's concept of radical evil unless we think in terms of such a "totalitarian project," one that radically accelerates the superfluousness of human beings in the modern, mass age. I suggest that Arendt rejected this concept when she realized that she had endowed totalitarian regimes with a Faustian grandeur (and metaphysical meaning) they hardly deserved. In so doing, she did not deny the possibility that evil can be "extreme," even "infinite." But she did deny the supposition that behind monstrous deeds there lies a monstrous or transhuman doer, a force or agency that transcends human individuals or which expresses some deep, subterranean current of the West. Arendt's political thinking as a whole takes no small cue from Nietzsche's declaration that "God is dead."[87] In *Eichmann in Jerusalem* and in her letter to Scholem, she showed herself ready to dispense with the Devil, ready to face the problem of evil in entirely secular terms.[88]

. . . . .

Eichmann in Jerusalem raises what Arendt called "the fundamental problem of postwar intellectual life in Europe"—the problem of evil—but it does so indirectly. Arendt focused narrowly on Eichmann and his deeds, deliberately excluding more general questions.[89] That she was misunderstood—that her adversaries took the subtitle of her "trial report" as a denial of the Holocaust's infinite evil—is not surprising. She failed to clarify sufficiently not only how the concept of the "banality of evil" was rooted in the particularity of Eichmann, but also what led her to generalize this notion—not with regard to the motivations of the perpetrators, but in her philosophical reflections on the nature of evil. As a result, her critics failed to grasp the distinction between the "banality of evil" considered as a *reflective judgment* and as a *philosophical thesis*.

But Arendt cannot be faulted, as Goldhagen charges, for presenting Eichmann, the "desk murderer," as the archetypal perpetrator. That so many, including Goldhagen, have read her as doing just that testifies to a deeply rooted need for a picture of the "representative perpetrator." I want to conclude with a few remarks on what lies behind this need.

Goldhagen is not entirely wrong in saying that Arendt was somehow "responsible" for the image of the perpetrators as "one-dimensional men, performing their tasks reluctantly." But the truth of his remark has nothing to do with what Arendt argued or described in *Eichmann in Jerusalem*; rather, it flows from the fact that so many of her (admiring) readers *desired* a generalizable portrait, one that could be applied across cultures.[90] The image of the perpetrator as faceless bureaucrat is one that readers anxious to highlight contemporary forms of authoritarian socialization created from their own (not particularly attentive) encounters with the book.

On the other hand, the image of the perpetrators drawn by Goldhagen—as "ordinary," that is to say, *representative*, Germans—reduces the dimensions of the Holocaust to the peculiarities of a national culture. It confirms the stereotypes of many American and European readers, enabling them to keep the idea of extreme political evil at arm's length ("genocide and concentration camps have nothing to do with people *like us*"). It also provides some younger Germans the morally questionable opportunity to take on guilt for deeds they did not commit.[91]

In the case of Arendt, the desire to turn Eichmann into a symbol of the "authoritarian personality" destroys the dimension of particularity which is the book's *raison d'être*. Arendt's focus on *this* man and his deeds is forgotten, the better to narcissistically worry about "the Eichmann in each one of us." In the case of *Hitler's Willing Executioners*—a book that *does* aim at supplying a portrait of the "representative" perpetrator—the idea that an eliminationist anti-semitism was the "common sense" of the vast majority of "ordinary Germans" offers a comforting distance. Goldhagen's opening anthropological analogy is all too apt: German society is presented as radically other, subject to modes of magical thinking which render it as remote to we heirs of the Enlightenment as a primitive Amazonian tribe.[92]

If *Eichmann in Jerusalem* has any relevance for the historiography of the Holocaust, it resides in its steadfast avoidance of this dialectic of too near and too far. The desire for a portrait of the "representative perpetrator" is understandable. Depending on one's mood, politics, or background, such a portrait can undermine complacency or provide reassurance in the face of unbearable fears. Yet this desire necessarily does violence to a complex subject matter, and it impedes, rather than aides, the work of understanding and judgment. This, I think, is the lesson of *Eichmann in Jerusalem*'s unremitting focus on the particular, a lesson available only to those who are able to read the book carefully, in a cool hour.

The Anxiety of Influence

ON ARENDT'S RELATIONSHIP TO HEIDEGGER

INTRODUCTION

The fact that Hannah Arendt was Martin Heidegger's student was never a secret. Nor was his philosophy's influence upon her analysis of totalitarianism and her thinking about politics. What *was* a secret, at least until the publication of Elisabeth Young-Bruehl's biography in 1982, was that she and Heidegger were lovers while Arendt was his student in Marburg during the period 1924–29 (she moved to Heidelberg to work with Karl Jaspers in 1926).[1]

Young-Bruehl's revelations raised some eyebrows, but they were set in the context of a remarkable life story, together with an account of Arendt's intellectual development and her primary contributions to political thought in the twentieth century. As a result, no controversy was engendered. Indeed, the overall effect of the revelation about the relationship with Heidegger was merely to make an already colorful life appear that much more dramatic.

Things took a sharply different turn in 1995, when Elzbieta Ettinger published her brief account of the relationship. Because Ettinger had been able to peruse the Arendt-Heidegger correspondence, which had been off limits to scholars for years, she could claim that something new was being revealed: the "fact" of Arendt's life-long, seemingly self-effacing devotion to Heidegger. According to Ettinger, this devotion led Arendt to become Heidegger's "agent" in the U.S. after the war, generating translations of his work and "whitewashing" the nature and extent of his complicity with the Nazis. Such, at least, were the conclusions Ettinger had drawn from materials which were finally published in German in 1998.[2]

Reviewers of Ettinger's book hostile to Arendt seized upon the slim reed of her psychologizing restatement of Young-Bruehl's basic facts, charging that Arendt was a German-Jewish intellectual snob, more in love with German *Geist* and its representative (Heidegger) than with "her own people," the Jews. Richard Wolin, writing in *The New Republic*, drew a dark parallel between Arendt's alleged exculpatory treatment of the "banal" Adolf Eichmann in *Eichmann in Jerusalem* and her supposed "exoneration" of Heidegger in her 1969 birthday tribute, "Martin Heidegger at Eighty." A debate about the damage to Arendt's moral and intellectual reputation spilled over into the popular press, with articles in *The New York Times*, *The Nation*, and *The Chronicle of Higher Education*, to name only the most prominent.

I will refrain from rehashing the details of the so-called "Hannah Arendt scandal." I do, however, want to challenge the primary idea which the controversy put into wide circulation, namely, that Arendt was a disciple of Heidegger, a thinker without any critical distance on the master's thought. This idea, the basis of Ettinger's account, helped revive the charge that Arendt was (in Wolin's phrase) a "left Heideggerian," a thinker as hostile to democracy and constitutional government as was her teacher. It also made plausible Ettinger's contention, amplified by Wolin, that a good deal of Arendt's energies in the 1950s and 1960s were devoted to restoring Heidegger's badly damaged reputation.

I cannot give a detailed biographical account of Arendt's distanced and often skeptical view of Heidegger the man (readers anxious for such an account will find Young-Bruehl a much more reliable guide to the ups and downs of their personal and intellectual relationship than Ettinger). What I propose to do in this chapter is provide an overview of the evolution of Arendt's critical view of Heidegger the thinker. This overview falls into two parts. First, I will look at Arendt's published assessments of Heidegger before and after 1950, the year of Arendt and Heidegger's supposedly complete reconciliation (if we are to believe Ettinger). Second, I will examine the two moments in Arendt's work where Heidegger's philosophical legacy is most strongly felt. These are *The Human Condition* (generally described as her most Heideggerian book) and the essay in which she allegedly exonerates Heidegger, "Martin Heidegger at Eighty."

What we find in these writings, and in her voluminous correspondence with Karl Jaspers, is a far more complicated and critical attitude toward Heidegger than Arendt's critics have allowed. *The Human Condition* is, in its own way, every bit as critical of Heidegger as it is of Plato or Marx. Similarly, "Martin Heidegger at Eighty" turns out to be less an exercise in apologetics than a rumination on the dangers of "extraordinary thinking." While Arendt took Heidegger seriously as a thinker (perhaps too seriously), she never approached his work or actions uncritically—even when she was paying tribute to his philosophical achievement.

BEFORE AND AFTER 1950

Absolutely central to both Ettinger's story and the moral judgment Wolin derives from it is the idea that Arendt's postwar meeting with Heidegger in 1950 led her to fall back under the personal spell of the "magician from Messkirch." From this point forward, we are told, her capacity to render objective judgments on either the man or the thought, let alone his Nazi involvement, ceased. As Ettinger puts it, in 1950 Arendt swiftly forgave Heidegger his sins, "not as much out of loyalty, compassion, or a sense of justice as out of her own need to save her pride and dignity."[3] Or, as Wolin puts it, "in 1950 her tone changed completely."[4] Gone was the bitter criticism of Heidegger found in her 1946 *Partisan Review* essay, "What Is *Existenz* Philosophy?" Its place was taken by a series of self-deluding apologetics, culminating in "Martin Heidegger at Eighty," where, Wolin tells us, Arendt "copped a plea on behalf of her embattled mentor."[5]

A survey of Arendt's writings and reflections on Heidegger during these years casts this tidy narrative of love, disillusionment, and renewed self-deception (not to mention intellectual self-sacrifice) in doubt. To be sure, Arendt is most acidly critical of Heidegger right after the war. However, the critical stance does not disappear after 1950; rather, it modulates, gaining substance, depth, and power. Beginning with the 1954 lecture on "Concern with Politics in Recent European Thought" and ending with the chapter-long Heidegger critique in the posthumously published *The Life of the Mind*, Arendt's public statements on Heidegger display what is, considering the circumstances, a remarkable impartiality. Her attitude toward Heidegger after 1950 is one of qualified respect for the work combined with a penetrating sense of the extent of his human failings and his political stupidity.

The *Partisan Review* essay is more accessible if we look first at Arendt's review of Max Weinreich's book, *Hitler's Professors*, also published in 1946. Weinreich's primary thesis was that "German

63

scholarship provided the ideas and techniques which led to and justified unparalleled slaughter." This is, as Arendt laconically put it, "a
highly controversial statement."[6] While contending that the "majority of German professors" fell in line "for the sake of their jobs,"
she singles out a few "outstanding scholars" who "did their utmost
to supply the Nazis with ideas and techniques."[7] Among these (including the legal theorist Carl Schmitt and the theologian Gerhard
Kittel) she counts "the existential philosopher Martin Heidegger."

Arendt criticizes Weinreich's book for concentrating on academic mediocrities, thereby diverting attention from these "outstanding" cases. At the same time, however, she notes that the Nazis
had remarkably little use for thinkers like Schmitt or Heidegger,
since they were far more interested in obtaining the veneer of
"scientificality" for their racial theories than they were in packaging
themselves as the latest installment of the *Weltgeist*. Anticipating her
analysis of the role ideology in *The Origins of Totalitarianism*, Arendt
writes:

> So while it is perfectly true that quite a few respectable German profes-
> sors volunteered their services to the Nazis, it is equally true—which
> was rather a shock to these gentlemen themselves—that the Nazis did
> not use their "ideas." *The Nazis had their own ideas*—what they needed
> were techniques and technicians with no ideas at all or educated from
> the beginning in only Nazi ideas. The scholars first put to one side by
> the Nazis as of relatively little use to them were old-fashioned national-
> ists like Heidegger, whose enthusiasm for the Third Reich was matched
> only by his glaring ignorance of what he was talking about.[8]

This paragraph articulates a perspective that Arendt adheres to with
remarkable consistency over the course of her career.[9] She holds
Heidegger and other "outstanding scholars" responsible for their
political choices, while questioning the notion that Heidegger's
ideas played even a minimal role in shaping or contributing to Nazi
ideology. This was, in her view, a vulgar idealist fantasy, one predicated on an almost total ignorance of the nature of the regime and
its leading ideas. To be sure, Heidegger, Schmitt, and others sought
to influence the regime, perhaps hoping to become its philosopher-
kings.[10] Yet such hopes revealed the enormous gap between the
mentality of an "old-fashioned nationalist" (Heidegger) anxious to
lead the leader in the cause of German renewal, and the reality of
Hitler's totalitarian mass movement. Arendt's phrase about Hei-

degger's enthusiasm in 1933 being matched only by "his glaring ignorance of what he was talking about" is thus hardly exculpatory.[11] It points to a kind of moral as well as political stupidity, to an *absence* of judgment for which the individual must be held accountable.

With these comments in mind, we can turn to "What Is *Existenz* Philosophy?" This is, as its title suggests, a mostly philosophical account of the currents in post-Kantian thought leading to the development of Heidegger's and Jaspers's existentialism. Arendt's ultimate concern in the essay is to contrast the "solipsistic" existentialism of Heidegger's *Being and Time* with Jaspers's focus on communication as the irreducible medium of the quest for truth and human freedom.

Arendt's critique of Heidegger, and her praise of Jaspers, are notable on a number of counts. First, she criticizes Heidegger for a kind of radical humanism, claiming that the "existential analytic" of *Being and Time* is actually philosophical idealism by other means. According to Arendt, Heidegger's turn to temporality as the "meaning of Being"—as the irreducible horizon through which human beings understand the is-ness of what is—leads him to focus on the negating or nihilating character of human existence. Where there is no preestablished harmony of thought and being (and Kant's critical philosophy had destroyed this illusion), and where the Being which I am not is irreducibly given, something I did not create—there the "nothingness" of human existence provides a medium in which such sheer facticity can be dissolved or negated. Arendt argues that the idea that "Being is really nothingness" has been of "inestimable value" to post-Kantian philosophy, since "proceeding from this idea, man can imagine that he stands in the same relationship to Being as the Creator stood before creating the world, which, as we know, was created *ex nihilo.*"[12] In addition to putting man into the traditional place of God, Arendt finds Heidegger guilty of a kind of ontological functionalism, one that reduces man to his modes of being or functions in the world.[13] Eschewing a normative conception of man such as we find in Kant, Heidegger gives an ontological description of the modes of being available to the abstract "Self." From Arendt's perspective, the descriptive thrust of Heidegger's fundamental ontology "dispenses with all those human characteristics that Kant provisionally defined as freedom, human dignity, and reason, that arise from human spontaneity, and that therefore are not phenomenologically demonstrable. . . . "[14] Or, to put it more straightforwardly, because Heidegger rejects any positing of a nature of man separate from his existence, he winds up denying human freedom and spontaneity. This, Arendt suggests, is the price paid for moving from an ideal or noumenal self to an existential or phenomenological "Self."

Taken together, these criticisms boil down to accusing Heidegger of radicalizing the already schizophrenic character of Kant's conception of the human subject. On the one hand, the God-like character of Heideggerian *Dasein* takes the Kantian notion of autonomy several steps further (just as the German Idealists had done); on the other, fundamental ontology "debases" man by reducing him not to his phenomenal existence (in the "mechanism of nature"), but to a conglomeration of "arbitrary" modes of being, which he has no way of ranking or choosing among.[15] Arendt underlines the paradoxical implications of her own critique when she writes that "apart from Nietzsche, . . . Heidegger's is the first absolutely and uncompromisingly this-worldly philosophy," immediately adding that Heidegger's authentic "Self" demands a virtual isolation from both the world and our fellow men: "The essential character of the Self is its absolute Self-ness, its radical separation from all its fellows."[16] It would be easy to accuse Arendt here of neglecting Heidegger's emphasis on being-with-others (*mitdasein*) as a structural characteristic of human existence. Indeed, Arendt minimizes the import of Heidegger's description of human being as "being-in-the-world," arguing that the worldly and intersubjective dimensions of the Heideggerian "Self" are consigned to the realm of inauthenticity, or fallenness (*Verfallenheit*). This is a controversial and somewhat slanted interpretation of *Being and Time*, one that Arendt will later modify. The moral-political point of her polemical exaggeration of tendencies in Heidegger's early philosophy is clarified by the following passage, where she plays the Heideggerian "Self" off the Kantian conception of man:

> What emerges from this absolute isolation is a concept of the Self as the total opposite of man. If since Kant the essence of man consisted in every single human being representing all of humanity and if since the French Revolution and the declaration of the rights of man it became integral to the concept of man that all of humanity could be debased or exalted in every individual, then the concept of self is a concept of man that leaves the individual existing independent of humanity and repre-

sentative of no one but himself—of nothing but his own nothingness.
. . . The Self in the form of conscience has taken the place of humanity,
and being-a-Self has taken the place of man.[17]

This passage reveals the real critical thrust behind Arendt's interpretation. Heidegger is "the last (let us hope) Romantic." He earns
this sobriquet not simply because of any delusions of genius, but
because of the subjectifying approach to individual and social existence found in *Being and Time*. However problematic the Kantian
conception of humanity or Mankind might be, it at least retained a
worldly referent, a sense of reality untainted by the expansive Romantic conception of the self. Thus, in the *Existenz* philosophy essay
Arendt is accusing Heidegger of contributing to the "world alienation" which she will later describe (in *The Human Condition*) as one
of the defining characteristics of the modern age.

In stark contrast to the weird mixture of romanticism, functionalism, and subjectivism she detects in Heidegger, Arendt's treatment
of Jaspers emphasizes how *his* version of *Existenz* philosophy retains
a focus on communication as "the pre-eminent form of philosophical participation," as well as giving human freedom priority over the
category of existence. In Jaspers's thought, according to Arendt,
"Existence is not man's being as such and as a given; rather, 'man is,
in *Dasein*, possible existence.'"[18] For Jaspers, the "thrown" or irreducibly situated character of our being-in-the-world and our being-
with-others is the guarantee of, rather than an obstacle to, our existential freedom.[19] The gap between Being and thought, the sheer
contingency of human existence, opens a space for freedom, a space
denied by the contemplative philosophical tradition (with its fixa-
tion on an order of Being) *and* Heidegger's notion of an authentic Self.

It is only in a note to "What Is *Existenz* Philosophy?" that Arendt
addresses directly the question of Heidegger's political engagement,
linking it to his allegedly solipsistic version of existentialism. I cite
this note in its entirety, since it is Arendt's first published statement
on the relationship between Heidegger's philosophy and his politics. (It also led to an important exchange between Arendt and Jaspers on the question of Heidegger's support of and obedience to the
Nazis, which I discuss below.) Arendt writes:

> Another question and one certainly worthy of discussion is whether
> Heidegger's philosophy has not been taken unduly seriously because it

concerns itself with very serious matters. In his political behavior, in any case, Heidegger has provided us with more than ample warning that we should take him seriously. As is well known, he entered the Nazi party in a very sensational way in 1933—an act which made him stand out pretty much by himself among colleagues of the same calibre. Further, in his capacity as rector of Freiberg University, he forbade Husserl, his teacher and friend, whose lecture chair he had inherited, to enter the faculty because Husserl was a Jew. Finally, it has been rumored that he placed himself at the disposal of the French occupational authorities for the reeducation of the German people.

In view of the truly comic aspect of this development and in view of the no less genuinely abysmal state of political thought in German universities, one is tempted simply to dismiss the whole business. What speaks against such a dismissal is, among other things, that this entire mode of behavior has such exact parallels in German Romanticism and that one can hardly believe them to result from sheer coincidence of a purely personal failure of character. Heidegger is (let us hope) the last Romantic—an enormously talented Friedrich Schlegel or Adam Müller, as it were, whose complete lack of responsibility is attributable to a spiritual playfulness that stems in part from delusions of genius and in part from despair.[20]

One is struck by how this stinging indictment says both too much and too little. On the one hand, Arendt refuses to acknowledge Heidegger's philosophical importance. If this "immensely talented Friedrich Schlegel or Adam Müller" is to be taken seriously, it is only because of the symptomatic character of his political affiliation. But this actually begs the question of the relation between his philosophy and his politics, reducing it to a mere function of the adolescent political posture of Romanticism, with its "spiritual playfulness," "delusions of genius," and indulgence of despair.

Arendt's attempt to diminish Heidegger's philosophical stature is not very convincing, one suspects not even to herself. Nevertheless, writers like Ettinger and Wolin stress the importance of the 1946 essay, seeing in it a clear-eyed condemnation of Heidegger the Nazi and antisemite, the betrayer of Husserl. Both Ettinger and Wolin stress how, at this point in her life, Arendt thought of Heidegger as a "potential murderer." And, from their point of view, the subsequent moderation of her views can only represent moral backsliding.

The phrase "potential murderer" comes from a letter Arendt sent to Jaspers in July 1946, after she had sent him a copy of "What Is *Existenz* Philosophy?" Jaspers had pointed out that "the facts in the note on Heidegger are not exactly correct."[21] While agreeing with the substance of the note, Jaspers had indicated that Arendt's description of the process through which Husserl was barred from the university was misleading. The letter sent by Heidegger informing Husserl of his exclusion from the faculty was in fact not the fruit of a personal initiative on Heidegger's part, but rather a circular "that every rector had to write to those excluded by the government [from the university by law]."[22] Arendt responds to Jaspers as follows:

> Regarding the Heidegger note, your assumption about the Husserl letter is completely correct. I knew that this letter was a circular, and I know that many people have excused it for that reason. It always seemed to me that at the moment Heidegger was obliged to put his name to this document, he should have resigned. However foolish he may have been, he was capable of understanding that. We can hold him responsible for his actions to that extent. He knew that the letter would have left Husserl more or less indifferent if someone else had signed it. Now you might say that this happened in the rush of business. And I would probably reply that the truly irreparable things often—and deceptively—happen almost like accidents, that sometimes from an insignificant line that we step across easily, feeling certain that it is of no consequence anymore, that a wall rises up that truly divides people. In other words, although I never had any professional or personal attachment to old Husserl, I mean to maintain solidarity with him in this one case. And because I know that this letter and this signature almost killed him, I can't but regard Heidegger as a potential murderer.[23]

Read in context, Arendt's judgment is more nuanced than either Ettinger or Wolin present it. The moral condemnation of Heidegger is severe, but it is a condemnation not of an ideologue or fanatical antisemite, but of a professor who, flush with his new power as rector and excited by the possibilities for restructuring the university opened by the Nazi regime, willingly signs off on a document that represents the most profound personal betrayal of his friend and mentor, Husserl. Heidegger is a "potential murderer" not because his letter to Husserl exposed a hitherto concealed "eliminationist" antisemitism, but rather because he allowed himself to cross a seemingly insignificant line when his duties as rector demanded it. (Anyone familiar with academic life, or administrative structures generally, will recognize this human, all too human evasion of moral responsibility.) The moral judgment Arendt clarifies in her letter to Jaspers points to what she will later refer to as Heidegger's "lack of character," a lack that prevented him from seeing how friendship *should* have placed clear limits on the extent of his coordination (*Gleichschaltung*) with the regime.[24]

The correspondence between Arendt and Jaspers proves an invaluable resource for those interested in the nature and evolution of Arendt's view of Heidegger. For the most part, it reveals a remarkable consistency over time in her judgment of Heidegger's political ignorance and lack of character. Both Arendt and Jaspers viewed Heidegger as (in Alan Ryan's phrase) a "political idiot," prone to lying and self-delusion. Their (often quite strained) friendship with him hardly made them less critical.[25] Yet despite their ample personal reasons for not trusting Heidegger, both acknowledged the obvious: here was one of the great thinkers of the twentieth century (a judgment shared by such fierce critics of Heidegger as Leo Strauss). The resulting ambivalence toward Heidegger is nicely expressed in a 1966 letter from Jaspers, who writes "It seems to me that there is something appealing about Heidegger at the moment. I've experienced this and think back on it with nostalgia and horror. There is something in him, and something substantial, but you can't rely on anything with him. And awful things happen."[26]

The *Correspondence* shows that, far from being helpless under Heidegger's spell (like the hapless Mario in Thomas Mann's parable of fascism, "Mario and the Magician"), both Arendt and Jaspers spent a good deal of time wrestling with the question of his personal behavior, his engagement with National Socialism, and the tendency toward kitsch and self-indulgence which threatened the quality of his philosophical work.[27] Given Jaspers's conception of philosophical activity as a direct expression of the *Existenz* of the thinker, it is not surprising that the relation between the personal and the philosophical in Heidegger preoccupied him more than Arendt (the *Correspondence* shows him frequently broaching the idea of a book on Heidegger's life and thought, and—just as frequently—deferring the task). For Arendt, the question of Heidegger's character (or lack thereof) was important, not because it expressed itself directly in the content of his work, but because his submission to the cult of his own genius threatened the quality and depth of his philosophical writing. Ettinger and Wolin are correct in noting that Arendt was concerned for Heidegger after their 1950 "reconciliation" meeting. However, this concern was animated more by anxiety about the fate of Heidegger's "passionate thinking" than it was by any nostalgia for an old romance.[28]

In 1954, four years after the supposed "transformation" in Arendt's attitude toward Heidegger, she delivered an address to the American Political Science Association. This lecture, "Concern with Politics in Recent European Thought," is an important marker in the evolution of her public evaluation of Heidegger. While the remarks on Heidegger in the *Existenz* philosophy essay were (in Young-Bruehl's phrase) "overwrought and acerbic," Arendt's consideration of the interest his philosophy holds for political science in this lecture is balanced yet critical. Reading it, the fact that she had gained a certain distance on Heidegger becomes clear. This distance allowed her to measure the significance of his philosophical work in relation to both the tradition and contemporary thought.

Arendt's address focuses on the "sea-change" in recent (postwar) continental thought. If the hallmark of the Western philosophical tradition had been a lofty, deprecatory attitude toward the entire realm of human affairs, then the experience of two world wars, totalitarian regimes, and the prospect of nuclear war had made such a posture impossible to maintain. Politics, the realm of human affairs, emerged as a domain "in which genuine philosophic questions arise," questions that cannot be answered from the traditional philosophical standpoint of the "wise man" or *sophos* who affects to stand above this realm, communing with the Absolute. *Events*, not timeless Being, gave rise to a new mode of philosophical thought, one that was essentially noncontemplative.[29]

As Arendt tells it, Hegel's concept of history prepared the way for this revolutionary turn by giving "the realm of human affairs a dignity it never enjoyed in philosophy before."[30] Yet Hegel maintained the philosopher's traditional contemplative stance (the "standpoint of the Absolute"), viewing history as the medium in which a larger, speculative truth appears. Heidegger's importance is that he radicalizes the Hegelian concept of historicity (*Geschichtlichkeit*), to the point where "no transcendent spirit and no absolute" is revealed in human history to the philosophical spectator. In this regard, Arendt cites a sentence from Heidegger's essay "*Das Ding*:" "We have left the arrogance of all Absolutes behind us." This, she states, "means

71

that the philosopher has left behind him the claim to being 'wise' and knowing eternal standards for the perishable affairs of the City of men, for such 'wisdom' could be justified only from a position *outside the realm of human affairs* and be thought legitimate only by virtue of the philosopher's proximity to the Absolute."[31]

Heidegger's concept of historicity thus makes a fundamental reorientation of philosophical thought to the political world possible. Arendt calls the abandonment of the position of the "wise man" "perhaps the most important and most fruitful result of the new philosophical concern with politics." The reason why is that

> The rejection of the claim to wisdom opens the way to a reexamination of the whole realm of politics in the light of elementary human experiences within this realm itself, and implicitly discards traditional concepts and judgments, which have their roots in altogether different kinds of experience.[32]

But, Arendt hastens to add, "such a development does not proceed unequivocally." In the case of Heidegger, the ancient philosophical hostility to the *polis* recurs in the phenomenological descriptions of *das Mann* (the "they") and *Offentlichkeit* (publicness or publicity) as fallen modes of being. Arendt no longer views these descriptions as utterly negative, in the manner of her *Existenz* philosophy essay. While condescending, they do not create an irreducible gap between the authentic (or philosophical) self and its "fallen," everyday world. Indeed, from a certain perspective, they offer "penetrating insights into one of the basic aspects of society," namely, the rule of public opinion.[33]

This is certainly a switch from the earlier essay. Yet "Concern for Politics in Recent European Thought" can hardly be seen as an attempt to proselytize for Heidegger. In focusing on his concept of historicity, Arendt is not saying that Heidegger's thought contains anything like adequate resources for founding the "new political science" demanded by the unprecedented political events of the twentieth century. The moment the concept of historicity is extended beyond society and public opinion to the analysis of the realm of politics proper, its limitations become all too clear.

Like the older Hegelian notion of history, Heidegger's concept of historicity approaches the political realm, but always manages to miss what Arendt calls "the center of politics—man as an acting being."[34] To be sure, Heidegger's concept emphasized the connect-

THE ANXIETY OF INFLUENCE

edness of thought and event to a degree unparalleled by Hegel and the rest of the contemplative tradition. Yet it ultimately created a conceptual framework "better prepared to understand history than to lay the groundwork of a new political philosophy."[35] Thus, Heidegger's philosophy is "highly sensitive to the general trends of the time" (such as "the technicalization of the world, the emergence of one world on a planetary scale, the increasing pressure of society upon the individual, and the concomitant atomization of society"), while remaining disturbingly forgetful of what Arendt calls "the more permanent questions of political science": "What is politics? Who is man as a political being? What is freedom?"[36]

Somewhat surprisingly, Arendt holds that such questions have been better preserved by Catholic philosophers like Etienne Gilson and Jacques Maritan and neo-Platonists like Eric Voegelin. Immune to Hegelianism and historicism, these thinkers awaken an "awareness of the relevance of the classical and permanent problems of political philosophy." Yet their return to religion and tradition, motivated by the trauma of recent events, hinges upon a denial of the full novelty of the crimes committed by totalitarian regimes, and thus upon a denial of the extent of the moral breakdown which led to the ordinary individual's complicity with these crimes. Arendt praises the antitraditionalist, action-focused response of French existentialists like Sartre and Camus, which avoids this form of bad faith. However, she is extremely dubious about their tendency to look "to politics for the solution of philosophic perplexities," to seek "salvation from thought through action."

The limitations of these alternative paths in continental thought lead Arendt, at the conclusion of her lecture, to turn once more to the existentialism of her teachers, Jaspers and Heidegger. As in the *Existenz* philosophy essay, Arendt praises Jaspers's focus on communication. Philosophy, conceived not in contemplative terms but rather as a special kind of communicative practice, "becomes the mediator between many truths, not because it holds the one truth valid for all men, but because only in reasoned communication can what each man believes in his isolation from all others become humanly and actually *true*."[37] So conceived, philosophy is stripped of its arrogance "toward the common life of men." But Jaspers's communicative paradigm, while appropriate for the activity of philosophy, is of limited political relevance. Its phenomenological roots are found "not in the public political sphere, but in the personal

73

encounter of the I and the Thou. This relationship of pure dialogue is closer to the original experience of thinking—the dialogue of one with oneself in solitude—than to any other."[38] Reversing the judgment she made in the *Existenz* philosophy essay, Arendt now says that Jaspers's dialogical paradigm "contains less specifically political experience than almost any relationship in our average, everyday lives."

Heidegger's philosophy scarcely holds the key to this dilemma, the dilemma of how to think political experience in its own terms once the contemplative standpoint has been abandoned. However, his philosophy does have one notable advantage over Jaspers's attempt to generate a political form of intersubjectivity out of the experience of personal communication or the dialogue of thought with itself. It is in Heidegger's concept of "world," and of *Dasein* as being-in-the-world, that Arendt now sees a possible "step out of this difficulty" and the persistent tendency of philosophers to think the political realm from the standpoint of thoughtful solitude. Heidegger's descriptions of the existential structures of a being who is essentially a being-in-the-world, a being with others, attributes "philosophical significance to structures of everyday life," structures that are "completely incomprehensible if man is not primarily understood as being together with others."[39] Here, for the first time, Arendt signals her awareness that Heidegger's project of overturning a whole raft of Cartesian prejudices about a subject detached from the world and others is of the greatest interest to any political theory that takes *worldliness* and *human plurality* as fundamentally constitutive of political experience itself.

These second thoughts about the relative value of Jaspers and Heidegger's approaches for political thinking reveal Arendt struggling to find a philosophical precedent for her own concept of human plurality (what she will call in *The Human Condition* the *conditio sine qua non* of the public realm). The postwar philosophers had tried to overcome the contemplative prejudices of the tradition. In the end, however, their various alternatives reproduced the characteristic deficiencies of the tradition (the tendency to interpret political experience in terms of solitary, philosophical experience; the inability to recognize or understand genuine novelty). Although spurred to engage politics by "the sheer horror of contemporary political events," none of the postwar philosophers actually succeeded in coming to terms with this horror. As a result, their thinking continued to express "the traditional refusal to grant the realm of human affairs that *thaumadzein*, that wonder at what is as it is, which, according to Plato and Aristotle, is at the beginning of all philosophy, yet which even they had refused to accept as the preliminary condition of political philosophy."[40]

This incapacity to experience wonder, rather than horror or bemused contempt, at the realm of human affairs is what limits the postwar philosophers' capacity to provide a new foundation for political philosophy. The "rejection of the claim to wisdom" underlying these efforts may have opened, in principle, the way to a "reexamination of the whole realm of politics in the light of elementary human experiences within this realm itself." However, none of the philosophers Arendt discusses in her lecture, Jaspers and Heidegger included, proved capable of actually performing such a reexamination.

At the conclusion of her address, Arendt rhetorically asks "who else is likely to succeed [in creating an authentic political philosophy] if they [the philosophers] should fail us?"[41] Arendt did not wait for an answer, for she had already begun the reexamination of the fundamentals of political experience suggested, but never directly engaged, by *Existenz* philosophy. The result of this reexamination was, of course, *The Human Condition*, the next stage in Arendt's critical dialogue with Heidegger's thought.

THE APPROPRIATION OF HEIDEGGER IN
THE HUMAN CONDITION

Thanks to Ettinger, we know that Arendt intended to dedicate *The Human Condition* to Heidegger. Indeed, she wrote Heidegger a letter to this effect, noting that "the book evolved directly from the first Marburg days, and it owes you just about everything in every regard."[42] This certainly sounds like the kind of statement a disciple would make, and taken at face value it seems to support Wolin's contention that Arendt was nothing more than a "left Heideggerian."

There is little doubt that *The Human Condition* is a work deeply influenced by Heidegger. The real question is: what is the nature of this influence? Does Arendt slavishly follow in the master's footsteps, jettisoning only his reactionary politics and cultural sensibility? Or does she use Heidegger violently, twisting his thought in directions he would neither have recognized nor endorsed, overcoming her teacher in a manner similar to the creative appropriations of such other Heidegger students as Leo Strauss, Hans-Georg Gadamer, and Herbert Marcuse?

Heidegger's thought aids Arendt's project of reexamining "the whole realm of politics in light of the elementary experiences within this realm itself" in several ways. First, the "existential analytic" of *Being and Time*, with its rebellion against the subject/object problematic of Descartes and Kant, suggested not only a revised conception of our fundamental relation to the world, but also a reformulation of the question of human freedom. Heidegger's conception of human being as being-in-the-world displaced both the cognitive subject and the practical subject as abstract entities standing over against the world. In their place, Heidegger stressed the essentially *involved* character of *Dasein* as both acting and understanding being. This revolutionary turn was clearly of great importance to Arendt, in that it helped her to surmount the monistic, subject-centered conception of freedom as freedom of the will (or "practical reason") which dominated the Western tradition of philosophical and political thought.[43] Heidegger's conception of *Dasein* as primordially both a being-in-the-world and a being-with-others helped her to place worldliness and human plurality at the heart of human freedom rather than at the extreme margins.

Second, Heidegger's work after *Being and Time* exposed the will to power or mastery underlying the traditional view of freedom as a form of sovereignty and action as an essentially goal-directed activity. For Arendt, Heidegger's insight into the tradition's rebellion against the finitude and frailty of the human condition provided the departure point for a critical reading of the Western tradition of political thought from Plato to Marx. This tradition, with its persistent misinterpretation of political action as a kind of making or fabrication, repeatedly tried to overcome what Arendt calls the "frailty, haphazardness, and contingency" of action in the public realm, with disastrous moral and political results. Heidegger's critique of the tradition's will to dominate Being through a "science of grounds" (metaphysics) thus sets the pattern for Arendt's critique of Western political philosophy's tendency to efface human plurality and spontaneity, which are typically seen as obstacles to the realization of the just society. (Think, in this regard, of the radical devaluation of

THE ANXIETY OF INFLUENCE

moral disagreement we find in Plato, Aristotle, Augustine, Hobbes, Rousseau, Hegel, and, of course, Karl Marx.)

Third, Heidegger's diagnosis of the pathologies of the modern age, however mired in cultural conservatism and images of pastoral wholeness, provided Arendt with the frame for her own critique of modernity in *The Human Condition*. Heidegger's account of how the modern age places the knowing and willing subject in the structural place of God (reducing the dimensions of reality to that which can be known and represented by such a subject) enabled Arendt to question the Promethean tendency of modern science and technology, along with the idea that a completely "humanized" reality will be one in which alienation is overcome.[44] "Resentment of the human condition" is seen to drive both modern science and technology, two forces that contribute mightily, in Arendt's view, to our increasing "alienation from the world" and from political action (for Arendt, the most worldly of human activities).

These three themes constitute what *The Human Condition* owes positively to Heidegger. But what has made the book a classic is hardly its reformulation of abstruse Heideggerian notions into more accessible language. Its startling originality is evident in the way Arendt uses Heidegger against Heidegger, in the service of ideas he would have condemned. Arendt's subversion of Heidegger's thought is every bit as profound as her philosophical debt.

Thus, while Heidegger opened the way to a more worldly conception of freedom, he severely limited the political relevance of his conception of human being by framing it in terms of the broad distinction between authentic (*eigentlich*) and inauthentic (*uneigentlich*) existence. One can live one's life by adhering to the given and the everyday, or one can resolutely eschew the false comfort of everything public and established and confront the groundlessness of one's own existence. While authentic existence can never wrench itself free of "fallenness" and is, in fact, dependent upon it, Heidegger leaves little doubt that the public world is the privileged locus of inauthenticity. The "light of the public obscures everything" because it covers over the fundamental character of human existence as groundless, finite, and radically open or atelic.

In *The Human Condition* Arendt appropriated Heidegger's conception of human existence as disclosedness, as open possibility divorced from any pregiven hierarchy of ends, and turned it inside out. The *public* realm, which for Heidegger had signified the every-

77

dayness of *Dasein*, became, in Arendt's phenomenology, the arena of human transcendence and freedom, of *authentic* existence. According to Arendt, it is through political action and speech on a public stage that human beings achieve a unique identity and endow the "human artifice" with meaning. The realm of opinion and public talk—what for Heidegger had been the sphere of "idle chatter" (*Gerede*)—is recast by Arendt as the space of disclosure par excellence; the space where human beings are engaged in a form of initiatory, intersubjective activity; the space which reveals both a unique self and a meaningful "human artifice" or world.

Arendt's appropriation of Heidegger's deconstruction of the tradition is every bit as critical and transformative as her appropriation of his conception of existence as disclosedness. While Heidegger's story was built on quasi-idealist presuppositions and asserted a dubious linearity (an "inner logic") from Plato to Nietzsche, Arendt's radical revision was far more limited in its claims. She hardly thought that the "destiny of Being" (*Seinsgeschick*) came to language in the words of the great thinkers, who in Heidegger's metahistory of philosophy provide a kind of x-ray vision into the "essential" yet hidden history of the West.[45] She retained the phenomenologist's focus on concrete experiences and events. Thus, her concern with the language of theory focused, instead, on how it imposed an alien metaphorics upon the realm of human affairs, a set of structuring metaphors taken from other domains of human activity (such as thinking or fabrication) in which the condition of human plurality played little or no role.

For Arendt, the fact that the public political world has been conceptualized by a tradition originally fixated upon the experiences of contemplation and fabrication meant that essential phenomena of this realm (for example, human plurality) have never received their theoretical due. Moreover, it meant that political thinkers and actors had repeatedly construed action as a form of making, casting human beings as the "material cause" of the just state. The result is the baneful identification of action with violence ("You can't make an omelet without breaking eggs") and an enormous increase in the temptation for the best to do the worst as they attempt to "sculpt" human material into something ordered, beautiful, whole. From Plato to Marx, the tradition gives ample evidence of *this* tendency, the tendency of theorists to transpose political experiences and judgments into aesthetic or productivist terms. The result has been, and continues to be, moral horror.

While Arendt shared Heidegger's trepidation about the way modern science and technology act into nature, setting into motion processes that undermine the integrity of the human artifice, she hardly subscribed to his solution. For Heidegger, the escape from the "power trip" of Western metaphysics, science, and technology was to be found in an attitude of releasement (*Gelassenheit*): we must abdicate the "will to will," the will to human self-assertion and the domination of nature. For Arendt, in contrast, the danger posed by the existential resentment driving modern science was not (simply) that it objectifies nature or even human nature; rather, it was that by increasing our alienation from the world, it leads us to substitute the will to increased power for a politically engaged (and morally concerned) "care for the world."[46] Thus, while the later Heidegger's diagnosis of the pathologies of modernity led him to a "will not to will" and an intensified "thinking withdrawal," Arendt's critical appropriation of his diagnosis led to a renewed emphasis upon the importance of political action, moral judgment, human freedom, and an engaged worldliness. It led her to reiterate the importance of constitutional or republican government as a frame for sane political action and to emphasize the very human capacities which Heidegger had rejected in the mistaken belief that the only *true* form of action was thinking.[47]

But what about the charges of elitism and "political existentialism" which have hounded Arendt and which Wolin repeats in his review of Ettinger's volume? After all, doesn't *The Human Condition* celebrate heroic, agonal action over more associational forms of political engagement? And doesn't Arendt's Heidegger-inspired focus on the disclosive or revelatory quality of "great" deeds come at the expense of justice, rights, and more democratic forms of solidarity? Finally, doesn't Arendt's insistence on the relative autonomy of the public realm lead her to espouse an existentialist call for action for the sake of action?

There is no denying that *The Human Condition* is Grecophilac, or that Arendt's strenuous effort to distinguish political spaces and modes of action from social, economic, and other forms of activity broadly parallels the efforts of Carl Schmitt in his *The Concept of the Political*. Nor can it be denied that Arendt "aestheticizes" politics, describing action with the help of metaphors taken from the performing arts, theater in particular.

But before we charge her with being an elitist (or worse) in democrat's clothes, we need to be clear about her theoretical motivations. Arendt turned to the Greeks, not out of a Germanic longing for an idealized past, but because she sought an understanding of political action prior to the Greek philosophical or Christian view of politics as a *means* to the attainment of a predetermined (natural or divinely ordained) end. It was the experience of free political action in a realm of civic equality, a realm marked out and guaranteed by law, which Arendt wanted to preserve through her political theory. Wherever politics is understood primarily as a means, even to an ostensibly moral end, there the experience of a plurality of equals is bound to be devalued if not altogether effaced. Political action conceived as the vehicle to a preestablished end tempts good men to treat their fellows not as peers, but as means to the ultimate end of an eschatological form of justice. Thus Arendt rejects the moralizing interpretation of action laid down by Plato and Christianity, *for moral reasons*. (The parallel to Kant, and to liberalism generally, should be clear.)

It is for this same reason—the moral desire to respect and preserve human plurality—that Arendt aestheticizes action and rejects various forms of rationalism. Her "existentialism" consists in the rejection of the deeply ingrained Western assumption that there is or can be one correct or true answer to the question of how one should live, and that reason is the faculty which will deliver this answer to us. Arendt shares with liberals like Isaiah Berlin and conservatives like Michael Oakeshott a deep suspicion of rationalism in politics and the pretenses of theory to guide a transformative practice. From Plato's "tyranny of reason," to the French Revolutionary terror, to Marxism's catastrophic fulfillment in Stalinist totalitarianism, political rationalism has shown itself every bit as capable of generating moral horror as either religion or romantic nationalism. Arendt is certainly not "against" reason as such in politics. Rather, she demands that we view *opinion* as one of our primary rational faculties, thereby facilitating a deliberative politics from which the tyrannizing claim to a singular moral or political truth has been eliminated.[48] Again, the preservation of civic equality and human plurality—of human dignity—is at stake. Hence her view of the public realm in *The Human Condition* as a kind of stage on which plural actors appear, engaging in strenuous debate as well as concerted action.

Finally, Arendt's desire to view the political realm as relatively autonomous has nothing to do with establishing its hegemony as the field in which the life-and-death struggle between friends and enemies is played out, as in Schmitt's Hobbesian existentialism. If politics and political action are, for her, "existentially supreme" it is because they provide the most adequate vehicles for the human capacity to begin, to initiate. Viewed as relatively autonomous—as not subject to the dictates of economic, biological, or historical necessity—the political realm stands forth as the realm of human freedom. *The Human Condition* and Arendt's other major theoretical statements are devoted to reminding us of *this* fact, a fact obscured by rationalist philosophies of history, schools of economic determinism, and liberal celebrations of "negative freedom" (a liberty largely confined to the private sphere).[49] When, in her essay "What is Freedom?," Arendt writes that "freedom is the *raison d'être* of politics," she succinctly sums up her hopes for the political sphere, a potential space of "tangible freedom." The distance between these hopes and Heidegger's philosophy and politics is, obviously, vast.

"MARTIN HEIDEGGER AT EIGHTY": A "WHITEWASH"?

As the Arendt/Jaspers correspondence indicates, Heidegger did not take kindly to the violent appropriation (and implicit critique) of his thought which *The Human Condition* represented. His response to receipt of a copy of the German translation was frosty silence, and Arendt was subject to a "burst of hostility" from him and his circle, including a pointed snub by Eugen Fink during her 1961 visit to Freiberg.[50] For all intents and purposes, contact between Arendt and Heidegger broke off until 1967, when, with the mediation of Arendt's friend J. Glenn Gray, she gave a lecture in Freiberg and struck "a new accord" with Heidegger.[51] This was followed, a year later, by her agreement to contribute to Heidegger's eightieth birthday *Festschrift*. This contribution was subsequently translated and published in *The New York Review of Books* in 1971 under the title "Martin Heidegger at Eighty."

Both Ettinger and Wolin view this essay as a scandalous whitewash, typical of what they see as Arendt's desire to exonerate "the master" of his political past. Ettinger writes: "Arendt went to extraordinary pains to minimize and justify [sic!] Heidegger's contribution to and support of the Third Reich. . . . In her tribute to Heidegger, the last act in a drama started almost half a century ago, Arendt displayed the same unquestioning generosity, loyalty, and love she had shown since the beginning."[52] Wolin attacks as "blind devotion" what he reads as a defense of her "embattled mentor," a defense that hinged upon disputing "any essential relation between Heidegger's thought and his support of Hitler" and the denial that the "gutter born" ideology of Nazism owed anything to representatives of German *Kultur* such as Heidegger.[53]

Arendt certainly did not agree with Theodor Adorno's judgment that Heidegger's philosophy was "fascist down to its most intimate components." Indeed, any impartial reader of Heidegger's seventy-plus-volume *Gesamtausgabe* will be impressed by just how resolutely apolitical his philosophy generally is. (I am deliberately excluding the nonphilosophical public speeches he made in his capacity as rector of Freiberg during 1933. These are, of course, craven harangues, blatant attempts to coddle up to the new regime.) But if the question of an "essential relation" between Heidegger's thought and politics is a highly contentious (and by no mean obvious) one, what about the charge of "whitewash," of minimization and justification of Heidegger's engagement with National Socialism? What does Arendt actually *do* in her tribute essay?

The reader seeking a nest of "exculpatory" statements by Arendt will be disappointed. It is only in a long note that Arendt makes the following statement, in parentheses: "Heidegger himself corrected his own 'error' more quickly and more radically than many of those who later sat in judgment over him—he took considerably greater risks than were usual in German literary and university life during the period."[54] This statement accepts Heidegger's own account of his reasons for resigning from the rectorship and the nature of his subsequent philosophical activity under the Reich.[55] The biographical work of Hugo Ott and Rudiger Safranski enable us, in hindsight, to charge Arendt with excessive credulity on this score.[56]

The bulk of Arendt's essay is given over not to apologetics, but to an account of Heidegger's early fame as a teacher, and to an extended description of the nature of his "passionate thinking." With regard to the latter, Arendt emphasized the noninstrumental, noncognitive nature of thinking as practiced by Heidegger, a thinking which had "a digging quality peculiar to itself," an *active* (as opposed to contemplative) thinking which yields no results and is constantly beginning again.[57]

Such passionate thinking, so different from scholarship *about* philosophical doctrines or philosophical "problem solving," begins in wonder at that which is, and demands an abode in which such wonder can be experienced and extended. As Arendt puts it, the "abode of thought" is one of essential seclusion from the world, while thinking itself "has only to do with things absent."[58] The famous Heideggerian thesis about the "withdrawal of Being" was, according to Arendt, a function of thinking's need to create a "place of stillness" withdrawn from the world, where the distractions of everydayness prevent both thoughtful solitude and the experience of wonder. In Arendt's words:

> Seen from the perspective of thinking's abode, "withdrawal of Being" or "oblivion of Being" reigns in the ordinary world which surrounds the thinker's residence, the "familiar realms . . . of everyday life," i.e., the loss of that which thinking—which by nature clings to the absent—is concerned. Annulment of this "withdrawal," on the other side, is always paid for by a withdrawal from the world of human affairs, and this remoteness is never more manifest than when thinking ponders exactly those affairs, training them into its own sequestered stillness.[59]

One can see where Arendt is going with this passage, and how it might provide grist for those who charge her with being an apologist for Heidegger. In her view, the greatness of Heidegger's thinking was manifest in its purity, in the thoroughness of his withdrawal to thinking's "sequestered abode." When worldly events draw the thinker out from his abode, back into the realm of human affairs, he experiences a disorientation similar to that described by Plato in the *Republic's* famous allegory of the cave. Egregious "errors" of political judgment may result. Thus, Arendt concluded her tribute by retelling the story from Plato's *Theaetetus* about the pre-Socratic philosopher Thales, whose upward glance to contemplate "higher things" led him to stumble into a well, to the amusement of a Thracian girl who witnesses the thinker's fall. Heidegger, Arendt seems to be saying, also "stumbled" when he gave in to the temptation to "change his residence and get involved in the world of human affairs."[60] Yet, according to Arendt, "he was still young enough to learn from the shock of the collision, which, after ten short hectic months thirty-seven years ago drove him back to his residence, to settle in his thinking what he had experienced."[61]

Thanks to Hugo Ott, we know that the "collision" lasted more than ten months: twelve years is more like it. In accepting Heidegger's account of the span of his engagement with National Socialism as coterminous with his rectorship, Arendt can again be charged with excessive charity and credulity. But more troubling is the description of Heidegger's engagement as an "error." This, more than the mistaken statements about the length of his support of the Nazis, appears to support Ettinger and Wolin's charges of whitewash.

Yet the surface is deceptive. If we put Arendt's tribute essay together with the lengthy Heidegger critique found in the penultimate chapter of *The Life of the Mind*, we see that what at first glance appears to be an apology is, in fact, an indictment. For what Arendt draws attention to in both places is the way Heidegger's thought focuses on the absent: Being in it withdrawal, obscured by everyday ("fallen") reality. As a "pure activity" that issues in no concrete, useful result, Heidegger's passionate thinking resembles that of Socrates', but with one crucial difference. Socrates *performed* his thinking in the agora: the aporetic arguments of the dialogues are deployed by a "citizen amongst citizens." Socratic thinking points to a kind of *ordinary* thinking we should be able to demand of everyone: a capacity to reflectively dissolve conventional moral pieties and socially given rules, the better to activate the faculty of judgment and the voice of conscience. In opposition to such "ordinary" or Socratic thinking, Arendt posed the example of Heidegger's *extraordinary* thinking, a thinking utterly divorced from the world of appearances which is, for Arendt, the world of politics.

What is the force of this distinction between "ordinary" Socratic thinking and "extraordinary" Heideggerian thinking? The answer emerges when we consider the relation of thinking to judgment. For Arendt, as for Kant, judging and thinking are two different faculties. The former, in its reflective mode, ascends from particulars to universal concepts; the latter is neither a form of judgment nor a mode of cognition, but a quest for meaning beyond appearances. In the case of Socrates, the activity of thinking dissolves all ready to hand standards and rules for conduct. Yet Socratic thinking, because it is performed in the agora, retains its link to the world of appearances, the *public* world of plural human being. Thus, Arendt can claim that

Socratic thinking, which refuses to tell us *how* to judge or provide us with shortcuts that might avoid the labor of judgment, stimulates the capacity for judgment precisely because it throws our everyday derivation of conduct from preestablished rules out of gear. The perplexity induced by Socrates' "dissolvent " thinking is the prelude to a genuinely reflective, that is, *moral*, exercise of judgment. In "emergency situations" where most are carried away by their enthusiasm for a popular political regime or their unthinking identification with a group, it is this capacity to think for oneself—for judging "without banisters"—which can provide salvation.[62]

Arendt's point in "Martin Heidegger at Eighty" and the Heidegger critique in *The Life of the Mind* is that the activity of thinking, when purified of the "taint" of the world of appearances, loses its link to the activity of judging. Her surprising thesis is that pure thought is the death of judgment. This thesis, the result of her consideration of Heidegger's political idiocy, resonates with her suspicion of philosophy's traditional attitude toward the realm of human affairs. Moreover, it resonates with her portrait of the "thoughtless" Adolf Eichmann in *Eichmann in Jerusalem*, whose conduct she saw as a function of the unthinking application of clichés and "language rules" to every new situation. Heidegger and Eichmann, it turns out, are linked: pure thought and thoughtlessness are two sides of the same phenomenon, the incapacity for judgment. Heidegger's "error" was no error in judgment, his engagement with National Socialism no "mistake"; rather, what it testified to, in Arendt's view, was the *absence* of judgment.

This is a shocking and far-reaching claim. It constitutes a more profound and objective indictment of Heidegger than Ettinger's narrative of a nasty manipulative male or Wolin's reiteration of Adorno's charge. Of course, Heidegger was no Eichmann: he was not part of the killing apparatus. Nor was he, as Ettinger and Wolin both claim, an ideologue of the Party (his naive and silly idea that the National Socialist revolution could, in 1933, be given spiritual direction by a return to the thought of the pre-Socratics notwithstanding). He was a *genuine* philosopher—in Arendt's view, a great one—whose life is an object lesson in how pure thought can be, from a political point of view, indistinguishable from the greatest thoughtlessness.

The thematic of thought, thoughtlessness, and the absence of judgment I have just outlined does not lessen either Heidegger's responsibility for his support of the Nazi regime or Eichmann's responsibility for the central role he played in the genocide. In typically original fashion, Arendt focuses our gaze on two representative Germans under National Socialism. Her unsettling lesson is that moral and political judgment can be extinguished by extraordinary thinking as well as by no thinking at all. We see how far she is from any attempt to exempt genius from the responsibility inherent in citizenship (as Wolin charges) or "justifying" Heidegger's involvement (as Ettinger wrongly asserts). If Arendt is guilty of anything, it is failing to draw more explicitly the connections between her reflections on Heidegger, the nature of thinking, and the capacity for moral and political judgment. Her failure to do so enabled her critics to take phrases out of context and construct an apology where, in fact, one finds a worldly and wise moral judgment about the "philosopher's philosopher," Heidegger.

. . . . .

The story of Arendt's relationship to Heidegger cannot be reduced to the stuff of soap opera or to the category of unthinking discipleship. From 1946 on, her public and private reflections on Heidegger, as well as her theoretical work, show an uncanny ability to arrive at an impartial judgment of a thinker to whom she had once been intimately attached. For Arendt, as for Kant, distance and impartiality were the hallmarks of judgment. Arendt's ability to appreciate Heidegger's philosophical achievement while remaining critical of its content; her intense awareness of his failings as a human being and his idiocy as a political actor; her respect for his passionate thinking and her fear of its radical unworldliness—all these things testify to a faculty of judgment which remained remarkably unclouded, even when confronted by the "magician from Messkirch."

CHAPTER FOUR

Thinking and Judging

> I think that commitment can easily carry you to a
> point where you no longer think.
> (*Hannah Arendt*[1])

INTRODUCTION

Few issues in the thought of Hannah Arendt have drawn as much
criticism as her strict distinction between thinking and acting. Many
political theorists, anxious to link theory and practice, have been
frustrated by her insistence that "thinking and acting are not the
same," that "they occupy two entirely different existential positions."[2] To Arendt's critics, this insistence reflects a misplaced clas-
sicism, one inscribed in her fundamental distinction between the
vita activa and the *vita contemplativa*. This distinction underlies her
phenomenology of human activities, providing the basic architec-
ture for her consideration of the active life in *The Human Condition*
and mental activities in *The Life of the Mind*.

Arendt was convinced that action took place in the world, with
others, while thinking involved a withdrawal from the world into
the solitude of an "internal dialogue between me and myself." This
institutionalization of the gap between thinking and acting has
driven her more sympathetic critics to her fragmentary and unfin-
ished work on judgment. Their hope has been that her analysis of
this faculty would provide the "missing link" between the life of the
citizen and the life of the mind. Arendt encouraged such hopes by
referring to the faculty of judgment as "the most political of man's
mental abilities" and "the political faculty par excellence."[3] Indeed,
her observation of the "thoughtless" Adolf Eichmann at his trial in
Jerusalem in 1961 led her to suspect the most intimate of links between thinking and judgment. Reflecting on Eichmann's "extraordinary shallowness" in her 1971 essay "Thinking and Moral Considerations," Arendt was impelled to ask, "Is our ability to judge, to
tell right from wrong, beautiful from ugly, dependent upon our

faculty of thought? Does the inability to think and a disastrous failure of what we commonly call conscience coincide? "[4]

Such formulations, when coupled with her descriptions of political or "representative" thinking in several essays from the 1960s, certainly seem to point to the faculty of judgment as a kind of bridge between thought and action. Yet Arendt remained adamant about keeping them distinct. She also continued to insist upon the distinction between thinking and its "by-product" judgment, as well as that between judgment and action.[5]

The purpose of this chapter is to make sense of these distinctions and to answer why it was so important to Arendt to maintain them. I want to dampen the tendency among political theorists to view her theory of judgment as the crowning synthetic moment of her political philosophy, the moment in which the gap between thinking and acting is finally overcome, *aufhebung*. In my opinion, Arendt had very good reasons for preserving the distinction between thinking and acting, along with the related distinctions between judgment, on the one hand, and either action or thought, on the other. Although she certainly acknowledged that "thinking has some influence on action" and spent a good deal of energy specifying the nature of this influence, she remained intensely skeptical of the ideal of a unity of thought and action (or theory and practice), an ideal pursued by Marxism and other theory- or ideology-driven movements.[6]

In Arendt's view, this ideal is a chimera, and a dangerous one at that. It grows out of and enforces an "instrumental" configuration of theory and practice, one which originated with Plato and which threatened the autonomy of judgment by framing action as the *means* through which an end posited by reason is realized. In such a cognitively based account, judgment is reduced to the activity of subsuming particulars under theoretically derived universals: the "open space" needed for its reflective and independent exercise is eliminated. This tendency to reduce judgment to a deductive exercise in which pregiven truths or theoretically derived standards are applied to "the realm of human affairs" reaches its *reductio ad absurdum* in totalitarian ideology. Here the most basic prerequisites of both thought and independent judgment are effaced, and reality itself is absorbed in the *a priori* "truth" of totalitarian fictions.[7]

Arendt's response to the instrumental configuration of thought and action and the degradation of the faculty of judgment was to focus on the very different phenomenological grounds of thinking, acting, and judging. Above all, she wanted to show how the basic experience of these activities had been obscured by the tradition's insistence upon a deductive relation between theory and practice, the universal and the particular. She therefore took great pains to contrast philosophical thinking and argument with political thinking and judgment. In her view, the former derived from the solitary reasoning process of the philosopher and aimed at truth, while the latter concerned the formation of opinion by a political actor who always found himself or herself in the context of human plurality. The essays from the 1960s which highlight this contrast ("The Crisis in Culture" and "Thinking and Politics") are also the place where she develops the notions of "representative thinking" and an "enlarged mentality," specifically political modes of thought geared to human plurality and opinion rather than solitude and truth.

In Arendt's presentation, these modes of political thinking evidently culminate in the activity of judgment, understood as an essential part of political debate and deliberation. It is Arendt's "rescue" of the faculty of judgment from domination by theoretical wisdom, scientific knowledge, or ideology that prompts many to view her theory of judgment as the "other side" of her theory of political action, as providing a bridge between reason and thinking (on the one hand) and deliberating and acting with others (on the other).[8] As Richard Bernstein has pointed out, judgment emerges as a form—perhaps *the* form—of political action in these essays.[9] This apparent rapprochement of thinking and acting is particularly attractive to those who want to assimilate Arendt's thought to a quasi-rationalist politics, such as we find in Habermas's version of critical theory.

Yet, I shall argue, the appearance is deceptive. For Arendt, good judgment is not, finally, a form of political action, nor is there a "method of thinking" that renders it continuous with the activities of debate and decision-making with others. On the contrary, thinking prepares for judgment in a largely negative fashion: it purges us of "fixed habits of thought, ossified rules and standards," and "conventional, standardized codes of expression." Through its destructive activity, thinking liberates the faculty of judgment, creating (in Ronald Beiner's phrase) an "open space of moral or aesthetic discrimination and discernment."[10] It is the existence of such an open space, born of "the wind of thought," that enables us to appreciate the novelty of a particular event or phenomenon, and which makes

89

genuinely independent judgment (free of "leading strings," as Kant would say) possible.

Critical or "Socratic" thinking (Arendt uses the terms interchangeably) enters the world, then, through the judgment of particulars. Judgment brings the negative "results" of the thinking process to bear on the "world of appearances."[11] In Arendt's striking formulation, "the manifestation of the [destructive] wind of thought is no knowledge; it is the ability to tell right from wrong, beautiful from ugly."[12] So understood, thinking and judging are indeed political, but in the limited sense that they help the individual break free of the strictures of public opinion, strictures which often permit or underwrite political evil. Thinking and judgment are prophylactic faculties in the world of politics, faculties that may help "prevent catastrophes, at least for myself, in the rare moments when the chips are down."[13] They prepare us, as individuals and citizens, to say no to policies or narratives which present themselves as necessary, unquestionable, irresistible.[14]

A major objection to this argument against viewing judgment as an essentially deliberative faculty (one manifest in the course of debate and decision-making) is that what Arendt calls "representative thinking" cannot be reduced to "critical thinking." There appear, in Arendt's work, to be two different accounts of how thinking prepares for judgment, accounts that correspond to two distinct phases of her thought about this "mysterious" faculty. As Beiner suggests, it is quite plausible to speak of not one, but *two* theories of judgment in Arendt.[15] The first (earlier) theory considers judgment from the perspective of the *vita activa*; the second, later theory considers it from the standpoint of the life of the mind. Thus, as we move from Arendt's essays of the 1960s to her writings of the 1970s, the emphasis in her account of judgment "shifts from the representative thought and enlarged mentality of political agents to the spectatorship and retrospective judgment of historians and storytellers."[16]

I don't want to deny this shift in emphasis. As both Beiner and Bernstein have shown, it is textually demonstrable. But I do want to argue that Arendt's emphasis on independent or autonomous judgment, while perhaps more pronounced in the later writings, in fact underlies both phases. When viewed in the light of "thinking (and judging) for oneself," her articulations of political and critical thinking turn out to be more closely related than often assumed. Indeed, interpretations of "representative thinking" which present it as encapsulating a method of public deliberation and decision-making fundamentally distort Arendt's intention, which is to show how such thinking facilitates individual judgment.

This judgment may be that of the actor, of a "citizen among citizens," or it may be that of the (spatially or temporally removed) spectator. It is always, however, the expression of how the world and the things in it (actions, events, phenomena) appear to me, the engaged practioner of "enlarged thought" or the detached renderer of impartial judgment. While judging is "one, if not the most important, activity in which . . . sharing the world with others comes to pass," it is also the activity by which we express our moral "taste"— our capacity for discrimination and discernment—and choose our company.[17] In Arendt's case, the expression of her moral "taste" put her at odds with many who placed solidarity at the head of the political virtues, who viewed fundamental political commitments as entailing the abdication of the privilege of independent judgment. Arendt clung fiercely to this privilege, holding it to be the core of any defensible idea of human dignity.[18]

The Dangers of Directly Linking Thought and Action

In order to understand why Arendt maintained the distinction between thought and action, insisting on their relative autonomy, we must turn to her analysis of ideology in the concluding chapter of *The Origins of Totalitarianism*. There she writes:

> An ideology is quite literally what its name indicates: it is the logic of an idea. Its subject matter is history, to which the "idea" is applied; the result of this application is not a body of statements about something that *is*, but the unfolding of a process which is in constant change. The ideology treats the course of events as though it followed the same "law" as the logical exposition of its "idea." Ideologies pretend to know the mysteries of the whole historical process—the secrets of the past, the intricacies of the present, the uncertainties of the future—because of the logic inherent in their respective ideas.[19]

Ideologies work by positing a single idea (for example, the idea of race or class struggle) as an axiomatic premise, and then unfolding it in a manner that apparently comprehends the totality of the historical process. The chief characteristic of this unfolding is the logical deduction of the whole of history from the initial premise. Arendt identifies the coercive force of logic as the backbone of totalitarian ideologies, the source of their evident persuasiveness for huge numbers of people. Hitler and Stalin may have contributed nothing new to the *content* of racist doctrine or Marxist ideology, but they did perfect the coercive logicality of their respective ideologies, driving the process of all-explaining deduction to merciless, but eminently logical, extremes.[20]

As instruments of total explanation, ideologies emancipate their believers from experience by violently reducing reality to an "inner logic" at work behind multifarious appearances. Ideological thinking "orders facts into an absolutely logical procedure . . . [one that] exists nowhere in reality."[21] Once it has established its premise, the tyranny of logicality prevents ideological thinking from ever being disturbed by experience or instructed by reality.

The total submission to the coercive force of logic demanded by totalitarian ideologies extends to the relation of theory to practice. Just as the explanation of the past and present proceeds by deductive reasoning, so future-oriented action derives from a crude form of practical syllogism. Thus, as Arendt observes, "whoever agreed that there are such things as 'dying classes' and did not draw the consequence of killing their members, or that the right to live had something to do with race and did not draw the consequence of killing 'unfit races,' was plainly either stupid or a coward."[22] The activism of totalitarian regimes springs from the logical imperative inherent in their schemes of total explanation: "You can't say A without saying B and C and so on, down to the end of the murderous alphabet."[23]

This strict deduction of action from ideologically given premises eliminates the need for judgment, and, as a habit of mind, shuts down the space for thinking (which Arendt describes as "the freest and purest of all human activities," as "the very opposite of the compulsory process of deduction").[24] In submitting to the logical coercion of totalitarian ideology, the individual "surrenders his inner freedom [just] as he surrenders his freedom of movement when he bows down to outward tyranny."[25] Ideology is the means by which human beings are stripped of the primary source of their freedom and spontaneity. They are rendered calculable and docile through their internalization of the "logical necessity" of the totalitarian idea and its consequences.

While the claim to total explanation of past, present, and future posed by totalitarian ideologies is relatively novel, the pattern by which action is derived from an idea is not. Indeed, much of Arendt's work subsequent to *The Origins of Totalitarianism* attempts to trace the genealogy of the totalitarian denial of freedom back to the basic categories of Western political thought itself. In *The Human Condition* Arendt identifies the desire to overcome the "contingency, haphazardness, and moral irresponsibility" born of a plurality of actors as in large part determining how freedom, action, and judgment have been formulated by the Western tradition of political theory, from Plato to Marx.

The central moment in this genealogy is Arendt's analysis (in *The Human Condition*) of what she calls "the traditional substitution of making for acting." Plato's antipathy to the "chaos" of democratic politics (burned in deep by the trial and condemnation of Socrates) led him to seek a way by which the wisdom of the few might dominate the passions and opinions of the beastlike *demos*.[26] If people could be convinced that there were immutable standards governing the realm of human affairs, standards available only to the philosopher, then the wisdom of the few could take precedence over the fluctuating opinions and beliefs of the many. Truth would replace opinion, moral conflict would disappear, and an agonistic, chaotic plurality would give way to a harmonious unity.[27]

According to Arendt, the problem for Plato was how to come up with a way of making the *sophia* of the philosopher seem pertinent to the world of the citizen. This he did by adapting his theory of ideas (originally, "the things which shine forth most," the beautiful) so that they could become unvarying "yardsticks" for the realm of human affairs.[28] By appealing to an analogy with the craftsman, who "sees" his product first as an ideal model guiding the fabrication process, Plato was able to present political action as the means through which an independently given model or standard of the just *polis* could be realized.[29] The distinction between the artisan's model and his application of this "idea" becomes the basis for a thoroughgoing separation of knowing and doing, one that replaces the transient *doxa* and endless deliberations of plural equals with a relation of command and obedience.

Plato's substitution of making for acting proves foundational for the Western tradition, in which "consciously or unconsciously, the concept of action is interpreted in terms of making and fabrication."[30] This subsumption of *praxis* (action) by *poiesis* (making) places theory in a hegemonic relation to action, a relation which receives various articulations in the tradition but which never fundamentally changes. Throughout the history of political thought, the faculty of reason is called upon to identify the idea or *telos* of justice, and to show how this idea can be realized concretely in the world. In Plato, Hobbes, Hegel and Marx, the "theoretical analysis" first isolates the (ideal) end, and then reveals the means by which it will be—or has been—produced (by philosopher-kings, a sovereign definer of rights and duties, world history, or proletarian revolution).

As Jean-Francois Lyotard has pointed out, this configuration of theory and practice hinges upon an essentially mimetic logic: theoretical science (*episteme*) provides an accurate description of the "true being" of the just society or human nature, from which various prescriptions for action are derived. These, presumably, will bring imperfect reality into accord with what Nature or History demands.[31] And—as opponents of an *episteme* of justice from Aristotle and Burke to Gadamer and Arendt have noted—such a logic leaves little room for the faculty of judgment. Reason elucidates the universal, which is then applied to the particular (present conditions) by theory-guided action. A pattern is set in which judgment is utterly marginalized by the syllogistic deduction of action (the machinery of Kant's Categorical Imperative is a good, if largely benign, example). The questions of what practical virtues are appropriate in *these* circumstances, or what examples of good action or judgment might guide us in *this* context, are rendered superfluous.[32] This deeply rooted tendency to efface both plurality and judgment, deliberation and context, reaches its murderous extreme in the ideological deductions of totalitarian regimes.

The dangers of this direct, instrumentalizing linkage of thought and action should be obvious. If political action is really the means by which a theoretically just state of affairs is produced, then it becomes imperative that the main causes of the "contingency, haphazardness, and frailty" of human affairs be isolated and removed. As Arendt repeatedly points out, it is human plurality—the fact that "men, not Man, live on earth and inhabit the world"—which lies at the root of this peculiar frailty. Thus, action can be the "instrument"

94

of thought or theory only if it is not continually frustrated by the unpredictable and disruptive effects invariably produced by a plurality of actors. If we judge action according to whether it successfully achieves its goal, then radical measures are in order for restricting these effects and the plurality that generated them. From this perspective—by and large the perspective of the tradition—the end justifies the means, as Plato, Hobbes, Hegel, and Marx all agree.[33] It is, therefore, hardly surprising that virtually all the great theorists (with the notable exceptions of Aristotle, Machiavelli, and Mill) have nothing good to say about plurality, faction, or moral pluralism, and that they tolerate difference only as a functional necessity of the state. Even those who, like Aristotle, insist that the political community is made up of different kinds of individuals, and that judgment (*phronesis*), rather than *sophia*, is the first political virtue, in the end radically restrict the significance of human plurality and the scope of independent judgment.[34]

From Philosophical Thinking to Political (or Representative) Thinking

Arendt's rescue of the faculty of judgment from its theory and ideology-induced oblivion begins by bracketing this instrumental configuration of thought and action. In self-conscious opposition to the tradition, she foregrounds human plurality as the phenomenological ground not only of freedom and action, but of judgment as well. She attempts to break the stranglehold of rational truth on political thought by rehabilitating opinion, the plurality-based faculty persistently maligned by the tradition.

In Arendt's view, the degradation of judgment and opinion go hand in hand, and have their roots in the Platonic war against plurality and the rule of the many. In the essay "Philosophy and Politics" (written, but not published, in 1954), Arendt argued that Plato's "furious denunciation of *doxa*" (opinion) and his desire for absolute standards by which the philosopher could dominate the *polis* were direct results of the trial and condemnation of Socrates, which revealed in dramatic fashion the inadequacy of persuasive speech as a medium for philosophical truth.[35] The Platonic transformation of the ideas into atemporal standards for action was intended to back up the claim that the philosopher's truth, born of

95

solitary thought and reasoning, actually possessed an unquestionable validity in the realm of human affairs, where the relativity of
perspective and opinion had previously ruled.

As Arendt observes, "the opposition of truth and opinion was certainly the most anti-Socratic conclusion that Plato drew from Socrates' trial."[36] Socrates' philosophical activity was not that of a withdrawn thinker, but of a "citizen amongst citizens" trying to "help
others give birth to what they themselves thought anyhow."[37] Socratic dialectic aimed not at destroying or transcending *doxa*, but
rather at "talking something through" so that his partners in dialogue could clarify their perspective and improve their opinion. In
this way, they became aware of the truth *in* their opinion. Thus,
Socratic dialectic, as the conversation of citizens in the agora,
"brings forth truth *not* by destroying *doxa* or opinion, but on the
contrary reveals *doxa* in its own truthfulness."[38]

It is the continuity between truth, perspective, and opinion revealed by Socrates' "maieutic" activity that Arendt returns to again
and again in a series of essays written in the 1960s. "The Crisis in
Culture," "Truth and Politics," "Thoughts on Lessing"—all argue
that the public realm is the realm of opinion; that truth in this realm
is never univocal, but rather perspectival; that the process of opinion
formation and judgment are among the most woefully neglected
rational activities of man as a thinking, public being. As Arendt put
it in *On Revolution*, "opinion and judgment obviously belong among
the faculties of reason, but the point of the matter is that these two,
politically most important, rational faculties had been almost entirely neglected by the tradition of political as well as philosophical
thought."[39] Philosophy neglected opinion because its conflict with
the *polis* convinced it that reason and logic were to be found solely in
the solitary thought process of the philosopher. Arendt reclaims the
dignity of opinion in these essays, assailing the Platonic hierarchy
while questioning the idea that the "mode of asserting validity"
common to the "rational truths" of philosophy, mathematics, or science has any place whatever in the public, political realm.[40]

It is in the course of this anti-Platonic argument that Arendt describes the kind of rationality and validity peculiar to opinion formation and judgment. Political (as opposed to philosophical) thinking is characterized not by the rigorous logical unfolding of an
argument, but rather by imaginative mobility and the capacity to
represent the perspectives of others. The (rational) formation of an

opinion hinges upon this capacity for what Arendt calls "representative thought." In an oft-cited passage from "Truth and Politics" she writes:

> Political thought is representative. I form an opinion by considering a given issue from different viewpoints, by making present to my mind the standpoints of those who are absent; that is, I represent them. This process of representation does not blindly adopt the actual views of those who stand somewhere else, and hence look upon the world from a different perspective; this is a question neither of empathy, as though I tried to be or to feel like somebody else, nor of counting noses and joining a majority but of being and thinking in my own identity where actually I am not. The more people's standpoints I have present in my mind while I am pondering a given issue, and the better I can imagine how I would feel and think if I were in their place, the stronger will by my capacity for representative thinking and the more valid my final conclusions, my opinion.[41]

Richard Bernstein has argued that this passage shows that "opinion formation is not a private activity performed by a solitary thinker" and that it involves "a genuine encounter with different opinions," one which can only occur in "a political community of equals" who have the imagination to represent other viewpoints and the "courage to submit opinions to public exposure and test."[42] In this interpretation of Arendt, representative thinking is presented as inseparable from an idealized form of *public argument* in which judgments are formed through the submission of opinions to the judgments of others.[43] The peculiar validity of an opinion or judgment is thus a function of the "communication, testing, purification" that takes place in the process of public dialogue.

Support for Bernstein's interpretation can be found in Arendt's invocation of the Kantian idea an "enlarged mentality" (*eine erweiterte Denkungsart*) in both "Truth and Politics" and "The Crisis in Culture." In the latter essay she writes:

> The power of judgment rests on a potential agreement with others, and the thinking process which is active in judging something is not, like the thought process of pure reasoning, a dialogue between me and myself, but finds itself always and primarily, even if I am quite alone in making up my mind, in an anticipated communication with others with whom I know I must finally come to some agreement. From this potential

agreement judgment derives its specific validity. This means, on the one hand, that such judgment must liberate itself from the "subjective private conditions," that is, from the idiosyncrasies which naturally determine the outlook of each individual in his privacy and are legitimate as long as they are only privately held opinions, but which are not fit to enter the market place, and lack all validity in the public realm. And this enlarged way of thinking, which as judgment knows how to transcend its own individual limitations, on the other hand, cannot function in strict isolation or solitude; it needs the presence of others "in whose place" it must think, whose perspectives it must take into consideration, and without whom it never has the opportunity to operate at all . . . judgment, to be valid, depends on the presence of others.[44]

In Bernstein's estimation, this passage is "the culmination of Arendt's thinking about action and politics."[45] It not only elucidates the specific brand of thinking essential for political life, it also reveals how the activity of judgment is itself the consummate form of political action. For it is in the process of judgment captured by the notions of "representative thinking" and "enlarged mentality" that plurality is preserved, opinion redeemed, and deliberative rationality enthroned as the political faculty par excellence. To judge is to engage in rational public dialogue, deliberating with others with whom I must finally come to an agreement and decision. This, in a nutshell, is the Arendtian vision of democratic politics as a politics of judgment and debate, one whose principle of legitimacy is found in the idea of unforced public dialogue.[46]

THINKING AS PREPARATION FOR JUDGMENT

But is this really the way that thinking prepares for judgment? And should we view the judgment that it prepares for as intrinsically a part of public debate and decision-making?

As Bernstein notes, it is precisely at the moment Arendt comes closest to a quasi-Aristotelian account of judgment as *phronesis* that she veers toward Kant and the notions of taste, distance, impartiality, and spectatorship so important to his aesthetics. For Bernstein, as for Beiner, this indicates a fundamental tension in Arendt's thought about judgment, the presence of two very different perspectives on the same mental ability. The more Arendt thought about judgment, the more she identified it, not with the *political* ability to "think in the place of others," but rather with the ability to think for oneself, without reliance upon customs, rules, and habits. If the passages cited above point to judgment's dependence upon a "common sense" (the *sensus communis* invoked by Kant in section 40 of *The Critique of Judgment*), which enables the judge *qua* actor to persuade or "woo" his peers, then Arendt's later work seems to present judgment as a faculty that "comes into its own when politics breaks down."[47]

Is there a tension here, or (worse yet) a "flagrant contradiction"?[48] I think not. Of course, the faculty of judgment looks different depending on whether we take the perspective of the actor or the spectator. But it is simply not the case that Arendt counseled "common sense," persuasion, and consensus for those in the game, and critical thinking, impartiality, and autonomy for those who were out of it. If we step back and examine the passages cited above in context, and relate them to Arendt's account of critical or Socratic thinking in "Philosophy and Politics," "Thinking and Moral Considerations," and her Kant lectures, we see the underlying continuity in her thought on judgment.[49]

One reason why critics like Bernstein and Beiner see an irreducible gap between Arendt's early, actor-centered account of judgment and her later, critical or historical one is that they fail to take sufficient account of Arendt's overarching narrative about the destruction, loss, or decline of the public realm in the modern age. This narrative, developed in detail in *The Human Condition*, serves to make any appeal to community-based judgment (whether Aristotelian *phronesis* or Kant's judgments of taste) highly complex, if not downright ironic. Where "common sense" can no longer be counted upon to fit us into the world, subjectivism, ideology, or various kinds of moral objectivism try to fill the gap. The question then becomes: how can disinterested, impartial judgment be preserved in a world without a *sensus communis* or agreed upon criteria for what constitutes "the better public argument"? To put this another way: how can plurality, as Arendt conceives it, survive in an age of irreducible moral pluralism?

There is no easy answer to this question. But it does force us to take another look at Arendt's various statements about judgment. When we put these in the context of the "crisis in judgment" implied by the narrative in *The Human Condition* (a crisis she explicitly addresses in the essays "Understanding and Politics" and "The Crisis in Culture"[50]), Arendt's statements on judgment as a form of acting are revealed to be highly conditional. From the very beginning—indeed as far back as *The Origins of Totalitarianism*—Arendt emphasized the dissolution of modern Europe's moral groundwork, the "break in our tradition" and the "loss of common sense," events that yield a staggering growth in stupidity (understood in the specifically Kantian sense as the inability to judge). If *phronesis*, representative thinking, and an "enlarged mentality" were ever characteristics of active citizens, they are no longer: their basic conditions of possibility have been destroyed by "the moral and spiritual breakdown of occidental society," on the one hand, and the rise of mass culture, on the other.[51]

Arendt writes about judgment, then, in a historical situation weirdly parallel to the one Socrates confronted in fifth-century (BCE) Athens. There, too, traditional morality had fragmented or been hollowed out to yield a bastard morality of success. As the Socratic confrontations with Polus and Callicles in the *Gorgias* or Polemarchus and Thrasymachus in the *Republic* demonstrate, one can hardly rely on "common sense" or society's account of the virtues in such situations. These have become mere customs or clichés, complacently exchanged and unthinkingly applied. It scarcely comes as a surprise when they are denounced as patent illusions by "strong" individuals like Thrasymachus or Callicles, who draw the logical conclusion and worship power instead.[52] The way out of this situation, for Arendt as well as Socrates, is no return to a shattered tradition, nor a simple call to action, but a radical questioning of all the old "yardsticks" for action and judgment. What is called for in such situations is not activism, but independent judgment, "thinking without banisters " (*Denken ohne Gelander*).[53]

It is because of the modern crisis in judgment, of the staggering growth of stupidity and the inability to judge, that Arendt explicitly turns to Socrates as a model in "Philosophy and Politics," "Thinking and Moral Considerations," and in the *Lectures on Kant's Political Philosophy*. In these texts, she poses Socrates as a model of "critical thinking" or *Selbstdenken*, a model which captures the negative and public dimensions of how thinking prepares for independent, impartial judgment.

In all three texts, Arendt emphasizes the purgative quality of Socratic thinking. Socrates did not *teach* anything; rather, he exposed unexamined prejudgments to the "wind of thought," dissolving prejudices but putting no "truths" in their place.[54] Hence "critical thinking"—as performed publicly in Socratic dialectic—is an essentially destructive activity. It has a "destructive, undermining effect on all established criteria, values, measurements for good and evil, in short on those customs and rules of conduct we treat of in morals and ethics."[55] Socrates is not merely (as the famous figure of the *Apology* has it) a "gadfly" to the complacent Athenians. He is also (as the simile from the *Meno* reminds us) something of an "electric ray" or stinging fish, in that his aporetic arguments interrupt the everyday activities of his dialogical partners, "paralyzing" them with thought and doubt. Such doubt, if sustained, makes the ordinary conduct of life impossible, since the general rules and received notions on which it is based have all been exposed to the destructive wind of thought.[56]

The Socratic dialogues can hardly be characterized as deliberation aiming at decision and action. Socratic thinking, while a "public exercise of reason," undercuts action: its unstated goal is to slow people down. Yet this kind of thinking prepares for judgment precisely insofar as it has the effect of suspending all "fixed habits of thought, ossified rules and standards." As Arendt put it at a conference on her work in 1973:

> . . . I think that this "thinking". . . —thinking in the Socratic sense—is a
> maieutic function, a midwifery. That is, you bring out all your opinions,
> prejudices, what have you; and you know that never, in any of the [Pla-
> tonic] dialogues, did Socrates ever discover any child [of the mind] who
> was not a wind-egg. That you remain in a way empty after thinking. . . .
> And once you are empty, then, in a way which is difficult to say, you are
> prepared to judge. That is, without having any book of rules under
> which you can subsume a particular case, you have got to say "this is
> good," "this is bad," "this is right," "this is wrong," "this is beautiful,"
> and "this is ugly". . . . we are now prepared to meet the phenomena, so
> to speak, head on, without any preconceived system.[57]

It is the negative preparation that thinking provides for judgment which Arendt valued above all, and which she feared was vanishing from the world. Judgment of a particular phenomenon or event can be the "by-product" of thinking, not because it is in any sense the direct result of thought, but rather because thinking clears the space which makes it possible.[58] The testing and examination of opinions that is the heart of critical thinking as practiced by Socrates (and articulated by Kant) creates the mental space necessary for independent, impartial judgment.[59]

With the help of Arendt's Kant lectures, we are now in a position to re-examine the passages on representative thinking and "enlarged mentality" cited above, passages which seem to provide unequivocal support for viewing judgment as a form of action. In fact, as the lectures make clear, "representative thinking" and "enlarged mentality" are not really models for public deliberation and rational will formation at all. They are, rather, the necessary vehicles of critical thinking. As habits of mind—exceedingly difficult to learn and master, even with the aid of Socratic dialectic or Kantian critique—they proceed imaginatively, drawing on the *possible* standpoints and opinions of others in order to "abstract from the limitations which contingently attach to our own judgment."[60] As Arendt puts it in the *Lectures*:

> The "enlargement of the mind" plays a crucial role in the *Critique of Judgment*. It is accomplished by "comparing our judgment with the possible rather than the actual judgments of others, and by putting ourselves in the place of any other man." The faculty that makes this possible is called imagination. . . . Critical thinking is possible only where the standpoints of all others are open to inspection. Hence, critical thinking, while still a solitary business, does not cut itself off from "all others." To be sure, it still goes on in isolation, but by the force of imagination it makes the others present and thus moves in a space that is potentially public, open to all sides. . . . To think with an enlarged mentality means that one trains one's imagination to go visiting.[61]

Dialogue in the agora, or the "public use of one's reason," are good ways of "enlarging" one's mentality, of "training one's imagination to go visiting." But neither representative nor "enlarged" thought have decision or action as their *raison d'être*. The "abstraction from contingent limitations" enables the attainment of a "general standpoint," which Arendt characterizes as "a viewpoint from which to look upon, to watch, to form judgments, or as Kant himself says, to reflect upon human affairs."[62] It "does not tell one how *to act*"; rather, it enables one to judge—impartially, independently.

The more "detached" version of representative thinking we encounter in the Kant lectures points back to the earlier formulations of "Philosophy and Politics." There, Arendt had emphasized how

Socratic "thinking something through" was intended to "bring out the truth" of each individual's *doxa*, his "it appears to me." What links Socratic dialectic and Kantian enlarged thought for Arendt is the way both yield not *the* truth or an Archimedean standpoint, but a more impartial (and hence more valid) "it appears to me."[63] If we view Arendt's thoughts on judgment in terms of a broader perspectivism, the standpoints of the actor and the spectator emerge not as two radically different species of judgment (engaged and political vs. detached and historical), but rather as two poles of the more inclusive phenomenon of independent judgment.[64] To be sure, the "general standpoint" of the impartial judge is different from the seemingly more robust standpoint of the citizen's "it appears to me." Yet, as Kant's great enemy Nietzsche reminds us, "the more eyes, different eyes, we can use to observe one thing, the more complete will our 'concept' of this thing, our 'objectivity,' be."[65] Impartial judgment, as conceived by Arendt, remains perspectival in character: it is opinion in its highest form.

If, in the end, the standpoint of the spectator takes precedence over that of the actor for Arendt, it is because the former is more distanced and impartial, and thus more open to the particularity of an event or phenomenon. And while, from the Greek perspective, the Kantian spectator has in fact given up the *dokei moi*, the it appears to me, along with the desire to appear to others, Arendt is willing to pay the price.[66] In a world in which the opportunities to be a "participator in government," to share words and deeds on a public stage, have been dramatically curtailed, we still have the choice between being passive consumers of media-packaged spectacle, or independent judges of the events which constitute the "spectacle" of the public world and history.

THE LIMITS OF JUDGMENT

Judgment, then, is not action, nor does it produce a substitute for action. Thinking and judging for oneself remains in tension with "acting with others." Nor should we look to judgment for a bridge between political theory and political practice. Yet even when judgment is distinguished from the kind of debate and deliberation that goes on in the public realm, it remains a distinctly political faculty, and not just "by implication."[67] When "liberated" by thought, the faculty of judgment is free to confirm the being of what is, or what was. That is to say, the judgment of the semi-alienated citizen or detached spectator is what recognizes and preserves the particularity and novelty of a given phenomenon or event. Arendt thinks that Kant was right to insist that it was not "the deeds and misdeeds of the actors but the opinions, the enthusiastic approbation, of spectators" which singled out the French Revolution as a world historical event, a "phenomenon not to be forgotten."[68] The uninvolved spectator is free to say what is, just as the historian is able to say what was.

It is the capacity of judgment (whether in the form of "critical thinking" or historical narrative) to say what is, to "judge particulars without subsuming them under those general rules which can be taught and learned until they grow into habits," that makes it "the most political of man's mental abilities."[69] We are not here concerned with the establishment of facts (absolutely essential for judgment to even begin[70]), but with the actual process of discriminating and discerning the new, of preserving singular "appearances" from effacement by clichés, universal rules, and ingrained habits of thought. Arendt's work on the phenomenon of totalitarianism and the nature of Adolf Eichmann's evil stand as towering examples of judgment so conceived. I want to conclude by briefly considering the political implications of her controversial thesis about the "banality of evil," a concept she was "put in possession of" when confronted "in the flesh" with Eichmann's "extraordinary shallowness."

In the penultimate chapter of *Eichmann in Jerusalem*, Arendt closes her description of Eichmann's comic, self-contradictory remarks under the gallows (the *Gottglaubiger* informed his hangmen that they would all "soon meet again") with the sentence: "It was as though in those last minutes he was summing up the lesson that this long course in human wickedness had taught us—the lesson of the fearsome, word-and-thought-defying *banality of evil*."[71] With these words she put into circulation a concept which has been essential for grasping the peculiar evil of twentieth-century bureaucracies of murder. Twenty years later she wrote that by the "banality of evil" she meant "no theory or doctrine, but something quite factual, the phenomenon of evil deeds, committed on a gigantic scale, which could not be traced to any particularity of wickedness, pathology, or ideological conviction in the doer, whose only personal distinction was a perhaps extraordinary shallowness."[72] In the case of bureaucratic evil, motives become superfluous: "The trouble is precisely that no wicked heart, a relatively rare phenomenon, is necessary to cause great evil. "[73]

While the furor surrounding the Eichmann book was largely the result of Arendt's brief discussion of the unwitting complicity of some Jewish ghetto leaders with the Nazis, her concept of the banality of evil was scarcely less controversial. Many found her description of a thoughtless, patently undemonic Eichmann too much. The gap between the crimes and the man seemed somehow to diminish the horrors and the guilt.[74] Only a monstrous Eichmann could fully live up to the enormity of the crime.

Both the novel, paradoxical quality of Arendt's concept and the outraged response to her judgment are of interest here. "The banality of evil" is, first of all, a perfect example of detached, impersonal judgment, the judgment of the spectator. A particular— Eichmann—is not subsumed under ready-to-hand ideas about the nature of evil; rather, Arendt practiced a form of reflective judgment, ascending from the particular (Eichmann in the flesh) to a concept. This concept, "the banality of evil," enabled her to disclose not only the specific nature of Eichmann's evil, but also the increasingly widespread phenomenon of evil detached from wickedness, evil committed by the most ordinary or "normal" of men, men who were neither ideological fanatics nor beasts in human form.[75] The precondition of this disclosure was the purging of a traditional theological and philosophical ways of thinking about evil as a phenomenon with deep roots in the sinful, proud, or envious character of the doer. Only then, when the concept of evil had been unfrozen (so to speak), could the recognition and naming of a new phenomenon occur.[76]

We must not forget, however, that this very judgment elicited the most outraged of responses. Following Kant's dictum, Arendt had resisted enormous pressure and made her judgment public.[77] The price of "publicity" was not "testing and purification," but virtual excommunication. Her judgment revealed her moral sense, her moral "taste," yet there could be little question of "wooing the consent" of others in *this* instance.[78] The philosophical and moral challenge implicit in Arendt's judgment was too great. Her independence of mind was deemed "perverse," the reflection of (in Gershom Scholem's words) a lack of *Ahabath Israel*, love of the Jewish people.[79]

Indeed, in making her judgment, Arendt self-consciously took the standpoint of the outsider: a nonparticipant in the trial, to be sure, but also an outsider when it came to the immediate political stakes of the process. In her view, it was far more important to focus attention on "the central moral, legal, and political phenomena of our century" than to align herself in solidarity with the narrative (and tactics) of the prosecution in the case. But like Socrates, Arendt was not very good at the persuasive speech that convinces the many. (To this day, *Eichmann in Jerusalem* remains her most controversial and persistently misunderstood book, largely because the judgment it renders does not fit preconceived categories.[80])

Just as Socrates' public performance of thinking led him to be charged with "corrupting the youth," so Arendt's public judgment was seen as a betrayal of her people. This is the risk run by *anyone* who dares to truly think and judge in public, a risk which is glossed over by the neo-Aristotelian presentation of judgment as a stately form of deliberation, as well as by the liberal formula of "the public use of one's reason." The more genuine judgment is, the less it respects the pregiven "yardsticks" that are appealed to by "common sense" in retreat. Independent judgment "brushes history against the grain."[81] As a creative activity (and Arendt's shared emphasis with Kant on the role of imagination in judgment leaves little doubt that it is), it will most likely be misunderstood and resented.

This is not to say the truly independent judge must become a martyr like Socrates. However, it will be difficult to avoid becoming something of a pariah, especially if one has the courage to make one's judgments public. Indeed, for Arendt, looking at things from "the pariah's point of view" was a lifetime vocation. It is an admirable vocation, but one which cannot (for obvious reasons) provide the basis for political action nor a bridge between theory and practice.

If we desire, then, to do justice to Arendt's insights concerning the interrelations of thinking, judging, and acting, we must avoid the twin temptations of existentialist *engagement* and philosophical withdrawal. For, in the end, what Arendt teaches is the irreducible need to be both in and out of the game—as the times and situation demand, and as personal talents dictate.

CHAPTER FIVE

Democratizing the Agon

NIETZSCHE, ARENDT, AND THE
AGONISTIC TENDENCY IN RECENT
POLITICAL THEORY

> It seems to me that those who criticize the conflicts between the nobles and the plebeians condemn the very things which were the primary cause of Roman liberty, and that they pay more attention to the noises and cries raised by such quarrels than to the good effects that they brought forth; nor do they consider that in every republic there are two different inclinations: that of the people and that of the upper class, and that all the laws which are made in favor of liberty are born of the conflict between the two. . . .
> (*Machiavelli*, The Discourses, *Bk. 1, chap. 4*)

> Every talent must unfold itself in fighting. . . .
> (*Nietzsche*, Homer's Contest)

> Politics means conflict.
> (*Max Weber*, Parliament and Government)

INTRODUCTION

To speak of an agonistic politics in a liberal democratic context invites skepticism, given the traditional liberal fear of stirring up the moral passions and conflicting visions of the good that divide citizens of a pluralist society. To speak of a "democratic agonism" is, perhaps, to push this skepticism to outright disbelief, given the heroic/aristocratic virtues associated with the agonal ideal articulated by both Friedrich Nietzsche and Hannah Arendt. Yet many contemporary political theorists (Sheldon Wolin, William Connolly,

Chantal Mouffe, and Bonnie Honig among them) have turned to a broadly agonistic model of politics as *the* way of advancing a radical democratic agenda. These theorists worry that modern democracies are hardly democratic at all; that the bureaucratic edifice of the state has usurped the space of the political, rendering citizens the passive recipients of policy decisions; and that liberal theory has contributed to this state of affairs by promoting a conception of politics which is essentially juridical/administrative, one which seeks ways of diminishing, if not eradicating, the contest and debate that is the life blood of a robust democratic politics.[1]

Concerning the last point, agonistic democrats worry that John Rawls and other advocates of a broadly proceduralist liberalism are so anxious to avoid conflict that they construct a set of public institutions, and a code of public argument and justification, which leave precious little space for initiatory or expressive modes of political action.[2] What Rawls calls the "domain of the political" is seen as so strictly circumscribed that it marginalizes not only substantive moral argument, but essential questions of economic power and political identity. Agonistic democrats share Michael Sandel's fear that "fundamentalists rush in where liberals fear to tread" and his suspicion of the hard distinction between public and private which Rawls' political liberalism is (apparently) built on.[3] While skeptical of Sandel's civic republican remedy (and his call for a frankly moralistic public discourse), agonistic democrats tend to agree with his basic point that political liberalism has been all too successful in separating the *homme* (or *femme*) from the *citoyen*.[4]

Viewed against the background of a liberalism that desires, above all, to remain neutral with respect to controversial views of the good life, agonism appears to provide a much-needed life- and reality-restoring corrective to political theory. Contemporary agonists remind us that the public sphere is as much a stage for conflict and expression as it is a set of procedures or institutions designed to preserve peace, promote fairness, or achieve consensus. They also insist (*contra* Rawls) that politics and culture form a continuum, where ultimate values are always already in play; where the content of basic rights and the purposes of political association are not the objects of a frictionless "overlapping consensus," but are contested every day, in a dizzying array of venues. With its battlecry of "incessant contestation," political agonism seems to provide a welcome return to the repressed essence of democratic politics: conflict.

The political agonist is, however, open to an array of equally compelling liberal objections. Isn't a politics of rules, interests, and accommodation infinitely preferable to a politics of action, passions, and ideological conflict? Doesn't a more expansive and expressive public sphere, one in which ultimate values and questions of group identity are actively engaged, exacerbate the divisions within society, threatening to burst the fragile integument of liberal secularism asunder? Finally, doesn't an agonistic politics, even a "radically democratic" one, make the friend/enemy distinction the core of political life? Doesn't it threaten to turn us all, if not into Carl Schmitts, Rush Limbaughs?[5]

One need not be a Rawls or a Madison to worry about the consequences of an "incessantly contestatory" (and presumably more ideological) politics, even if one shares the sense that Americans, at least, are deeply alienated from political life. Indeed, the trouble with recent formulations of an agonistic politics is that they have tended to celebrate conflict, and individual and group political expression, a bit too unselectively. One can agree with their diagnosis of some of the ills of liberal theory and practice (the tendency to overvalue consensus, order, and rational deliberation, for example) without being entirely persuaded by their cure. Making citizens more expressive, and demanding that their expressions be heard in the public realm, may not, in the end, make them any less subservient to the rule or any more resistant to "normalization" (so much, at least, is suggested by the analyses of Richard Sennett and Michel Foucault).[6] Moreover, it is hardly the case that liberalism itself has been free of the worry that citizens of a constitutional order, democratic or otherwise, will gradually come to think and act as docile subjects of that order, rather than as vigilant watchers over political authority (think of Locke in the *Second Treatise on Government*, Thoreau in "Civil Disobedience," or Mill in *On Liberty*). This suggests that the real problem is not how to encourage and make room for expression, unruly or otherwise. Rather, it is how to promote an ethos of independent thought and action, one that is sufficiently impersonal to be both morally serious and publicly oriented.

As Honig has argued, one can learn much from Nietzsche in this regard. But one can learn even more, I would argue, from the selective appropriation of Nietzsche performed by Hannah Arendt. More than any other theorist, Arendt demonstrates the political relevance of Nietzsche's agonistic stance. At the same time, her reading of Greek political experience, along with her appreciation of the lessons of Socrates and Kant, made her acutely aware of the need to set limits, both institutional and characterological, to the agon that *is* political life. If Arendt goes much further that any liberal would go in her advocacy of an agonistic ethos in politics, she distinguishes herself from contemporary agonists by her emphasis upon the impersonal dimensions of such an ethos. Impersonality does not denote the effacement of the individual under his civic mask or persona (Arendt is not the champion of an unvarnished civic republicanism that many have made her out to be). Her agonism, like Nietzsche's, is surprisingly individualistic. But, unlike his, it is not particularly expressive. This creates an instructive tension with the formulations of contemporary agonists. In my view, the impersonality of Arendt's agonistic ethos makes it preferable to these more recent formulations.

In what follows, I present Arendt's selective appropriation of Nietzsche in light of current debates. First, I sketch the concerns that inform Nietzsche's agonism, and Arendt's. I then turn to consider the difference between her appropriation of Nietzsche and that of the advocates of "incessant contestation."[7] I conclude with some reflections on the limits of the agonistic strand in contemporary political theory.

Agonism in Nietzsche and Arendt

Throughout his work, Nietzsche addresses the problem of a modern, "democratic" culture that has inherited the prejudice of "slave morality" against heroic or individualizing action. While *Beyond Good and Evil* (1886) and *On the Genealogy of Morals* (1887) provide the most profound meditations on this theme, the broad problematic is already established in the essay "On the Use and Abuse of History for Life" (1874). Nietzsche's critique of historicism—his insistence that great action demands a protective, partly closed horizon—prefigures his later polemics against philosophical skepticism and both religious and scientific versions of the "ascetic ideal." Indeed, the theme that "knowledge kills action" goes back to *The Birth of Tragedy*. From the beginning, "Socratism," understood as a will to truth that dissolves life-sustaining illusions, is under indictment.[8]

What makes the later texts interesting, however, is Nietzsche's specification of what constitutes a "healthy," action-promoting moral horizon. In *Beyond Good and Evil* (*BGE*) and *On the Genealogy of Morals* (*GM*) Nietzsche leaves the exhortatory rhetoric of *Lebensphilosophie* behind, focusing instead on those structures that inhibit independent action and which stand in the way of fashioning the self as a work of art.

In *GM* Nietzsche argues that the *moral epistemology* set in place by the "slave revolt in morality" is one that is intrinsically hostile to action and the active life. If the aristocratic Greeks lacked a developed distinction between an actor and his acts, a subject and his "effects," it was because they could not conceive of the noble man as *other* from his deeds. To be and to act were, from their perspective, the same.[9] It is only the reactive man, the "slave," the man who *cannot* act, who needs the comforting fiction of a subject entirely separate from its actions or "effects." Thus, in his famous parable of the lamb and the bird of prey (*GM* I, 13), Nietzsche writes that "to demand of strength that it should *not* express itself as strength, that it should *not* be a desire to overcome, a desire to throw down, a desire to become master, a thirst for enemies and resistances and triumphs, is just as absurd as to demand of weakness that it should express itself as strength."

Yet despite the absurdity, this is how we, "masters" and "slaves" alike, come to think of the relation between the doer and his deed. Thanks to the "fiction" of a neutral subject "behind" the actions of the "strong man" or the reactions of the "weak," human agents are rendered morally accountable for *all* their actions. Such accountability is a lighter burden for those who abstain from action; indeed, it turns their abstention into a kind of virtue. For the agent predisposed to manifest his virtues in action, to individualize himself through the *performance* of great or noble deeds, such accountability shifts the standard of judgment of action away from its beauty or greatness, and towards its presumably disruptive consequences for the social whole. Through the "fiction" of the subject—the basic element of the moral epistemology of "slave morality"—action is moralized and the actor rendered subservient to a code of conduct that applies universally to society as a whole. "Active," agonistic agents cease to compete with their peers in order to demonstrate their excellence. They become, like the rest of us, "responsible"

111

subjects, self-surveilling and slow to initiate anything, ever conscious of the code of conduct of the "herd."

Nietzsche does not hold out the possibility, or even the desirability, of re-creating the state of almost animallike health that he ascribes to the Homeric Greeks. The bulk of *GM* is devoted to telling the long, bloody story of how responsibility originated. Despite all the gruesomeness of the "morality of mores" and the "social straitjacket," Nietzsche leaves no doubt that what he calls the moralization and internalization of man is the price paid for creating an "interesting" animal, an animal capable of autonomy and self-legislation (*GM*, II, 2). The problem is that so many of us get stuck in the intermediate stage of bad conscience, the stage of an internalized social code that encourages continual self-monitoring and condemnation of the strong passions essential to initiatory action. To frame what is typically considered *the* moral life as a transitional phase, one all too dependent on the myth of a divine surveillance apparatus in the sky, is one aim of *GM*'s materialist history of morals.

Of course, liberal democracy sees itself as making enormous contributions to the project of autonomy, to the creation of a social space in which more and more individuals not only live the life they please, but also attain a degree of moral maturity and independence of judgment previously undreamt of. The goal of the second and third essays of *GM*, and of much of *BGE*, is to shatter this self-conception. If the morality of mores had to make men "to a certain degree necessary, uniform, like among like, regular, and consequently calculable" in order for responsibility to emerge, the democratic age accelerates rather than reverses this process. Democracy doesn't create the conditions for the "sovereign individual"; on the contrary, it represents the triumph of *ressentiment* and the will to sameness and unconditionality that characterizes slave morality. As Nietzsche writes in *BGE*:

> *Morality in Europe today is herd animal morality*—in other words, as we understand it, merely *one* type of human morality beside which, before which, and after which many other types, above all *higher* moralities, are, or ought to be, possible. But this morality resists such a "possibility," such an "ought" with all its power: it says stubbornly and inexorably, "I am morality itself, and nothing besides is morality." Indeed, with the help of a religion which indulged and flattered the most sublime herd-animal desires, we have reached the point where we find

even in political and social institutions an ever more visible expression of this morality: the *democratic* movement is the heir of the Christian movement.[10]

The democratic subject is, according to Nietzsche, the herd animal par excellence, the living embodiment of the "morality of timidity." His virtues—the virtues of "public spirit, benevolence, consideration, industriousness, moderation, modesty, indulgence and pity"—stand in direct opposition to the virtues manifest in the masters' agonal striving. Indeed, these latter virtues (and the passions that underlie them) are seen as the greatest threat to the democratic community.[11]

When we ask how Nietzsche envisions nonslavish, nonconformist virtues (the virtues of the "sovereign individual"), the answer does little to soothe democratic sensibilities. Nietzsche's ethos of self-overcoming and his hostility to universalizing moral codes lead him to laud not simply action over passivity, but all those characteristics that distinguish the "healthy" from the "sick." Great passions, great energies, the will to command oneself and others, the willingness to sacrifice oneself and others: these, together with an intense appreciation of the Greek valuation of "struggle and the joy of victory," delineate a masculine aestheticism that stands in the greatest possible tension with the democratic repudiation of rulership.[12] For Nietzsche, the affirmation of life requires the affirmation of rule, of rank and "the pathos of distance."[13] One must rule oneself by focusing one's energies with the severest discipline; one can achieve greatness in politics only insofar as one is willing to *command*. Whether discussing the self or the polity, Nietzsche invariably deploys the metaphor of the work of art, with its implication of violence toward the "raw materials" (internal or external) that need shaping.[14] His examples of "sovereign individuals," those who are "autonomous and supramoral," tend either to be virtuosic artists (like Goethe or Beethoven) or political actors of great, but ruthless, *virtu* (Cesare Borgia, Napoleon).

Given Nietzsche's coupling of the "herd animal" with democracy, and his aristocratic conception of the agonistic virtues, it is hardly surprising that his critique of the "responsible subject" fell on deaf ears for so long. Foucault's *Discipline and Punish* changed all that by showing how the modern state produced "docile subjects" through the proliferation of "microtechniques of power." Quite

113

self-consciously, Foucault provided a *Genealogy of Morals* for the democratic age, one which attempted to demonstrate that rights and disciplines are two sides of the same coin.[15] From a Foucauldian point of view, our ostensibly greater freedom masks an ever more profound internalization of norms; indeed, it is possible only on the basis of our becoming "self-surveilling" subjects.

Foucault's analysis provides an essential touchstone for most contemporary agonists. Their calls for "resistance" and "excess" presuppose that liberal democracy has been all too successful in "taming" its citizens, diminishing or diverting their potentially political energies. Again, the general theme is hardly new: recall Machiavelli and Rousseau's civic republican critiques of Christian passivity, or Mill and Tocqueville's prescient analyses of democratic conformity (it was, after all, Mill who called for a strong dose of "pagan self-assertion" to balance the inherited burden of "Christian self-denial"[16]). Foucault's unique contribution to this thematic was to suggest not only that power permeated everyday life (in the form of the disciplines), but that the very process of producing "docile subjects" created resistances and multiple sites of struggle in places hitherto relegated to the extreme margins of political life (hospitals, schools, factories, prisons). Thus, precisely when the agon seemed like the most ancient of history, it reemerged in the interstices of the welfare state itself.[17] Agonistic subjectivity—the subjectivity of Nietzsche's "masters" and his elite of "sovereign individuals"— returned in the democratized form of the politics of resistance.

But Foucault's updating of Nietzsche remained insufficient from the standpoint of the radical democratic project. While generating a "politics of everyday life," its center of gravity was, in fact, ethical rather than political; its foremost concern, resisting the imposition of identities on groups and individuals. And for this reason the "radical democrats" have turned to Arendt's expressly *political* reformulation of Nietzsche's agonism. What attracts them to Arendt?

First, she gives a central place to action in her conception of the political. This sets her at odds with the liberal focus on institutions, procedures, interests, and "negative freedom" (the freedom *from* politics).[18] But Arendt goes far beyond the affirmation of "public freedom" and "public happiness" that we encounter in the civic republican tradition. Like Nietzsche, she affirms the initiatory dimension of all genuine action, its radically innovative character.[19] And, like Nietzsche, she affirms the contingency of human (and especially political) affairs, disdaining all teleological orderings and utilitarian criteria. For Arendt, the freedom of action is manifest in its capacity to transcend both the needs of life and the supposed necessity of history. The Nietzschean formula "the deed is everything" holds for her, since it is through deeds—through initiatory political speech and action—that human beings tear themselves away from the everyday, the repetitive, the merely reactive.[20] *Unlike* Nietzsche, however, she insists that action properly occurs only in a public sphere characterized by relations of equality. Citing the Greek *polis*, she goes so far as to identify freedom with (political) equality.[21] Human plurality—the existence of diverse equals—is for her the *sine qua non* of political action. Indeed, all genuinely political action is, in fact, an "acting together."[22] *Contra* Nietzsche, rulership signals the end of political action, its dissolution into the instrumental and fundamentally unfree activity of command and obedience.[23]

Second, radical democrats are attracted by Arendt's endorsement of the "fiercely agonal spirit," which she sees as animating all genuine political action. Again like Nietzsche, Arendt turns to the Greeks in order to isolate the "immortalizing impulse," the passion for greatness, as *the* specifically political passion.[24] The impulse to distinguish oneself, to prove oneself the best of all, lies at the heart of action's tremendous individualizing power. But while Nietzsche's agonistic stance culminates in a heroic individualism, Arendt's expressly political version dovetails with what she calls the "revolutionary spirit" and the spirit of resistance.[25] Her examples are not virtuosic statesmen, but the spontaneous heroic action manifest in the American Revolution, the Paris Commune of 1871, the 1905 Russian Revolution, the French Resistance during World War II, and the Hungarian revolt of 1956. This makes it possible and plausible for contemporary agonists to assimilate her to "an activist, democratic politics of contest, resistance, and amendment."[26] And while radical democrats are generally quite skeptical of Arendt's Nietzsche-inspired distinction between the social and the political, viewing it as an aristocratic excrescence, they applaud the spirit behind pronouncements like the following (from *The Human Condition*):

> It is decisive that society, on all its levels, excludes the possibility of action, which formerly was excluded from the household. Instead, society expects from each of its members a certain kind of behavior, imposing innumerable and various rules, all of which tend to "normalize" its

members, to make them behave to exclude spontaneous action or outstanding achievement.[27]

Here Arendt mediates between Nietzsche's critique of the ascetic
regimes through which individuals are "tamed" and made useful to
the "herd," and Weber's savage depiction of the *Ordnungsmensch*
fostered by the bureaucratic penetration of everyday life. And, of
course, she prefigures Foucault's basic theme in *Discipline and
Punish*.

Third, Arendt draws out the specifically political consequences of
Nietzsche's anti-foundationalism, showing how the will to an extrapolitical ground in the modern age can only be nihilistic, antipolitical, and antidemocratic.[28] The will to find a transcendent
ground for politics is a will to escape the irreducible relativity of
human agreements and opinions; it is the will to discover an immov-
able authority which will put an end to the incessant debate and
contestation that *is* democratic politics. Arendt gives Nietzsche's
anti-Platonism a political (and democratic) twist by arguing for a
groundless "politics of opinion," one which recognizes the human
need for stability but which eschews (in Honig's words) a "law of
laws that is immune to contestation and amendment."[29] What
makes Arendt's conception of an agonistic public sphere so attractive to radical democrats is not that it puts everything up for
grabs (a viable public sphere depends on relatively firm laws and
lasting institutions), but that the meaning and authoritativeness
of its founding and basic institutions are determined by the clash
of conflicting interpretations. So conceived, the public sphere is,
above all, an institutionally articulated site of perpetual debate and
contestation.

If we add to Arendt's focus on action, praise of the spirit of resistance, and political "postfoundationalism" her ingenious adaptation
of Nietzsche's perspectivism for the demands of a democratic public
sphere,[30] it is easy to see why the proponents of a politics of "incessant contestation" turn to her just as often as to Nietzsche for inspiration. This is not to say, however, that they believe that Arendt
succeeds in stripping agonism of its aristocratic trappings. On the
contrary, Wolin, Connolly and Honig take her to task for maintaining distinctions which they view as either unjustifiably elitist or
essentialist. Thus, Wolin attacks Arendt's distinction between the
social and the political, charging that her desire for a "pure politics"

unsullied by economic concerns and the needs of the "masses" is, at base, deeply antidemocratic. An Arendtian politics of memorable deeds performed by virtuosic actors is, according to Wolin, scarcely compatible with democratic politics, the primary thrust of which is to "extend the broad egalitarianism of ordinary lives into public life."[31] Similarly, Connolly charges her with maintaining a "political purism" parallel to Kant's moral purism, one that purges "the social question and the body" from the public realm. The result is a "bleached and aristocratic" version of human plurality, one deprived of important "dimensions of diversity which might otherwise enrich and fortify it."[32]

From a somewhat different angle, Honig attacks Arendt's apparently unbending distinction between public and private, which she views as both arbitrary and self-defeating.[33] Arendt's conception of the public sphere is, according to Honig, overly formalistic; it is also deeply conservative insofar as it naturalizes the public/private distinction. It thereby seals off inherited race, class, gender, and ethnic identities from contest and reformulation.[34] Whereas Wolin sees Arendt's conception of agonistic action as entailing the social/political distinction, Honig suggests that action as theorized by Arendt is essentially destabilizing, boundless, and unpredictable. It mirrors the movement of Derridean *differance*. Hence, the public/private distinction as deployed by Arendt arbitrarily confines the unconfineable: it seeks to put the genie (disruptive, "excessive" action) back in the bottle. Arendt is blind to her own insight. Radical democrats must save her from herself.

ETHOS AND LIMITS OF THE POLITICAL AGON

These critiques and emendations of Arendt's agonism will strike a chord with all serious readers of her work. In the end, however, I think the criticisms are too easy; they ignore the underlying concerns that shape her political appropriation of Nietzsche. Arendt's distinctions between the social and the political, or the public and the private, are not motivated by a Nietzschean desire to keep the healthy, active few separate from the "sick," resentful masses; nor are they designed to erect a "nonnegotiable" barrier that confines and emasculates her account of "disruptive" action. Rather, these

117

distinctions (and the dramaturgical conception of action and the public sphere they underwrite), serve to focus attention on the central role that impersonality and self-distance play in the preservation of a (genuinely) agonistic ethos. What matters for her is less *where* political action takes place and *what* it concerns than the spirit in which it is undertaken. Let me explain.

To *act*, for Arendt, means appearing on a public stage, before diverse equals. In so doing, we leave behind the private self of needs, drives, and a diffuse interiority. We take on a public persona, create a public self, one whose words and deeds are judged by the "audience" of our civic peers. Arendt's insistence on the social/political and public/private distinctions highlights the discipline, stylization, and conventionality assumed by the virtuosic political actor in the presentation of such a self. Only if actor and audience are adept at distinguishing between their civic/political selves and the self driven by material and psychological needs can something like a relatively autonomous political sphere exist at all. Arendt's distinctions are designed not to exclude groups of agents from the political sphere, but to point out the dangers inherent in certain mentalities or approaches to the public realm. Insofar as action is driven by the immediacy of unbearable oppression or material want, it cannot hope to attain the degree of impersonality that is the hallmark of *political* action. The passions and needs that drive such desperate, often violent action have little to do with what Arendt calls "care for the world," by which she means concern for the artificial "home" that a political association provides for human beings. Concern for this "in-between," for the structure of institutions and terms of association it sets, is what marks the *political* actor.

In other words, action must have a constitutional referent for it to qualify as political for Arendt. If we are to be fair to her, we must understand "constitutional" broadly, in the Greek rather than the more restricted American sense. "Constitutional" in the former sense denotes a whole way of life, that of the democratic, oligarchical, or aristocratic regime.[35] Political action in a constitutional democracy would, in Arendt's understanding, be citizenly action aimed against the state and other forces that threaten to restrict or overturn the pluralistic and (politically) egalitarian terms of association the constitution sets out. Of course, the precise nature of these terms and their moral implications are the stuff of ongoing, open-ended debate and contestation.[36] The democratic political life, as

Arendt understands it, is agonistic, often raucous, and passionate in its moral commitments; it is neither narrowly legalistic nor top down in its functioning. It is, however, importantly limited to *public* issues and terms of discourse. It is also more interested in playing the game than winning (this is Arendt's definition of a *public-spirited* agonism, what she calls the "joy of action"). Of course, *public* issues are not set in stone, and much of the content of democratic politics is debate over what issues are, in fact, of public (and constitutional) concern.[37] From an Arendtian point of view, however, Wolin's identification of democratic politics with grass-roots struggles for social justice is far too restrictive in its redefinition of the "public," just as Honig's Derrida-inspired "radicalization" of action as the boundary-blurring force par excellence is far too indefinite.

This serves to highlight an Arendtian departure from Nietzsche, one that also distinguishes her from contemporary agonists. Arendt's understanding of institutions and law as marking out the boundaries of the public realm (an understanding equally indebted to the Greeks and the American founders), and her emphasis upon the artificiality and relative fragility of this "man-made realm," offer a marked contrast to the celebrations of democratic flux found in Wolin and Honig. For Wolin, democratic action is essentially transgressive and revolutionary. By its very nature, it stands in extreme tension with any "settled constitution." Indeed, democracy is "reduced" and "devitalized" by form; it is not a form of government at all, but "a mode of being," an "experience" of common action that can be, at best, episodic, momentary.[38] Honig does not go nearly as far down this vitalist path, stressing as she does Nietzsche's and Arendt's shared "reverence for institutions." Nevertheless, her voluntarist assertion that Arendt relies on the practice of promising to create "fragile stabilities" amidst the contingent, flux-filled realm of politics dramatically underplays the extent to which Arendt envisions agonistic politics as a function of a "relatively permanent" public sphere.[39]

Arendt also departs radically from Nietzsche in her reliance upon the Renaissance and eighteenth-century tradition of *theatrum mundi*, a tradition she traces back to her beloved Greeks. It is her appreciation of the theatrical dimensions of political action—of the artificiality and conventionality that make it possible for a person to don a public mask, and to be judged by criteria appropriate to their public role—that underlies her fierce critique of both voluntarism

119

and romantic expressivism in politics.[40] Both, she thinks, read the common public world back into the self, destroying its autonomy and relative permanence.[41] It is because she wants to combat expressivism and the "worldlessness" it promotes that she identifies freedom with *virtu*, that is, with the virtuosity of the performing actor.[42]

Arendt's agonist critics have uniformly ignored the worldly thrust of her theatrical model of political action, of action as *performance*.[43] Without exception, they dismiss her conception of the public sphere as a theatrical space where such (distanced, impersonal) freedom can dwell, the better to bring agonistic action in line with some version of the expressivist model. Thus, Wolin insists that moments of genuine democratic politics arise as expressions of "the common being of human beings," while both Connolly and Honig argue that agonistic action flows from the energies of "multiple selves."[44] While the emphases on "common being" and "the subject as multiplicity" are themselves in tension (one suited to the project of reviving the *demos*, the other to identity politics broadly construed), they share a profound devaluation of the *worldliness* of political action, its impersonal or theatrical character. For Wolin, Connolly, and Honig, democratizing the agon is inseparable from making agonistic action *expressive* action.

Why is this such a sin? What could possibly be wrong with overcoming the constricting conventionality assumed by Arendt's theatrical model in favor of a more transgressive, Nietzschean, conception? What do we lose by detaching the agon from Arendt's strong notion of a public world and a public self?

For one thing, we lose the ground of a "care for the world" which, in Arendt's view, animates all genuinely political action. In its stead, we find the demands for social justice and recognition of emergent identities. Such demands are not to be taken lightly. The problem is that they do little to promote an agonistic ethos that rises above interest group politics. This problem has not gone unnoticed by contemporary agonists, who point out the need for "an ethos of engagement" and an attitude of "agonistic respect." Connolly, for one, argues against both Arendt and Rawls by calling for a politicized form of pluralism, a pluralism freed from the myth of a single common good and from the split between *homme* and *citoyen*:

> In such a culture, participants are neither called upon to leave their metaphysical presumptions at home when they enter the public realm

nor to pursue a single common good to be acknowledged by all parties in the same state. Such a public plurality of religious/metaphysical perspectives fosters a democracy appropriate to the intercultural diversity of the late-modern world if and when an *ethos of engagement* is forged between numerous constituencies honoring different metaphysical assumptions and moral sources.[45]

Connolly thinks he can evade the charges that agonism is either a) dangerously irresponsible in its glorification of conflict or b) merely a dressed-up version of interest group politics by imagining a political culture that fosters such an ethos, a democratized version of the eristic virtues celebrated by Nietzsche. By deploying Foucauldian "arts of the self" to therapeutically dissolve our inner sources of envy and resentment, we are free to enlarge the political domain beyond the boundaries envisaged by the "aristocrat" Arendt and the liberal Rawls, without fear of exacerbating the latent conflict between our incompatible religious, moral and philosophical views.[46]

The problem is that this version of agonistic politics presupposes a culture in which no individual's or group's "fundamental metaphysical position" is *fundamental* in the sense that it is a truth which stands in irreconcilable conflict with other ultimate values. The pathos of the agonistic actor—his consciousness of the tragic dimension of value conflict, of his own "here I stand, I cannot do otherwise"—is replaced by an *agnostic* willingness to suspend the truth claim implicit in his own ultimate values. Connolly suggests that through "work on the self" the encumbered self can take on a new lightness of being, one untainted by the "will to the unconditional" and *ressentiment*. Thus, what Rawls calls the starting point of political liberalism, namely, the "absolute depth of that irreconcilable latent conflict" between controversial views of the good life, ceases to be a problem.[47]

Simply put, this is presuming a lot. Connolly's vision of an "impure" agonistic politics, one that no longer depends on a "hard" public/private distinction of the sort deployed by Arendt or Rawls, rests on the idea of a citizen body in which a sizeable proportion of individuals have "overcome" themselves in the Nietzschean sense.[48] "Work on the self" replaces the classical concern with political education. Connolly even suggests that the root of seemingly ineradicable moral and political conflict is in fact a psychologically rooted disgust at one's own materiality, a disgust that is then projected onto an anathematized "other."

Such an analysis illuminates one of the basic mechanisms of prejudice, to be sure, but it provides scant resources for recovering a sense of the public or cultivating a *civic* agonism. Indeed, the most striking thing about it is its poststructuralist assumption that all potentially violent conflict is a function of an overly bounded, substantialist conception of identity. As an abstract thesis, this may well be correct. However, the conclusion Connolly draws—that our most urgent political need is "work on the self"—fits all too well with the subjectivist assumptions of a therapeutic age.

Arendt's version of an agonistic politics is predicated on a completely different diagnosis of the pathologies of contemporary politics. For her, the identifying mark of the modern age is the loss of a robust sense of the public realm. In attempting to recover such a sense, she does not (*contra* Connolly) insist on a singular conception of the public good. Rather, she adapts Nietzsche's aestheticism and perspectivism to her own *political* purposes, suggesting ways we might think of the public world and political deliberation which break free of the civic republican tradition's focus on a univocal "common good." In *The Human Condition* she writes:

> . . . the reality of the public realm relies on the simultaneous presence of innumerable perspectives and aspects in which the common world presents itself and for which no common measurement or denominator can ever be devised. For though the common world is the common meeting ground of all, those who are present have different locations in it, and the location of one can no more coincide with the location of another than the location of two objects. Being seen and heard by others derive their significance from the fact that everyone sees and hears from a different position. *This is the meaning of public life*, compared to which even the richest and most satisfying family life can offer only the prolongation or multiplication of one's own position with its attending aspects and perspectives. . . . Only where things can be seen by many in a variety of aspects without changing their identity, so that those who are gathered around them know they see sameness in utter diversity, can worldly reality truly and reliably appear.[49]

It is not, in other words, a question of fostering an ethos of a unitary "common good" in opposition to the "corruption" represented by a multitude of interests, of juxtaposing a singular and abstract universal to myriad concrete particulars. Rather, what Arendt strives to impart is the need for distance and a certain minimum amount of self-alienation if the "public world" is to have any reality for us. It is the agonistic play of perspectives on *this* world, and the competing interpretations of the public good that inform and animate it, which Arendt wants to encourage. But, in order to be "free for the world"—in order to appreciate and value the play of perspectives for its own sake—one must, to some degree, be free of the most pressing concerns of life. Arendt's distinction between the social and the political, the object of so much critical fire, is intended to reinforce *this* point. One cannot value the "play of the game" if winning the game is crucial to the sheer survival of oneself or one's group; nor can one value this play of perspectives if the question of basic material subsistence looms larger than all others. For Arendt, an agonistic politics ends where violence, or the most basic demands of the body, intrude.

This brings us to what Arendt viewed as the "other side" of agonistic political action, namely, the capacity for disinterested, independent judgment. If the conflict of opinions that *is* political life is not to devolve into a struggle defined by Schmitt's friend/enemy distinction, it is imperative that action be informed by a faculty of judgment which is sensitive to particulars, which is not bound by a set of rules or an ideology. What contemporary agonists fail to appreciate is that while Arendt worries about the broad phenomenon of depoliticization, she is (nervertheless) hostile to all modes of civic engagement predicated on ideological mobilization or subscription to a *Weltanschauung*.[50] The formation of an opinion (and opinions, not interests, are the stuff of genuine politics for Arendt) presumes the capacity for what she calls representative thought, a capacity that is blocked by adherence to any ideology. To cite the important passage from her essay "The Crisis in Culture" once again:

> I form an opinion by considering a given issue from different viewpoints, by making present to my mind the standpoints of those who are absent; that is, I represent them. This process of representation does not blindly adopt the actual views of those who stand somewhere else, and hence look upon the world from a different perspective; this is a question neither of empathy, as though I tried to be or to feel like somebody else, nor of counting noses and joining a majority but of being and thinking in my own identity where actually I am not. The more people's

standpoints I have present in my mind while I am pondering a given issue, and the better I can imagine how I would feel and think if I were in their place, the stronger will be my capacity for representative thinking and the more valid my final conclusions, my opinion.[51]

This is Arendt's gloss on the Kantian notion of an "enlarged mentality" (*eine erweiterte Denkungsart*) found in the *Critique of Judgment*. Like Kant, Arendt considers the capacity for an enlarged mentality, for representative thought, essential to opinion formation and judgment. And, also like Kant, she insists that disinterestedness—the liberation from one's own private interests—is the crucial precondition for the kind of imaginative exercise we find in representative thinking.[52] Thus, Arendt's political actor displays not only initiatory energy, but detached judgment (what Max Weber, in his lecture "Politics as a Vocation," calls "a sense of proportion"). Similarly, the specific *meaning* of his or her actions—their justice or injustice, glory or baseness, beauty or ugliness—appears only to those capable of detached judgment.

Arendt's emphasis on detached judgment as a crucial component of any morally defensible agonistic politics seems to take us far from the Nietzschean focus on action and energy (the "will to power"), approximating instead Aristotelian prudence (*phronesis*). In fact, this is how many commentators on her theory of judgment have read her. Consider, however, Nietzsche's definition of a praiseworthy, life-enhancing form of intellectual "objectivity" as "the ability *to control* one's Pro and Con and to dispose of them, so that one knows how to employ a *variety* of perspectives and affective interpretations in the service of knowledge."[53] Arendt wants to pose a parallel norm for political judgment. And, as with her emphasis on the theatrical dimensions of political action, the focus on the distanced or disinterested quality of political judgment throws the expressivism underlying contemporary formulations of the agonistic ideal into sharp relief.

Arendt's conception of an agonistic politics thus stands at a crucial remove from the versions proposed by contemporary (Nietzsche-inspired) agonists. As I have tried to show, this difference has little to do with Arendt's admiration for the Homeric Greeks. Rather, it has to do with her stipulation that action and contestation must be informed by both judgment and a sense of the public if they are to be praiseworthy. The mere expression of energy in the form of political commitment fails to impress her. Of course, some will find this version of the agonistic ethos still too selective, still too aristocratic (or self-deluded) in its demand for "disinterestedness." How can victims of injustice and oppression be expected to rise to her standard, to forget their rage at what they have suffered? The answer is that Arendt doesn't expect them to, nor does she want them excluded from the public realm. What she emphasizes is the possibility, open to virtually everyone, that political action—debate and deliberation—can cultivate a public-spiritedness which is not limited by group affiliation or interest; which genuinely values a plurality of opinions on the same issue; and which is characterized by an independence of mind not typically celebrated by the civic republican tradition. The fact that interest-driven politics encourages none of these effects indicates that little is to be gained by stripping the agonistic ethos of its impersonal dimensions and making the self, multiple or otherwise, the center of politics.

Conclusion

Contemporary agonists applaud Arendt's politicization of Nietzsche's agonistic ideal; they decry the narrow set of boundaries they see her imposing on the public realm. The self, they argue, must be drawn in, in all its gendered, racial, and class-based concreteness. To fail to do so is to indulge in the aristocratic fantasy of a pure politics, a politics without substance and without relevance. If Arendt points the way to a politicization of Nietzsche, this politicization can be completed only by further "Nietzscheanizing" Arendt; that is, by stressing the boundary-blurring force of "boundless" political action. Only then will contemporary struggles for justice be given their due in an agonistic politics.

At one level, one can't but agree with these general points. But, as I've tried to indicate, there is also reason for disquiet. "Incessant contestation," like Foucauldian "resistance," is essentially reactive. What is contested or resisted are the "normalizing," identity-imposing practices of the bureaucratized welfare state, or of cultural representation. This is, in its own way, a remarkably constricted view of politics and political contestation. Moreover, its reactive quality insures that, disclaimers aside, there won't be much

125

"agonistic respect" for different views of the public good. A genuinely agonistic ethos presumes not merely pluralism, but plurality in Arendt's sense: a diversity of (distanced) views on the same object or issue. An agonistic politics that fails to sufficiently appreciate the specificity of the public sphere more or less insures that its claims to justice will be read by opponents as sheer ideological dogma. Politics, then, is merely fighting—as both Machiavelli and Weber suggested in their respective versions of *Realpolitik*.

Contemporary agonists are to be commended insofar as they remind us, with Arendt, that action is at the heart of politics. From an American perspective, this means recognizing daily that the Constitution is not a machine which "runs by itself." They should also be commended for reminding us (again with Arendt) that deliberation and consensus are *parts* of political action, but by no means its totality. Finally, they deserve praise for their attempts to prod a radically apolitical culture in a more political, and indeed more progressive, direction.

It is, however, the *localness* of their prescription that gives one pause, and which should prompt us to question whether their criticisms of Arendt really hit the mark. One often has the sense when reading contemporary agonists that they are rewriting the young Nietzsche. However, instead of worries about the life-dissipating effects of too much history, we get variations on the theme of the "use and abuse of legalism (or constitutionalism) for politics." The sense pervading their work is of a law- or rule-induced sclerosis, which has depleted the agonal energies of politics. Rawls serves as a handy theoretical manifestation of what the neo-Nietzscheans view as *our* "sickness." Anything that serves to loosen or question norms, inspire "resistance," empower historically oppressed groups, or build "more slack into the system" is given a warm welcome in the face of a liberalism that is perceived as increasingly "regularian."

This is merely to point out that the agonistic strand in contemporary political theory is of a particular time and an even more particular place. As such, it rebels against the very idea of boundary drawing and an overly stabilized distinction between public and private. In its more extreme forms, it even rebels against the "constitutionalization" of democracy.[54] However, unlike Arendt (and, indeed, unlike the mature Nietzsche), it takes the broad constitutionalist separation of public and private completely for granted. Like deconstruction, it is necessarily parasitic upon its "texts."

Arendt's agonism, informed by the experience of totalitarianism, transcends this problematic. It exercises greater caution because it takes correspondingly greater risks. Her theory of political action operates without a safety net of the sort her more "radical" critics assume. Hence her agonism focuses on public-spiritedness, independent judgment, and self-distance in addition to initiatory action. The limits and qualifications she attaches to the agonistic ethos remind us not only that politics has risks, but also that any humane politics has at its core a care for the world, a care for the public realm. Where such care is present, the world is indeed humanized by the "incessant and continual discourse" generated by a plurality of political opinions.[55] Where such care is absent—where the concerns of the self or the group dominate—politics is *simply* conflict. This is why Arendt, like the anti-agonist Rawls, wants to maintain a distinction between *homme* and *citoyen*. These two radically dissimilar theorists strictly delineate the "domain of the political," not out of a passion to exclude or homogenize, but precisely because they take difference so seriously. For it is only when differences are mediated politically, through shared institutions and shared citizenship, that they can be, as Machiavelli insisted, the "cause" of liberty.

CHAPTER SIX

Theatricality and the Public Realm

INTRODUCTION

What is the role of theatricality in the political theory of Hannah Arendt? Why does she persistently refer to the public space as a kind of "stage" upon which political *actors* disclose themselves "in word and deed"? Why does she rely so heavily upon the metaphors of performance and virtuosity in articulating her concepts of political action and freedom? More to the point: does Arendt's recourse to a theatrical metaphorics illuminate the nature of the public space and its problems in the modern age, or does it merely serve to obscure these by making the Greek polis the normative model of a robust public sphere?

Arendt's vision of the public realm as a "space of appearances" in which heroic individuals perform great deeds and speak memorable words is fully manifest in the Greek-inspired conception of political action set forth in *The Human Condition*.[1] However, there is another dimension to Arendt's conception of political action, one that emphasizes the deliberative speech of equals and the capacity to "act in concert." This dimension comes to the fore in *On Revolution* and the essays in *Crises of the Republic*, as well as the posthumously published *Lectures on Kant's Political Philosophy*.[2]

These two dimensions of Arendt's view of political action have led Maurizio Passerin d'Entreves and others to claim that there is "a fundamental tension in [Arendt's] theory between an *expressive* and a *communicative* model of action."[3] This tension introduces a basic ambiguity into how we interpret Arendt's broader conception of politics. As d'Entreves puts it:

> Insofar as Arendt's theory of action rests upon an unstable combination of both expressive and communicative models (or action types), it is clear that her account of politics will vary in accordance with the emphasis given to one or the other. When the emphasis falls on the expressive model of action, politics is viewed as the performance of noble deeds by outstanding individuals; conversely, when her stress is on the communi-

cative model of action, politics is seen as the collective process of delib-eration and decision-making that rests on equality and solidarity.[4]

As Seyla Benhabib demonstrates in her essay "Models of Public Space" (and, more recently, in *The Reluctant Modernism of Hannah Arendt*), Arendt's internally divided view of political action gener-ates two very distinct models of the public sphere: the agonistic and the associational.[5] The agonistic model of public space—an overtly *theatrical* model—"represents that space of appearances in which moral and political greatness, heroism, and preeminence are re-vealed, displayed, shared with others."[6] The associational, in con-trast, represents "the kind of democratic or associative politics that can be engaged in by ordinary citizens who may or may not possess great moral prowess but who acquire the capacities of political judg-ment and initiative in the process of self-organization."[7]

Benhabib leaves little room for doubt as to which of Arendt's models is the more relevant. "The distinction between the agonistic and the associational models," she writes, "corresponds to the Greek versus the modern experience of politics."[8] Arendt's theatrical, ag-onistic model places a premium on expressive action and the actor's achievement of a unique identity before his "audience." As such, it presumes, in Benhabib's view, a high degree of moral and political homogeneity; otherwise, the competition for excellence among peers could not take place in the *public* realm at all.[9]

Another drawback from Benhabib's perspective is that the ago-nistic model presumes a rigidly defined public realm, one that can serve its theatrical function of being a "stage where freedom can appear" only if it is spatially delimited and its "substantive content" severely restricted. Only narrowly *political* matters, those concern-ing the founding and preservation of the polity's constitution (in the broad, Greek sense), are fit to appear in public. "Household mat-ters"—which include a wide range of economic and social issues—introduce the taint of necessity, and so must be rigorously excluded, in Arendt's view, from this "theater" in which freedom can appear and become a "tangible reality."

Because "the distinction between the social and the political makes no sense in the modern world," and because modern polities conspicuously lack the kind of moral/political homogeneity neces-sary for purely agonistic action, Benhabib concludes that Arendt's theatrical model of politics must be abandoned: "Arendt's agonistic model is at odds with the sociological reality of modernity, as well as with modern political struggles for justice."[10] The associational model of public space presents itself as the only viable alternative under the conditions of modernity.

Is this conclusion warranted, or is it, perhaps, premature? Does Arendt's theatrical conception of the public sphere have anything to teach citizens of modern democracies, or does it merely sum up those aspects of her political thought that are no longer tenable, the residue of a Grecophilic, Heidegger-influenced "philosophy of origins"?

It is my contention that Arendt's emphasis on the theatrical dimensions of public space and political action has, *pace* Benhabib, much to teach us about the nature of a healthy public sphere and the reasons for its contemporary decline. These reasons have little to do with what Benhabib calls Arendt's tendency toward phenomenological essentialism and the kind of "nostalgic *Verfallsgeschichte*" (story of decline) we find in Heidegger.[11] By focusing on the theatricality of the public realm of the polis, Arendt is not positing a pure origin from which we moderns have fallen away. Rather, she is trying to teach us a lesson about the nature of *worldliness*—about a quality of human being-in-the-world that waxes and wanes in different societies and in different epochs. One reason Arendt so often appears to her critics as a nostalgic antimodern is that she felt the modern age unleashed forces (including capitalist expropriation, the "rise of the social," technological automatism, and a culture of authenticity) that have seriously, if not fatally, undermined our capacity for worldliness. Her emphasis on the theatricality of genuine political action and a robust public sphere is an attempt to get us to see how vastly different *our* "attitude toward the world" is from more political (read: worldly) cultures and times.

This chapter examines the close link between theatricality and worldliness in Arendt's writing. I hope thereby to demonstrate the continuing relevance of her "agonistic" model of public space.[12] In my view, following too closely Benhabib's advice on what is living and what is dead in Arendt's political theory would rob us of what is, perhaps, her most profound contribution to critical thinking about politics and the public sphere under contemporary conditions.

My argument proceeds as follows. First I set out what Arendt means by "worldliness" and how she sees the theatricality of public life as its chief, and perhaps most important, expression. Next, I turn to the question of the distinguishing characteristics of "theatrical" political action as theorized by Arendt. Does this conception serve primarily expressive ends, as both Benhabib and d'Entreves assert? In the third section, I contrast Habermas's description of the rise and decline of the "bourgeois public sphere" in his *Structural Transformation of the Public Sphere* with the quite different perspective provided by Richard Sennett's *The Fall of Public Man*.[13] My goal is to broaden our understanding of the theatricality of public life. Sennett's work is helpful because it approaches the nexus of theatricality and publicness in a way that makes up for Arendt's much-criticized "sociological deficit."[14] In the Conclusion I suggest some reasons why an associational model of the public space and a purely deliberative conception of democracy fail to provide an adequate critical model for the diagnosis of "the public and its problems" in contemporary society.

WORLDLINESS AND POLITICAL ACTION

There is a strong temptation (as the quote from d'Entreves shows) to view Arendt's Burke-derived definition of political action— "acting together, acting in concert"[15]—as juxtaposing a solidarity-based model of politics to the heroic individualism of the agonistic model. Yet it is a temptation we should resist, and not only because Arendt herself was highly skeptical about solidaristic models of political action. More to the point, this simple juxtaposition obscures the crucial role the idea of worldliness plays in Arendt's view of political life, a role we lose sight of the moment we reduce her thought to a variation on the civic republican tradition or an attempt to update this tradition for a social democratic politics.

This point is driven home if we turn to Arendt's essay "On Humanity in Dark Times: Thoughts about Lessing."[16] This remarkable essay, given as a lecture on the occasion of Arendt's receipt of the Lessing Prize in 1959, focuses on what happens to our feeling for the world during those "dark times" when the public realm either forcibly excludes us or becomes a source of shame and unease. Arendt plays the response of Lessing (who, as the subject of a monarch, was deprived of a public space for action) off the response of persecuted Jews and alienated Germans during the early (pretotalitarian) years of Nazi power.

131

What distinguishes Lessing from those closer to us in time is that he was never tempted to salvage meaning from his exclusion by means of a further self-withdrawal. Unlike victimized "pariah peoples," who could compensate for their exclusion from the public world by generating feelings of warmth and fraternity, or those who found this public world so stupid, base, and unendurable that they withdrew into the interior realm of thought and feeling, Lessing continued to uphold his "partisanship for the world."[17] Restricted to thought and writing, he attempted to humanize the darkened public world through discourse and argument and the peculiar "friendship" these engender. He eschewed the comforts of withdrawal, solidarity, and intimacy in order to remain "open to the world."

What is Arendt's purpose in drawing this contrast? It is, first and foremost, *not* a criticism of "pariah peoples" for being complicit in their exclusion (although Arendt's ambivalence about the "inner emigration" response—the response of her teacher and friend Karl Jaspers—is palpable). Rather, the example of these responses to "dark times" reveals an essential difference between the modern and late modern "attitude towards the world." For the early modern Lessing, a life lived in private or confined to a circle of intimates was not worth living. This attitude is similar to that of Arendt's beloved Greeks insofar as it values the human relation of friendship as mediated by the world (Aristotle's *philia*) over modern forms of intimacy and solidarity.

Like the Greeks, Lessing saw friendship as an essentially *worldly* phenomenon, born of discourse about the common world, rather than as an expression of intimacy or a brotherliness grounded in a shared humanity.[18] Arendt focuses on his response to "dark times" because it reveals an attitude toward the world fundamentally at odds with the late modern retreat from a hostile public world. Lessing's response is colored throughout by an intuitive awareness of the cost to our very sense of reality that such a retreat from the world involves. Toward the end of her essay, Arendt writes:

> Lessing, too, was already living in "dark times," and after his own fashion he was destroyed by their darkness. We have seen what a powerful need men have, in such times, to move closer to one another, to seek in the warmth and intimacy the substitute for that light and illumination which only the public realm can cast. But this means that they avoid disputes and try as far as possible to deal with people with whom they

cannot come into conflict. For a man of Lessing's disposition there was little room in such an age and in such a confined world; where people moved together in order to warm one another, they move away from him. And yet he, who was polemical to the point of contentiousness, could no more endure loneliness than the excessive closeness of a brotherliness that obliterated all distinctions. He was never eager really to fall out with someone with whom he had entered into a dispute; he was concerned solely with humanizing the world by incessant and continual discourse about its affairs and the things in it. He wanted to be the friend of many men, but no man's brother.[19]

What does it mean when our alienation from the world makes a figure like Lessing (at least as rendered by Arendt) seem infinitely remote, almost premodern? We can easily comprehend the desire for warmth that draws "pariah peoples" together; we have no trouble understanding the phenomenon of "inner emigration." But how to understand a passion for the world so intense that an individual would rather risk self-destruction than face the prospect of an *unworldly* existence? How to understand someone who, in the face of "dark times," eschews the solidarity of the oppressed or the warmth of intimacy for the "friendship" of argument and discourse?

These questions lead us to *The Human Condition* and its evocative passages about the nature of the public realm—"the common world." For it is here that Arendt draws out her understanding of the peculiar reality of the public realm—a reality that has become increasingly elusive to us, but whose traces Lessing doggedly clung to.

In section 7 of *HC*, Arendt states that "the term 'public' signifies two interrelated but not altogether identical phenomena." The first is that "everything that appears in public can be seen and heard by everybody and has the widest possible publicity."[20] In the public realm, "appearance . . . constitutes reality." The second phenomenon signified by the term "public" is "the world itself, in so far as it is common to all of us and distinguished from our privately owned place in it."[21] By "world" Arendt means neither the earth nor nature, but the "human artifact," the relatively permanent artifice created by "the fabrication of human hands."

The reason these two senses of "public" are interrelated is that both refer to something common, whether to appearances that are seen and heard by all, or to an "objective"artifice that is (in an extended sense) inhabited by all. The difference between these two senses and the phenomena they refer to is that public appearances depend not only upon the availability of a public realm, but upon the existence of a "human artifice" which "relates and separates men at the same time."[22]

Arendt's thesis in *HC* is that both phenomena designated by the term "public" have, in the late modern age, ceased to perform their characteristic functions. As a "space of appearances," the public no longer provides us with the same "feeling for reality" that it did for previous ages: "what appears to all" seems least real, while what is felt by the self or experienced in intimate settings becomes the benchmark of reality.[23] Yet, as Arendt points out, when the subjective or the private is deprived of a strong contrasting term, it too loses much of its force. Hence the "weird irreality" that attends these experiences in the present, as they lose the sharp definition that juxtaposition with the "bright light of the public" used to provide.

Similarly, according to Arendt, the man-made world of things, the "human artifice," no longer fulfills its function as an "in-between." Under the conditions of mass society, the public world no longer serves to gather humans together, to "relate and separate" us as individuals.[24] Indeed, as the human artifice is increasingly swamped by transient consumer goods and subjected to the rhythms of production and consumption, the "thing character" of the world becomes less and less tangible.[25]

These observations by Arendt raise the obvious question of why "the public" (in both senses) no longer seems able to play its characteristic roles in the modern age. I want to defer this question for now, focusing instead on Arendt's entry point into the discussion of the public realm. What is obvious in *HC*, but all too often overlooked by her critics, is that Arendt's discussion of the public realm centers on the experience of a particular sort of reality, a specific kind of "feeling for the world."

This feeling, born of a vivid "space of appearances" and the relative permanence of the human artifact, is what Arendt identifies with worldliness, which she sees as increasingly rare in the late modern age. This feeling cannot be reduced to public-spiritedness, a sense of community, or a participatory politics. Of course, all of these may be vehicles of worldliness, supports for a sensibility that is neither escapist/Romantic nor exploitative/capitalist. But what clearly matters for Arendt in these pages of *HC* is less politics than the "feeling for the world" itself. Indeed, one can say that Arendt's affirmation of political action as the existentially supreme human activity flows from her desire to preserve worldliness at all costs. In this sense, even political action turns out to be of secondary importance, something of a means rather than an end in itself.[26]

How does political action promote and sustain worldliness? In answering this question, the first thing to observe is that not all political action *does* contribute to worldliness. Arendt's highly selective approach to the question of what counts as genuine political action flows less from a misplaced purism than from an acute sense of the ways in which ostensibly political forms of action can contribute to our alienation from the world. Thus, in *HC* and "On Violence" she excludes violence, force, and domination as categories of *political* relations; in *On Revolution* she denies that struggles for liberation from domination, or the "instrumental" relationship between citizens and their representatives in contemporary democracy, constitute authentically political forms.

The common denominator linking all these "nonpolitical" forms of politics is that they undercut what Arendt, following Kant, calls our "common sense" of the world. Violence, force, and domination are mute: they are used to monopolize the public sphere, to control what is seen and heard in it (whether our examples are *ancien régime* monarchies or more up-to-date authoritarian regimes). By excluding the majority of subjects from any participation in the "space of appearances," they enforce and promote alienation from the world. Under conditions of total domination—totalitarianism—terror destroys the very possibility of an "in-between," throwing individuals back upon themselves and depriving them of even the simulacrum of worldliness.[27] More surprising is Arendt's contention that the politics of liberation struggles and representative democracy also contribute nothing to worldliness. The former is "prepolitical," concerned solely with the overcoming of domination that is but the prelude to the founding of a new public sphere, while the latter encourages an interest group politics, which undermines the sense of the common or public.[28]

When we turn to Arendt's conception of "genuine" political action, we begin to see how theatrical/agonistic action contributes to worldliness in ways that other, seemingly less exotic, forms do not.

Yet Arendt's formulations sometimes have the effect of strengthening rather than easing the doubts raised by Benhabib and d'Entreves.

In her essay "What Is Freedom?" Arendt establishes a strong link between the freedom made manifest in political action and the "virtuosity" of the political actor. She appeals to Machiavelli in order to illustrate the distinctive freedom of the political actor/performer:

> Freedom as inherent in action is perhaps best illustrated by Machiavelli's concept of *virtu*, the excellence with which man answers the opportunities the world opens up before him in the guise of *fortuna*. Its meaning is best rendered by "virtuosity," that is, an excellence we attribute to the performing arts (as distinguished from the creative arts of making), where the accomplishment lies in the performance itself and not in an end product which outlasts the activity that brought it into existence and becomes independent of it. The virtuoso-ship of Machiavelli's *virtu* somehow reminds us of the fact, although Machiavelli hardly knew it, that the Greeks always used such metaphors as flute-playing, dancing, healing, and sea-faring to distinguish political from other activities, that is, that they drew their analogies from those arts in which virtuosity of performance is decisive.[29]

If we combine this passage with those from the chapter on action in *HC*, we appear to have ample confirmation of Benhabib's objections to the agonistic model. The more we focus on the theatrical or performative character of political action, the more the quality of virtuosity (or performative excellence) takes precedence in our evaluation of the political actor. As Benhabib points out, such a perspective—in which the consequences of any action and the motives behind it are relegated to the status of secondary criteria—presupposes a high degree of "moral homogeneity." For it is only against the background of a substantive agreement on positive virtues that the question of the excellence of the performance can come to the fore.

The emphasis on "virtuosity of performance" as the most important manifestation of the freedom of political action has another drawback. Insofar as it encourages us to view political action as a competitive agon between virtuosic actors, it also encourages us to view action as primarily expressive in character. This consequence is noted by d'Entreves, and has been echoed by many of Arendt's critics.[30] She seems committed (at least in *HC* and "What Is Freedom?") to a view that frames political action as the most important vehicle of the agent's self-disclosure or self-expression.[31]

But is the expression of excellence, or the disclosure of one's "unique identity," in fact the main reason for Arendt's deployment of a theatrical metaphorics? Both Benhabib and d'Entreves equate the agonistic Arendt with an overtly Romantic Arendt, one perhaps overly influenced by Nietzsche. Yet if we turn to another of Arendt's texts, *On Revolution* (hereafter, *OR*), we see that the identification of agonism with expressivism is more than a little problematic. Arendt's appeal to theatrical metaphors in her discussions of political action and the public realm is, in fact, intended to demolish the presuppositions of the expressivist model of action.

AGONISTIC ACTION: IMPERSONAL OR EXPRESSIVE?

In an important but somewhat obscure discussion in *OR*, Arendt addresses Robespierre's politics of virtue and the hatred of *ancien régime* hypocrisy that energized it.[32] What, she asks, made hypocrisy such a monster for Robespierre? Why did the unmasking of *this* vice come to take absolute priority in the politics of the French Revolution, and with what consequences? In answering these questions, Arendt juxtaposes two models of theatrical self-presentation to the "corrupt" playacting of court society that Robespierre so reviled. Her examples, surprisingly, are Socrates and Machiavelli.

For Arendt, Socratic moral integrity is not the opposite of playacting, a Greek version of Luther's "Here I stand, I cannot do otherwise." Rather, she views Socrates as taking his departure from "an unquestioned belief in the truth of appearances. . . ."[33] Operating within, not against, this framework, Socrates urged his interlocutors to "Be as you would wish to appear to others." According to Arendt, by this he meant "Appear to yourself as you wish to appear to others."[34] Socratic conscientiousness consists in the demand for self-agreement, and exploits the phenomenon of the "two-in-one" of consciousness the better to internalize the audience to one's actions. For Socrates, according to Arendt, the agent and the onlooker "were contained in the selfsame person."[35]

Machiavelli, in contrast, operated within the assumptions of Christianity; that is, he assumed a gap between appearances (how we appear to our fellow human beings) and reality (how God perceives us). Hence he taught, "Appear as you may wish to be"—by which he meant (again in Arendt's paraphrase), "Never mind how you are, this is of no relevance in the world and in politics, where only appearances, not 'true' being, count; if you can manage to appear to others as you would wish to be, that is all that can possibly be required by the judges of this world."[36]

The point Arendt stresses is that neither Socrates nor Machiavelli, however radically divergent they were in all other respects, equated the theatrical presentation of self with hypocrisy. "Playacting"—the idea of a distinct public self, or the view of oneself as an actor performing for an internalized audience—had yet to gain the connotation of deceit or corruption. Only when such acting becomes merely a vehicle of deceit—of oneself and others—does the hypocrisy that Rousseau and Robespierre attacked so ferociously become the defining characteristic of the public sphere. As Arendt presents it, the court society of the *ancien régime* gave playacting— the conscious adoption of a role, the wearing of a public mask—a bad name. The response, manifest in Rousseau's theory and Robespierre's practice, was a cult of the "natural" man, of the authentic or roleless individual, coupled with a ruthless politics of unmasking.[37]

Arendt focuses on the way hypocrisy becomes a *political* topos for the French Revolution because she wants to reveal the relatively recent moment in our history when the ideas of playacting, maskwearing, and a distinct public self came to have a largely negative connotation. Once public role-playing or mask-wearing was no longer seen as the medium of a specific truthfulness—as the means by which the actor's voice could "sound through" while his private self remained protectively hidden—the notion of a public persona became permanently and irrevocably tainted. The very conventionality of the public realm now became the problem, with the result that an impersonal presentation of self became suspect and politically self-defeating. With the Revolution, we enter an epoch in which public words and deeds are seen as either self-serving appearances (and therefore false) or the expression of the actor's "true," authentic self.

This way of viewing actions and speech, Arendt maintains, was simply impossible for Socrates or Machiavelli, both of whom thought of acting in a theatrical sense that did not *obscure* truth, but rather enabled it to appear. Indeed, the example of Socrates' "theatrical" notion of conscience shows that there is no necessary connection between conscientious moral agency and the notion of an authentic self (however natural this connection seems to we heirs of the Reformation).[38] Even conscience can be theatricalized, divorced from the voice of God or the authentic (natural, virtuous) self.

Arendt's discussion of appearances, masks, and persona in Chapter 2 of *OR* is brief, but it highlights the assumption underlying Benhabib's and d'Entreves's characterizations of her "heroic" or agonistic model of action. The *last* thing Arendt wants to give us is a theory that identifies political action with self-expression. Such a notion derives from the politics of authenticity invented by Rousseau. It is, in Arendt's understanding, fundamentally at odds with the kind of impersonality fostered by a theatrical conception of the self as a performer on the public stage. The fact that we, unlike Socrates or Machiavelli, equate impersonality with hypocrisy or "mere" playacting leads us to demand the performance of authenticity by our contemporary political actors. The inevitable result, as I shall argue below, is a shallow cynicism which further undermines of our sense of the reality of the public world.

That Arendt's appeal to the theatrical dimensions of the public realm is directed *against* an expressive model of political action can be seen by returning to "What Is Freedom?" In a passage immediately preceding the one cited above, she explains what "acting from principle" means in terms of her theatrical conception. *Free* action, according to Arendt, "is neither under the guidance of the intellect nor under the dictate of will"; it is "free from motive on one side, from its intended goal as predictable effect on the other."[39] Arendt is not denying that intellect or will are necessary for the achievement of any action, nor is she claiming the motives and goals play a negligible role in an agent's deliberations. Rather, she is claiming that the *freedom* of action does not reside in any of these categories, its "determining" factors. The freedom of action is manifest in the performance itself and in the *principle* that inspires it.[40]

It is important to note here that Arendt's own inspiration on the question of principles is Montesquieu rather than Kant. In Book III of *The Spirit of the Laws*, Montesquieu analyzes forms of government and their respective inspiring principles (democracy and virtue, aristocracy and moderation, monarchy and honor). This analysis provides Arendt with a way of thinking about what it means to "act from a principle" that is perfectly suited to the worldly, theatrical quality of political action. Principles in her sense are not defining self-conceptions, one's "core convictions"; rather, "they inspire, as it were, from without."[41] Too general to prescribe particular actions, they become fully manifest "only in the performing act itself": "the manifestation of principles comes about only through action, they are manifest in the world as long as the action lasts, but no longer."[42] Following Montesquieu, Arendt cites honor, glory, love of equality, distinction or excellence as examples of "inspiring" (rather than determining) principles.

What is Arendt getting at with this idiosyncratic (and decidedly non-Kantian) rendering of "acting from a principle"? First, she is trying to reformulate "principled" action in a way that detracts nothing from the *performance* itself; which does not reduce the meaning of action to the motivations of the agent or his success in achieving his goal. "Principles" in her sense are immanent to action: they may inspire "from without," but they are fully real only when they are embodied in action. But the main reason Arendt links the freedom of action to the "inspiration" of principles is that she is looking for a way to *depersonalize* political action, to separate it from the inner determination of "the assertive will, the calculating intelligence, the impassioned heart, or the urges of the body or spirit."[43]

Arendt's dual emphasis on the depersonalized nature of principled action and the impersonal dimension of a public self or persona should make us question interpretations that see an expressive model of action lurking behind her agonism. Yes, "self-disclosure" is an undeniable part of what George Kateb calls the "existential achievement" of political action as theorized by Arendt. But this self-disclosure is not the externalization of an inner potential nor an expression of one's "true" self.[44] Arendt's focus on the impersonal qualities of political action is not intended to promote the idea of selflessness; rather, it serves to highlight the distinction between the public and the private self. This distinction is undermined by the expressivist model we have inherited from Rousseau and Romanticism, which stresses the achievement of an integrated, "whole" human being.[45] Arendt's understanding of the performance of political action certainly links it to the achievement of a "unique identity," but this identity is shaped by the discipline and depersonalization that comes from adopting a specific public role or mask.

This is why the distinction Benhabib draws between agonal and narrative models of action is somewhat misleading.[46] Benhabib deploys this distinction in order to distinguish the expressivist or "essentialist" Arendt from a more dialogical or discursive Arendt. Benhabib frames the contrast in the following terms:

> . . . whereas action in the agonal model is described through terms such as "revelation of who one is" and "the making manifest of what is interior," action in the narrative model is characterized through "the telling of a story" and the "weaving of a web of narratives." Whereas in the first model action appears to make manifest or to reveal an antecedent essence, the "one who is," action in the second model suggests that "the one who is" emerges in the process of doing the deed and telling the story. Whereas action in the first model is a process of discovery, action in the second model is a process of invention. In contemporary terms, we may say the first model of action is essentialist while the second is constructivist.[47]

The force of this contrast is to drive a wedge between the deliberative, plurality-oriented Arendt (who views meaning and identity as functions of intersubjective narrative constitution) and the agonal Arendt (who sees action on the public stage as the expression of an individual's unique identity). Benhabib draws attention to the fact that *all* action (including agonal action) is narratively constituted, which is to say that it is articulated and defined in terms of a "web of interpretations."[48] Her point is that Arendt's agonal model deliberately and mistakenly *obscures* this dimension by focusing so intently on the "rare deeds" of the virtuosic performer.

However, if we attend to the more impersonal dimensions of Arendt's theatrical conception, we see that Arendt's agonistic model of the public space does not really reduce to yet another expression of what Habermas has dubbed "the philosophy of the subject."[49] Arendt's emphasis on the importance of roles, masks, and principles demonstrates the presence of "intersubjectivity," but in the specific form of a theatrical conventionality. She is drawing our attention to a "narrative web of interpretations" of a very particular kind, one focused on a distinct set of phenomena: public words and deeds. She is *not* trying to make a general point concerning social epistemology, about what Benhabib calls the "the deep structure of human action as interaction."[50] Benhabib reads her as doing precisely this, the better to assimilate her insight into the "narrative structuration of action" to the social epistemology of Hegel, Marx, Mead, and Habermas.[51]

Once *this* move is made, the specific characteristics of agonal action—its manifest theatrical dimensions—are dissolved to make way for a larger point about the intersubjective constitution of the "lifeworld." According to Benhabib, "One of Arendt's fundamental contributions to the history of twentieth-century philosophy is the thesis that the human space of appearances is constituted by 'the web of relationships and enacted stories.'"[52] The stagelike "space of appearances" is thus read back into the linguistically constituted "horizon of human affairs." From here it is but a short step to questioning the need for Arendt's unpopular distinction between the political and the social. Not only does this distinction appear untenable under modern conditions; it ceases to do any important theoretical work once action is identified with social interaction *tout court*. According to Benhabib, nothing about *political* action distinguishes it, generically, from any of the other "narrative" modes of action, modes that exist and flourish without the presence of a theatrical "space of appearances."

In Benhabib's presentation, then, Arendt's agonistic model—the public realm as theater or stage—emerges as superfluous and needlessly constricting. If the important point about human action is that it is narratively constituted through a communicative web of interpretations, then the need for a bounded, ocular space of appearances dissolves. We are then free to use Arendt's insight into the narrative structure of action to discover public/political spaces throughout the social body. This is precisely what Benhabib does when, for example, she asks us to view Rahel Varnhagen's nineteenth-century Berlin salon as a proto-public sphere, one that brings different social types (women, Jews, intellectuals and aristocrats) together and establishes a quasi-egalitarian space of discourse between them.[53]

Turning to the present, Benhabib emphasizes how viewing action as interaction enables us to see various contemporary social movements for gender, wage, and racial justice as forms of *political* action. The thrust of her argument is that the shift from an agonistic to a communicative or "narrative" model of action fundamentally alters our sense of what a robust public sphere looks like. There is no longer any need to see a strong sense of the public as dependent upon the availability of a "holistic" or theatrical public space. Rather, we can view these social movements as initiating a process of moral-political *Bildung*, one that forces their participants to transcend the narrow (individual or group) interests that drove them into the public arena in the first place. As Benhabib puts it:

> Whichever class or social group enters the public realm, and no matter how class or group specific its demands may be in their genesis, the process of public-political struggle transforms the attitude of narrow self-interest into a more broadly shared public or common interest.[54]

The theatrical public space, then, no longer fulfills any important political function—or rather, it fulfills a function that is appropriate only to "face to face" societies, namely, it provides a venue in which a community "becomes present to itself and recognizes itself through a shared interpretive repertoire."[55] Benhabib proposes to drop Arendt's apparently antiquated desire for communal self-representation, extending her remarks about deliberation, judgment, and the Kantian enlarged mentality in order to "desubstantialize" our conception of the public sphere. Viewing the public sphere as "not just, or even principally, an arena for action but an impersonal medium of communication, information, and opinion formation" enables us to reconnect Arendt's theory of the public realm not only to the conditions of contemporary society, but to the question of democratic legitimacy as well.[56] According to Benhabib, such a critical updating and appropriation of Arendt has already been performed by Jurgen Habermas's *Structural Transformation of the Public Sphere*.

GENEALOGIES OF THE PRESENT: HABERMAS
VERSUS SENNETT

Habermas's study of the rise and decline of the bourgeois public sphere is at once Arendtian and at odds with the spirit of her work. It is Arendtian in that the story Habermas tells about the decline of the public realm in the nineteenth and twentieth centuries emphasizes the role played by the rise of the social welfare state and plebiscitary democracy.[57] In telling this story, he gives historical and sociological flesh to Arendt's somewhat vague thesis about "the rise of the social" in the modern age.[58] Yet the public sphere whose rise and decline Habermas charts is decidedly different in character from the agonistic, theatrical public realm depicted by Arendt.

What is the heart of this difference? There is the obvious point that Habermas's analysis focuses on the public sphere in Europe between 1640 and 1960, with nary a glance to the public sphere of the polis. But this difference in period is also a difference in the origins, character, and role of the public sphere. Unlike the public realm of the Greeks, the bourgeois public realm was, from its inception, a decentered public realm, occupying sites separate from both the state and the economy. It emerged when property-owning private subjects (the bourgeoisie) began to question the regulations laid down by autocratic rulers for the realm of civil society.[59] This non-political challenge, which took the form of subjecting such regulations to rational-critical public debate, gradually expanded to become a full-scale ideology of critical publicity and democratic legitimacy, in which the force of the better argument and public opinion informed by arguments rationalized the exercise of political power. Politically speaking, then, the bourgeois public sphere introduced a historically unprecedented medium for the confrontation with power: "people's public use of their own reason (*öffentliches Rasonnement*)."[60]

The first part of *Structural Transformation* is devoted to describing the process by which an independent, critically reasoning public begins to emerge in the coffeehouses, *salons*, and *Tischgesellschaften* of the eighteenth century. Excluded from participation in public decision-making, private individuals began to develop their capacity for critical judgment and public argument in these sites through the discussion of cultural and literary matters.[61] From its beginnings in a secularized world of letters and literary-cultural debate, the principle of critical publicity widened to include the rules governing civil society, giving rise to the idea of law as a body of abstract and universally valid rules.[62]

With the emergence of a critically reasoning public in the eighteenth century came the idea of public opinion as a critical filter, the carrier of a deliberative rationality that could distinguish between the parochial interests of elites and the common good.[63] "Publicity" became the test for all legislation and enactments: only those that could survive free and open discussion could claim legitimacy.[64] The great theorist of publicity as the moral test of policy was, of course, Kant, whose formulation in "What Is Enlightenment?" serves Habermas (despite its obvious limitations) as the normative ideal of the bourgeois public sphere. It was Kant who first showed how the "public use of one's reason" contributed to the formation of a critically reasoning public, one whose consensus would be built on the force of the better argument—now the "pragmatic test of truth" in moral-political affairs.[65]

The Kantian idea of a critical publicity deployed by a community of independent, rational citizens has, of course, never been fully realized in any political society. In terms of the story Habermas tells, however, the striking thing is how quickly the idea of public opinion as a force opposed to power became the object of theoretical anxiety as well as empirical skepticism. In Tocqueville and J. S. Mill, the idea of "public opinion" already begins to take on the negative connotation that it has today, the connotation of an irrational and conformist force, one that is easily manipulated and impossible to escape.[66] Stripped of its critical, rational form, public opinion quickly came to be seen as "one power among other powers."[67]

The fears expressed by nineteenth-century liberals do not render the ideal of a critically reasoning public obsolete for Habermas; rather, they anticipate what he calls the "structural transformation" of the public sphere that occurs in the context of mass society. Here, the instrumentalities of a bureaucratized, plebiscitary democracy combine with the media of mass culture to produce a "pseudo public sphere," one stripped of its critical (rationalizing, universalizing) function.

Habermas describes this transformation in the second half of *ST*, providing a peculiar synthesis of Arendt's arguments from *HC* with those of the "Culture Industry" essay from Horkheimer and Adorno's *Dialectic of Enlightenment*. In a section entitled "From a Culture Debating to a Culture-Consuming Public," he traces how the rise of mass culture destroys the sites of cultural discussion and debate in which the bourgeoisie had learned "the art of critical-rational public debate."[68]

"Since the middle of the nineteenth century," Habermas writes, "the institutions that until then had ensured the coherence of the public as a critically debating entity have been weakened."[69] The private arenas of reading and debate that developed an "audience-directed subjectivity" are either destroyed (as in the case of the salon) or colonized by the passive consumption of mass culture (as is the case with the family, which becomes the primary site of such consumption).[70] Moreover, the proliferation of panel discussions and media-staged debates turn public argument itself into yet

145

THEATRICALITY AND THE PUBLIC REALM

another commodity to be consumed. As Habermas notes (in Ador-
noesque tones), "today the conversation itself is administered."[71]
Critical debate, "arranged in this manner," may serve important
"social-psychological functions," but it is increasingly bereft of any
publicist (authentically critical) function.

As the public shifts from being an arena for critical debate and
argument to the passive consumption of prepackaged news (on the
one hand) and entertainment (on the other), we can no longer speak
of a *critical* publicity. In politics publicity now means the advertis-
ing efforts necessary to generate plebiscitary support for particular
leaders or policies, the manufacture of a (nonrationalized) consensus
from on high.[72] As Habermas puts it:

> Publicity is generated from above, so to speak, in order to create an aura
> of good will for certain positions. Originally publicity guaranteed the
> connection between rational-critical public debate and the legislative
> foundation of domination, including the critical supervision of its exer-
> cise. Now it makes possible the peculiar ambivalence of a domination
> exercised through the domination of nonpublic opinion: it serves the
> manipulation *of* the public as much as legitimation *before* it. Critical pub-
> licity is supplanted by manipulative publicity.[73]

Citizens are transformed into consumers in the political realm as
well as in private life. The public sphere is "refeudalized" in the
sense that publicity, bereft of its critical-rational function, increasingly takes on a purely symbolic role.[74] Worst of all, the public
sphere becomes a kind of "show" set up for "purposes of manipulation and staged directly for the sake of that large minority of the
'undecided' who normally determine the outcome of a election."[75]
Stripped of its active, argument-oriented character, public opinion
no longer plays a rationalizing role in the political arena, with the
result that what passes for consensus in contemporary democratic
societies has no real relation to the idea of justice implicit in "the
standard of a universal interest."[76]

The story of decline Habermas tells is by now a quite familiar
one, to the point of taking its place among the very media clichés we
passively consume. The point I wish to emphasize here, however, is
how Habermas's focus on the Kantian idea of the "public use of
one's reason" reduces Arendt's notion of the public sphere to its
formally deliberative dimensions. These are valued, while the agonistic or theatrical aspects are denigrated as either anachronistic or

mere "show." Publicity deprived of its rational, argumentative form, is, and can only be, manipulation. With this observation, Habermas tacitly evokes the original Socratic-Platonic critique of democratic politics as "mere" persuasion unrelated to truth, an emotional and irrational exercise performed by unscrupulous demagogues before an audience gathered in the assembly.[77] Habermas, in effect, provides an updated, democratic version of this critique, one in which the prospects for a more robust and democratic public realm hinge on our ability to "rerationalize" the public sphere, making it the scene of a critical, deliberative formation of popular will once again.

If Habermas strives, in this early work, to separate the deliberative kernel of Arendt's conception of the public realm from its theatrical shell, Richard Sennett draws our attention to the way theatricality is itself constitutive of public life. Moreover, he does so in a way which demonstrates that such theatricality is not dependent upon a "holistic" public sphere of the sort Benhabib describes. His historical analysis enables us to question the quasi-rationalist opposition of argument versus theater erected by both Habermas and Benhabib, for not all theatricality is spectacle, and not all performance is manipulation. Indeed, Sennett's thesis is that the manipulative forms of theatricality that Habermas points to are relatively late developments, functions of a pervasive personalization of the political realm.

Sennett's study, like Habermas's, traces the decline of public life in the period between 1750 and the present. Unlike Habermas, he is concerned with the health of public culture in a broad sense, and therefore is far less restricted in the range of phenomena he investigates. The presentation of self in everyday life; the rise of a culture of intimacy; the role that the "psychological imagination of life" plays in our constitution of public and private reality: all of these figure centrally in Sennett's work, while they appear peripherally, if at all, in Habermas's.[78]

The transformation Sennett depicts, then, is not the functional one of the role of public opinion in political life. It is, rather, the much larger change from an age of Enlightenment era society built on theatrical codes of self-presentation to a contemporary Western society in which a premium is placed on intimacy, directness of emotional expression (in public and private), and community. As Sennett notes toward the end of his book, "warmth is our god."[79] An ideology of intimacy, one which assumes that "social relationships of all kinds are real, believable, and authentic the closer they approach the inner psychological concerns of each person," rules our public as well as our private lives.[80] Indeed, it has contributed mightily to the dissolution of any strong sense of the distinctiveness of the public realm or self, to the point where political action is routinely read back to the "character" of the actor (his "real" self) and its evaluation made a function of the actor's personal characteristics and believability. The rise of a culture of intimacy systematically transmutes "political categories into psychological ones."[81]

It was not always so. In the first half of his book, Sennett describes the emergence of a secular "society of strangers" in the great urban centers of eighteenth-century London and Paris. The unprecedented concentration of strangers in one place created a "problem of audience": how to know and to judge the appearances—the words and deeds—of individuals encountered in this new, anonymous public. According to Sennett, the eighteenth century dealt with this problem by drawing on the venerable tradition of *theatrum mundi*, the image of society as itself a theater or stage. Expanding on this analogy, urban life in the eighteenth century built a "bridge" between the stage and the street, transferring a set of theatrical conventions and criteria of judgment (of dress, utterance, and believability) to the "theater" of the city.

To move in the public space of the eighteenth-century city was, almost by definition, to be an actor, a performer.[82] A shared set of conventions governed the presentation of self and emotion to strangers, enabling the growth of an "impersonal sociability" distinctive to the time. These conventions (of gesture, dress and speech) opened a communicative space that worked by creating a distance between the actor and his acts or appearances. Within this conventionally defined space, judgment and understanding focused on the act, the gesture, the word, rather than the agent behind them. If the "world is a stage," then "character of acts and the character of actors are separate, so that a man of the world 'can censure an imperfection, or even a vice, without rage against the guilty party.'"[83] When the common sense of public life was theatrical in this sense, one could disagree with the position held by another (often to the point of comical, polemical excess[84]) without feeling the need to demonize the *person* of the opponent.[85] One's opponent was simply an individual who had taken an evil or blameworthy role. In sum, it was the role that was condemned, not the person's *nature*.

This eighteenth-century notion of "man as actor" thus placed a premium on masks, role-playing, and appearances as the medium of an impersonal sociability. Such theatrical devices created a distance between the "natural" and social self, a distance that promoted an impersonal, but paradoxically easier and more expressive, sociability. As Sennett remarks, "Wearing a mask is the essence of civility. Masks permit pure sociability, detached from the circumstances of power, malaise, and private feeling of those who wear them. Civility has as its aim the shielding of others from being burdened with oneself."[86] With the aid of such conventions, the urban space of the eighteenth century created a distinctive public geography, one defined in large part by its highly artificial nature, its distance from the "natural" world of the home and family.[87]

The public space of the Enlightenment, then, was conventional through and through. Even the coffeehouses—one of Habermas's favorite examples of a proto-public space of rational discourse— "worked" as the result of establishing a strict set of conventions governing the form of discourse and sociality allowed within their doors: "The art of conversation [among social unequals in the coffeehouses] was a convention in the same sense as dressing to rank of the 1750's, even though its mechanism was the opposite, the suspension of rank."[88] The kind of impersonal sociability enabled by these theatrical devices is no longer available to us, for we have lost the art of playacting. Conventionality and theatricality are condemned, from Rousseau to the present, as inhumane and anti-egalitarian. The transition from the world of the eighteenth century to our own charts a dialectic of public theatricality and intimacy. In Sennett's words:

In the theater, there is a correlation between belief in the persona of the actor and belief in conventions. Play, playacting, and acting, all require belief in conventions to be expressive. Convention is itself the single most expressive tool of public life. But in an age wherein intimate relations determine what shall be believable, conventions, artifices, and rules appear only to get in the way of revealing oneself to another; they are obstructions to intimate expression. As the imbalance between public and intimate life has grown greater, people have become less expressive. With an emphasis on psychological authenticity, people become inartistic in daily life because they are unable to tap the fundamental creative strength of the actor, the ability to play with and invest feeling in external images of self. Thus we arrive at the hypothesis that theatricality has a special, hostile relation to intimacy; theatricality has an equally special, friendly relation to a strong public life.[89]

The rise of a culture of intimacy means the decline of (social) theatricality; the decline of social theatricality means the decline of public life. Focusing on the nineteenth century and the disruptions created by the rise of capitalism and an increasingly secularized culture, Sennett traces how the family ceased to be "a particular, nonpublic region" and became, instead, "an idealized refuge, a world all its own, with a higher moral value than the public realm."[90] As public life in the urban centers of the nineteenth century came to be seen as morally inferior to intimate life, public/political credibility became a matter of superimposing private upon public imagery.[91] Political actors still performed in public, but what they performed was their character, their feelings, the force of their personal convictions.

Sennett argues that this shift first comes to light in the revolutions of 1848, when virtuosos of Romantic subjectivity like Lamartine challenged and pacified hostile street audiences through the sheer force of their personality and charisma. Distrustful of convention, such audiences became passive spectators, convinced that what the truth of what any public speaker had to say reduced, finally, to the kind of person he was.[92] The more adept at performing "genuine" emotion—at displaying the private self in public—the politician is, the more believable he becomes. As Sennett remarks with regard to Lamartine: "The hidden power of a speaker like Lamartine is that he harnesses mystification. He has no text, and so escapes being measured by any standard of truth or reality. He can make the quality of his intentions and sentiments a self-sufficient basis of his legitimacy to rule. . . ."[93]

While the age of both proletarian revolution and the Romantic performer may be over, this distinctive cognitive structure survives. For us, as for the revolutionaries of 1848, "a believable public event is created by a believable public person rather than a believable action."[94] With the death of the dispersed, participatory theatricality of the eighteenth century, the performative dimensions of politics are confined to the calculated presentation of individual character to a silenced audience. "The genuine aesthetic qualities of the meeting of politics and the arts having disappeared, what remains is only the obscurantist, paralyzing effect of a 'politics of personality.'"[95] In contemporary politics, impersonality is death; the wearing of masks, deceit. In a culture of (faux) intimacy, politics reduces to what, for the eighteenth century, would have been a contradiction in terms: "personality in public."[96] While Americans may be a bit more savvy than they were when Nixon gave his Checkers speech, we remain firmly within the grid described by Sennett, one he equates with "the end of public life."

Conclusion

Sennett's description of the decline of social theatricality and the rise of an ideology of intimacy and community (or authenticity and what he calls "destructive *Gemeinschaft*") resonate powerfully with Arendt's observations on modern alienation from the world. Set against the backdrop provided by Sennett, her distinction between Lessing's "attitude towards the world" and the warmth sought by "pariah peoples" or the *fraternité* trumpeted by the French Revolution becomes even sharper. Neither intimacy nor solidarity, she is claiming, can provide a tenable substitute for lost worldliness. The public sphere is not merely the sphere of politics, of action or deliberation; it also has an irreducibly cultural dimension.[97] Hence the apparent paradox presented by both Arendt and Sennett's work: the spread of democracy in the modern age can coincide with the decline of the public realm.

Of course, neither Arendt nor Sennett blames democracy for this state of affairs, despite their common and profound debt to Tocqueville. Their shared point is that the decline of public culture, of worldliness in various forms, undercuts the promise of democracy. Benhabib and Habermas are also concerned with the public sphere's decline, but they view this sphere in terms so narrowly formal that the "recovery of the public realm" is identified with the achievement of a more "deliberative" democracy. This would, to be sure, be a great advance. However, the expansion of opportunities for public deliberation and debate in itself cannot guarantee a more robust sense of the public. Here, it seems to me, Benhabib and Habermas fall prey to a familiar delusion, namely, the idea that the more opportunities people have for debate and deliberation, the

151

more their moral horizons expand, the more likely (in the end) they will come to a reasonable consensus.

This faith in the power of public discourse to raise individuals from the merely personal and idiosyncratic to the common or universal runs deep in the Western tradition. One finds traces of it in the account of public judgment Aristotle gives in Book III of the *Politics*; it receives classic formulation in Rousseau and Kant (the former's phobia of factional argument notwithstanding); and it even inspires liberal theorists such as J. S. Mill (his worries about the tyranny of the majority aside). Yet, we must ask, is it really the case that (to cite Benhabib's formulation once again) "the process of public-political struggle transforms the attitude of narrow self-interest into a more broadly shared public or common interest"? Isn't it just as likely that, as Charles Larmore puts it, "the more we converse, the more we disagree"?[98] Recent appeals to a revived civic virtue or procedural forms of rationality are all attempts to offset both the pluralism and the privatism of contemporary society. Yet the possibility of generating consensus, whether through neo-Aristotelian or neo-Kantian means, cannot make up for our lost "feeling for the world." This, I take it, is the lesson that flows from both Arendt and Sennett, and we would be wise not to discount it.

Reading Arendt through the lens provided by Sennett does not merely make us skeptical of Habermas's and Benhabib's claim that the *sine qua non* of the public sphere is "the public use of one's reason." It also reveals just how off-target many of the objections to Arendt's "agonism" ultimately are. If Arendt's appeal to virtuosity and "rare speech and deeds" were merely a function of a misplaced hero worship, Benhabib's either/or of agonistic versus associational democracy would make sense. The heroic dimension is certainly there, but Arendt's focus on the impersonality of political action (a dimension Sennett's work serves to highlight) helps us see that an agonistic public need not be confined to the rare deeds of those who possess "great moral prowess," like Pericles.

Nor, for that matter, must such a public space be "holisitic" or "ocular." As Sennett demonstrates, theatricality can be every bit as dispersed as rational argumentation or information gathering, perhaps even more so. Reading Arendt's emphasis on the impersonal, theatrical quality of political action through Sennett, we are able to envisage multiple and fluid sites of public contest and debate. Indeed, Sennett's analysis warns us that our public sphere is becoming more "ocular," more bogusly "holistic," all the time. This is not to say that either Arendt or Sennett encourages us to find thriving public spaces where we least expect them (an activity currently popular among political and cultural theorists). By tying worldliness and theatricality so closely to culture and convention, both Arendt and Sennett deliver disillusioning news. They force us to acknowledge that the health of the political public sphere is inseparable from the health of public culture generally, and that no appeal to contemporary social movements or grass-roots politics can redress this fundamental shift in Western culture. The (currently depleted) energies of social democracy may be occasionally stimulated by such social movements as feminism or environmentalism, but the "return of the political" that so many expect to be generated by the associational life of civil society will be far less transformative than presumed.

Indeed, it may be doubted whether single-issue movements or identity politics do anything to transform the interests they articulate into "a more broadly shared public or common interest," at least in the quasi-Rousseauian sense both Benhabib and Habermas give this term.[99] It seems more likely that they contribute to the dialectic described by Sennett, largely by fostering an affinity group culture, one that is inclined to view moral-political virtues as a function of "who one is" in the most rudimentary sense. The inner connection between narcissism and the rhetoric of community has become increasingly apparent in virtually all forms of identity politics, as community is ever more tightly defined in terms of those like oneself. The psychic demands filled by the rhetoric of community also make it less likely that one's political opponents will escape demonization on the basis of who *they* are, whether male or female, straight or gay, white or black, and so on.

This returns us to the quandary raised by Arendt's characterization of Lessing in the passage cited above. Our inability to comprehend a figure like the one presented by Arendt flows from our inability to make the crucial distinction between actor and role, a distinction that both Sennett and Arendt identify as one basis of a *worldly* culture. We simply cannot understand how it is possible to "humanize the world by incessant and continual discourse about its affairs and the things in it." In a culture of intimacy/community, polemics and argument can only divide people; they cannot provide the medium of an impersonal sociability, let alone "friendship."

As long as we personalize the political in the sense described by Sennett, the ability to distinguish words, acts, and policies from a person's nature, character or "identity" will elude us. Slaves of the simplifying moral epistemology of the culture of intimacy/community, we have virtually eliminated the dimension of worldliness from our lives.

When Hannah Arendt focuses our attention on the agonistic "sharing of words and deeds" in the public realm of the *polis*, then, she is not promoting hero worship, nor is she yearning for the days of communal self-representation. Rather, she is trying to present this vanished dimension of worldliness in its most intense, theatrical and political form. The fact that she is so often misread as succumbing to the lure of Romantic subjectivity ("the performance of noble deeds by outstanding individuals" *à la* Burckhardt or Nietzsche) testifies to the accuracy of her diagnosis of modern alienation from the world. It may well be that *amor mundi* presupposes the "common sense" made possible by *theatrum mundi*. It is this possibility, rather than any "nostalgic *Verfallsgeschichte*," which makes Arendt (and Sennett) speak of the loss, destruction, or end of public life. The lesson they seek to teach us is that politicization as such has no particular connection to the recovery of the public sphere. This is a hard, and not particularly welcome, lesson, but one we would do well to learn if we really care about the fate of the public realm.

CHAPTER SEVEN

The Philosopher versus the Citizen
ARENDT, STRAUSS, AND SOCRATES

Introduction: The Problem

Viewed from the standpoint of liberal political theory, Hannah Arendt and Leo Strauss have much, perhaps too much, in common. There are, of course, the obvious similarities in background. Both were German-Jewish intellectuals who came of age during Weimar; both studied with Heidegger; both were refugees from Nazi terror; and both were intensely involved with Jewish thought and politics prior to their becoming celebrated political theorists in their new American home.

What stands out for the liberal theorist, though, is not biography, but the fundamental intellectual presuppositions shared by Arendt and Strauss. Indeed, one can persuasively argue, as John Gunnell has done, that they inhabit something like a common paradigm.[1] Arendt and Strauss both think in terms of something they call the "great tradition" of Western political thought, a tradition that begins with Socrates and Plato and enters a terminal stage of crisis with Marx and Nietzsche.[2] Both see this crisis in the tradition as reflecting a larger political-cultural crisis—the "crisis of modernity." Both find hope in the fact that the "end of the tradition" paradoxically provides the opportunity for new insight into the possibilities opened by ancient Greek political thought and practice, possibilities that had been obscured by the tradition.[3] Finally, both are fiercely critical of liberal democracy, decrying its underlying hedonism or utilitarianism. Despite the various expressions of allegiance to the American political system scattered throughout their works, neither is truly capable of appreciating what George Kateb has called "the moral distinctiveness of representative democracy."

Yet if Arendt and Strauss are, from the perspective of liberal theory, twin paragons of "antiliberal thought," what strikes their more patient readers is the range and depth of their differences. On any number of fundamental issues, Arendt and Strauss appear to be

155

poles apart, virtual antitypes. While Arendt wrote *The Human Condition* in order to question the devaluation of the political life performed by the "contemplative tradition," Strauss never ceased defending the philosophical life as indeed the best life. Politics had worth only insofar as it made such higher pursuits possible. Where Arendt insisted on thinking politics, political action, and "the realm of human affairs" in their own terms, with the greatest possible autonomy, Strauss maintained the need to subject political action and judgment to the moral certainties discoverable by reason. And whereas Arendt celebrated the spontaneous, initiatory quality of plural political action, Strauss upheld the classical-conservative virtue of moderation, *sophrosyne*.

All of these differences find expression in their respective (and radically divergent) images of a "healthy" politics. For Arendt, a healthy politics is an agonistic politics of open, never-ending debate; a politics that takes place in a public realm free of force and coercion, upon a "stage" suitable for the expression of human plurality and civic equality. For Strauss, a healthy politics is one in which the gentry or gentlemen rule; in which the passions of the *demos* are restrained by the virtues of their betters; in which enough order and freedom are present for the pursuit of philosophy; and in which philosophers can stand as potential "umpires" over political-moral disputes.[4]

This chapter focuses on the theme of the conflict between philosophy and politics, the philosopher and the citizen, as it emerges in the writings of Arendt and Strauss. Arendt's choice of sides in this conflict follows from her suspicion that philosophy—solitary thought concerned with invisibles—is, by its very nature, hostile to politics and human plurality. Indeed, she argues in a number of places that by far the greater part of philosophical thinking and writing about politics has been animated by an expressly antipolitical (and antidemocratic) impulse. Strauss emphasizes the fact of this conflict no less than Arendt, seeing it as rooted in man's fundamentally divided nature as a thinking and acting being. However, and in direct opposition to her, he turns to political theory, not to save politics from philosophical distortion, but to preserve the possibility of a philosophical politics.

Left at this, the theme of conflict between philosophy and politics seems merely to underline the basic opposition of Arendt and Strauss: in a world where the *demos* and the philosopher must always conflict, where the life of action and the life of thought are fundamentally at odds, Arendt sides with the citizen and Strauss with the philosopher. Yet, as any attentive reader of either thinker can testify, matters are less simple than the polarities of politics versus philosophy, or thought versus action, suggest.

My desire is to complicate our reading of the relation between philosophy and politics in the work of Arendt and Strauss. Like them, I begin by first sharpening the opposition between these activities. I then turn to the question of their possible, but necessarily episodic, harmony. There is, I shall argue, a curious intersection in the political theories of Arendt and Strauss. Both point to the possibility of a philosophical or Socratic form of citizenship, one that undercuts the dichotomy of philosophy versus politics which otherwise structures so much of their work. Ultimately, however, they both eschew this possibility. In so doing they betray their best insights, leaving us with the false alternative between a revised civic republicanism on the one hand and philosophical elitism on the other.

My aim is not to suggest that, despite appearances, Arendt and Strauss really agree on what Strauss called "the problem of Socrates." Nor is it to suggest that either of them pursued a synthesis of "theory and practice" via the figure of the "philosopher-citizen." Rather, I hope to show that Arendt and Strauss, despite their opposing loyalties to "politics" and "philosophy," contribute to the articulation of a distinctive mode of critical, distanced citizenship—what I have elsewhere called "alienated citizenship."[5] At the end of this chapter I offer some reflections on how such alienation informed Arendt's and Strauss's theoretical practice, at once fostering it and inhibiting it.

ARENDT: PHILOSOPHY AND POLITICS

As Margaret Canovan notes in her recent book on Arendt, there is more than a little ambiguity in the Arendtian characterization of the conflict between philosophy and politics.[6] Was the age-old tension the result of the specific events of Socrates' trial and death, or did it flow from the inherent characteristics of thought and action? The question Canovan poses is important as it sets the boundaries for Arendt's reflections on the possibility of harmonizing philosophy and politics. But regardless of whether the conflict is necessary or historically contingent, there is little doubt that Arendt believes *our* tradition of philosophical thought to be radically antipolitical. To understand why, we must look at the nature of the "public-political world" of the *polis* prior to its philosophical conceptualization (and distortion) by Plato and Aristotle.[7]

As is well-known, Arendt finds in the democratic Greek *polis* a well-defined public sphere, one characterized by the complete political equality of citizens.[8] Within this sphere, relations of rulership or coercion were unknown, as *political* relations were conducted through talk and persuasion. Whether in the assembly or the agora, the democratic Greek citizen knew a tangible, worldly freedom: the freedom to appear in public and be recognized by his peers; to exchange opinion; to debate and persuade; and to participate in decisions on matters of common concern. The essence of Arendt's view of Athenian politics is that it was one of incessant public talk.[9] Indeed, she goes so far as to claim that this was the Greeks' own understanding of politics: "To be political, to live in a *polis*, meant that everything was decided through words and persuasion and not through force and violence. . . . [It was] a way of life in which speech and only speech made sense and where the central concern of all citizens was to talk to each other."[10]

Such a politics of talk realizes the basic human condition of *plurality* in that deliberative speech among equals gives expression to individual perspectives on a common world. In expressing our opinion, our *doxa*, we give our formulation in speech of what *dokei moi*, of what appears to me.[11] According to Arendt, only in terms of such innumerable perspectives and aspects ("for which no common measurement or denominator can ever be devised") does the public realm come to presence and have its effective reality.[12] The politics of debate and persuasion is what generates the "shining brightness" of the public sphere, linking action and thought through reasoned speech (*logos*).

Viewed in these terms, the public realm is threatened from two directions: first, by an excess of agonal spirit, in which the will to shine before one's peers excels one's commitment to the "public thing"; second, by any attempt to privilege one perspective at the expense of all others. If the first threat describes the natural tendency of Greek politics to devolve into an unlimited competition for reputation and glory, the second describes what happens when philosophy or ideology attempts to transcend the realm of opinion and found a politics based on truth.

In her posthumously published essay "Philosophy and Politics" (written in 1954), Arendt credits Socrates with discovering a mode of philosophizing that did not oppose truth to *doxa*, but rather sought to deliver citizens of the specific truth of their opinions by forcing them to improve their *doxai*.[13] The essentially maieutic function of the philosopher, which reveals *doxa* in its own truthfulness, curbs the excesses of the agonal spirit through the exercise of "talking something through": dialogue or dialectic. Socrates, according to Arendt, "tried to make friends out of Athens's citizenry" through such dialogue.[14] If the greatest threat to the politics of talk was the tendency for agonistic political speech to degenerate into a competitive free-for-all and (thence) into mute violence, then Socratic dialogue attempted to create an understanding between friends that would serve as a counterweight to the agonistic spirit, providing a common ground for the expression of divergent opinions. The commitment to "talking something through," Socrates hoped, would limit the fragmentation and violence generated by an excess of agonal spirit. As Arendt puts it, "Socrates seems to have believed that the political function of the philosopher was to establish the kind of common world, built on the understanding of friendship, in which no rulership is needed."[15]

The Socratic project is not, however, reducible to the cultivation of *philia* through dialogue. As Arendt insists in "Philosophy and Politics," Socrates gives a highly distinctive twist to the idea of civic friendship, basing it on the individual's capacity for thought and self-knowledge. Unlike Aristotelian deliberation, Socratic dialectic aims not at revealing shared purposes, virtues, or character; rather, the primary effect of Socratic "talking through" is to *interrupt* our everyday derivation of judgment and action from unquestioned virtues, values or principles, and to throw us back on our "internal dialogue," the dialogue of thought, of me with myself. Arendt's claim, following the Socrates of the *Apology*, is that the experience of thought, of our inner plurality, is the true basis of conscience, and, as such, the ground of authentic citizenship. "Only someone who has had the experience of talking with himself," Arendt writes, "is capable of being a friend, of acquiring another self."[16] Living together with others "begins with living together with oneself."[17]

As Arendt understands it, then, the Socratic project aims at cultivating not solidarity, but thoughtfulness. The experience of the "two-in-one" of thought enables the individual to affirm the outer plurality of the world, the fact of different perspectives and moral disagreement. Moreover, thought itself is crucial to the development of the faculty of moral judgment, since only the "stop and think" urged by Socrates prevents judgment from proceeding in automatic fashion, along the lines suggested by the common sense of the community. In the 1971 essay "Thinking and Moral Considerations" Arendt argues that it was precisely the *absence* of thought which characterized Adolf Eichmann, and which prepared him for complicity with evil on an unprecedented scale.[18] One finds a different kind of thoughtlessness in the debates depicted by Thucydides in his *History of the Peloponnesian War* (the Mytilenian debate of 427 B.C.E. is the classic example), but it is thoughtlessness nonetheless. All too familiar with the dangers of collective enthusiasm, Socrates fosters a commitment to "talking through" in order to stimulate thinking, whose "by-product" is conscience and judgment—what Arendt elsewhere calls the "ability to think without rules." The original harmony of thought and action in reasoned speech is deepened through the cultivation of a conscientious citizenry—individuals who not only *talk* with each other in the agora, but who "stop and think," who are capable of slowing each other down in the relentless Athenian pursuit of glory.

Of course, the Socratic experiment failed miserably. Not only did the citizens of Athens fail to become "friends," they tried and condemned Socrates for his trouble. It is with this event that the hope to preserve the original harmony of action and thought manifest in *polis* politics comes to an end. And it is in response to the trial and death of Socrates that Plato and Aristotle attempt to make the world safe for philosophy by introducing the principle of authority into the plural, political sphere.[19] In so doing, they initiate our tradition of political philosophy, the greater part of which, in Arendt's view, ". . . could easily be interpreted as various attempts to find theoretical foundations and practical ways for an escape from politics altogether."[20]

What does Arendt mean by the principle of authority, and why are Plato and Aristotle the originators of it? To answer this question we must turn to what I regard as the companion piece to "Philosophy and Politics," namely, her 1956 essay "What Is Authority?"

At the beginning of this widely discussed (and much misunderstood) essay, Arendt claims that a "constant, ever-widening and deepening crisis of authority has accompanied the development of the modern world in our century."²¹ This has led many of her readers to assume that she is nostalgic for authority. In fact, nothing could be further from the truth. Arendt's essay is intended as a genealogy, not of authority in general, but rather "a very specific form which had been valid throughout the Western World over a long period of time."²² One mark of the current crisis is that, having lost touch with this form, we tend to conflate authority with power or violence. In "What Is Authority?" Arendt's goal is to recover the essence of this specific form.

Authority needs to be distinguished not only from power and violence, but from persuasion (the stuff of democratic politics) as well:

> ... authority precludes the use of external means of coercion; where force is used, authority itself has failed. Authority, on the other hand, is incompatible with persuasion, which presupposes equality and works through a process of argumentation. Where arguments are used, authority is left in abeyance. Against the egalitarian order of persuasion stands the authoritarian order, which is always hierarchical. If authority is to be defined at all, then, it must be in contradistinction to both coercion by force and persuasion by argument.²³

Authority defined in *this* way is obviously antipolitical, predicated as it is on a hierarchical distinction between "the one who commands and the one who obeys." Arendt's point is that in a specifically authoritarian political system, this hierarchy rests not on common reason or power, but on the recognition of the rightness and legitimacy of the relation itself by both parties.²⁴ Strictly speaking, the rule of authority means that both force and persuasion are superfluous.

But how could such a notion be introduced into the Greek world, particularly democratic Athens? Wouldn't any attempt to assert the centrality of the ruler/ruled distinction be seen as a transparently partisan argument for oligarchical domination, blatantly irreconcilable with the civic equality that was the essential precondition of a genuine politics? However much the trial and death of Socrates convinced Plato of the insufficiency of persuasion (*peithen*), there was no simple way of convincing his fellow citizens that rulership could be anything other than the *destruction* of political relations and a regress to prepolitical forms (the master of the household, say, or the tyrant).²⁵

Plato's solution was the discovery of a form of compulsion that did not rest on the use of violence, one that compelled without the resort to force. Such compulsion is found in the truths of reason and logical demonstration. As Arendt puts it, "very early in his search he [Plato] must have discovered that truth, namely, the truths we call self-evident, compels the mind, and that this coercion, though it needs no violence to be effective, is stronger than persuasion and argument."[26]

The problem with such compulsion, however, is that only the few are familiar with it. Hence, Plato had to find some way of reproducing this nonviolent form of coercion through reason in a manner that would command universal assent. According to Arendt, it was this demand that led him to reinterpret his doctrine of ideas so that they could be construed as transcendent standards for human conduct. If such standards existed, and if they were available only to those whose character and rational development enabled them to rise above the cave of human affairs, then thinking and action, knowing and doing, could be split apart along apparently natural hierarchical lines. The knowers—the philosopher-kings—give instructions based on these standards; their subjects merely execute them.

As Arendt emphasizes, the transformation of the ideas into standards or yardsticks for human conduct was by no means a matter of course. In their original incarnation, the ideas were "that which shines forth most," the beautiful (*ta kalon*). Plato was able to transform the beautiful into "unwavering, absolute standards for political and moral behavior and judgment" only by drawing on an analogy from the realm of fabrication, where the artisan relies on a "transcendent" model of his product, one which lies beyond the fabrication process yet which guides it at every step. The separation of thinking and acting—the placement of the philosopher in a position of command over the citizen—makes sense only insofar as political action and judgment are seen as the products of a similarly deductive application of more general principles.

Although Plato was hardly successful with respect to Athens, he was tremendously successful in installing the idea that there were absolute standards—transcendent "models"—for the realm of human affairs. Driven to posit such standards by "the spectacle of Socrates submitting his own *doxa* to the irresponsible opinions of the Athenians," Plato set the pattern followed by all subsequent authoritarian thought and government. Authoritarian rule is to be distinguished from tyranny by the fact that "its acts are tested by a code which was made either not by man at all . . . or at least not by those actually in power. The source of authority in authoritarian government is always a force external and superior to its own power; it is always this source, this external force which transcends the political realm, from which the authorities derive their 'authority,' that is, their legitimacy. . . ."[27]

While the idea of such a transcendent source of legitimacy has been a tremendously powerful one in the Western tradition, it is by no means the only, nor even the primary, effect produced by the Platonic appeal to atemporal standards. More long-lasting, and more deeply influential according to Arendt, was the relation Plato's fabrication analogy posited between such standards or measures and particular actions, events, and behaviors. As Arendt writes, ". . . the ideas relate to the varied multitude of things concrete in the same way as one yardstick relates to the varied multitude of things measurable, or as the rule of reason or common sense relates to the varied multitude of concrete events that can be subsumed under it."[28]

The resulting identification of *judgment* with the operation of subsuming a particular under a universal "had the greatest influence on the Western tradition," infecting even Kant, whose well-known distinction between determinate judgment (subsuming a particular under a pregiven concept) and reflective judgment (the imaginative operation of finding a concept for a particular) did not stop him from identifying *moral* judgment with the former.[29] Rightly or wrongly, Arendt sees the Categorical Imperative as an absolute in the Platonic/authoritarian sense, standing above men and the realm of human affairs, measuring them without any concern for context, specificity, or the "fundamental relativity" of the "interhuman realm."[30]

Arendt emphasizes this inheritance of Platonism because she sees it as inculcating a habit of mechanical, unthinking judgment. The more judgment is identified with the application of a rule, an unvarying standard or "yardstick," the more our powers of judgment atrophy, the less we are able to "stop and think" in the Socratic sense. Moreover, the insistence that judgment is dependent on such standards leads to a "crisis in judgment" when these standards are revealed to be without effective power. This, according to Arendt, is what happens in the course of the modern age, as new and unprecedented moral and political phenomena reveal the hollowness and inadequacy of the "reliable universal rules" the tradition had offered us. This process—call it the crisis in authority or, to use Nietzsche's symbolic formulation, the "death of God"—comes to its conclusion with the advent of the evils of totalitarianism, evils so unprecedented that they "have clearly exploded our categories of political thought and our standards for moral judgment."[31]

The failure of the inherited wisdom of the past, the fact of a radical break in our tradition, throws us back upon our own resources. Potentially, Arendt notes, the crisis is liberating, as it frees the faculty of judgment from its subservience to objectivist regimes such as Plato's ideas or Kant's Categorical Imperative. As Arendt puts it in "Understanding and Politics":

> Even though we have lost yardsticks by which to measure, and rules under which to subsume the particular, a being whose essence is beginning may have enough of origin within himself to understand without preconceived categories and to judge without the set of customary rules which is morality.[32]

The hope that the "crisis in authority" will lead to the rebirth of a genuinely autonomous faculty of judgment runs up against Arendt's own deeply ingrained sense that ordinary individuals will find it difficult indeed to wean themselves from pregiven categories, rules, and "yardsticks." Minus the presence of a Socrates (who, as the simile in the *Meno* has it, is like an stinging fish, paralyzing his partners in dialogue, forcing them to stop and think), the likely result of such a crisis is gratitude for anything that props up the old set of standards or provides the semblance of a new one. Responding to the philosopher Hans Jonas's call for a renewed inquiry into ultimate, metaphysical grounds for judgment at a conference on her work in 1972, Arendt declared her pessimism that "a new god will appear" and went on to observe:

> . . . if you go through such a situation [as totalitarianism] the first thing you know is the following: you *never* know how somebody will act. You have the surprise of your life! This goes throughout all layers of society, and it goes throughout various distinctions between men. And if you want to make a generalization, then you could say that those who were still very firmly convinced of the so-called old values were the first to be ready to change their old values for a new set of values, *provided they were given one*. And I am afraid of this, because I think that the moment you

give anybody a new set of values—or this famous "bannister"—you can immediately exchange it. And the only thing the guy gets used to is having a "bannister" and a set of values, no matter.[33]

Arendt thought that the natural tendency of the ordinary person, when faced with the destruction of one set of authoritative rules, will not be Socratic examination and perplexity (which only further dissolves the customary), but a grasping for a new code, a new "bannister." Thinking, especially Socratic thinking, dissolves grounds, it does not stabilize them. It is, as Arendt says, a "dangerous and resultless enterprise," one that can just as easily lead to cynicism and nihilism as to independent judgment and a deepened moral integrity.[34] Arendt here agrees with the analysis Kant gives in "What Is Enlightenment?": most people would simply prefer not to make the effort that independent judgment demands, let alone risk the taken-for-granted moral presuppositions of their existence.

Yet however real this aversion to thinking or "paralysis" is, Arendt holds onto the Socratic possibility that ordinary individuals will remain open to the "winds of thought." She profoundly agrees with Socrates that it is only through such examination that the individual is likely to avoid complicity with the moral horrors routinely perpetrated by popular political regimes. Socratic thinking—which, in its relentless negativity, is the very opposite of all foundational or professional philosophical thinking—liberates the faculty of judgment from the tyranny of rules and custom. In this way, it prevents the individual from being "swept away unthinkingly by what everybody else does and believes in."[35] Independent judgment is, according to Arendt, the "by-product" of this liberating effect of thinking; it "realizes" thinking "in the world of appearances."[36] Thus, while thinking may not be able to "make friends" of citizens as Socrates had hoped, it can "prevent catastrophes, at least for myself, in the rare moments when the chips are down."[37]

STRAUSS: PLATO OR SOCRATES?

Arendt's embrace of a Socratic conception of citizenship modifies the widespread view of her political theory as an extension or revision of the civic republican tradition.[38] Even in the chastened version of this ideal set forth in "Thinking and Moral Considerations," we find her valuing distance, reflection, and resistance over patriotism, will, and duty; conscience and independent judgment over shared purposes; episodic intervention over constant engagement. If Arendt remained suspicious of the enforced withdrawal from the world that pure philosophical thinking demands, she nevertheless celebrated the public performance of the thinking process by Socrates in the agora. Here, acting not as a teacher but rather as a kind of stinging fish or "electric ray," Socrates paralyzed his fellow citizens with his own perplexity, dissolving the solid ground of their unreflective opinions, making the unthinking application of general rules or customary definitions impossible.[39] By infecting his fellow citizens with thought, Socrates rendered them the morally salutary service of slowing them down, of making them less likely to channel their agonal energies into projects of injustice (such as Athenian imperialism).

In turning to Strauss, one is struck first by his general agreement with Arendt as to the *causes* of the conflict between philosophy and politics, the philosopher and the citizen. Philosophical thinking requires a withdrawal from the world of appearances; it is, essentially, the contemplative attempt to grasp the nature of the whole.[40] Such activity stands in the sharpest opposition to the active pursuit of glory or greatness in the political realm, a pursuit that never leaves the "conventional" world of the polity behind, which never concerns itself with the "invisibles" that are the object of the philosopher's "What is?" questions. The tension between *physis* and *nomos* (nature and convention) in Greek thought reflects the fundamental opposition between what Arendt calls the citizen's desire for worldly immortality (achieved through word and deeds) and the philosopher's experience of the eternal, which "can occur only outside the realm of human affairs and outside the plurality of men."[41]

But if Arendt's analysis in *The Human Condition* stresses the way the philosopher's concern with the eternal is "inherently contradictory and in conflict with the striving for immortality, the life of the citizen," Strauss stipulates a kind of continuity between the world of "the cave" and the philosopher's pursuit of wisdom. In his view, the philosophical project is not one of dissolving or negating *doxa*, but (to use the Platonic metaphor from Book VII of the *Republic*) of *ascending* from *doxa* or common sense to what is "natural," not merely conventional. As Strauss puts it, "even Socrates is compelled to go the way from law to nature, to ascend from law to nature."[42] Socratic dialectics is nothing other than the means by which the ascent from "common sense" is achieved.[43]

However, it is one thing to say that Socrates necessarily begins with "common sense," another to say that his mission is to maieutically tease out the truth of a particular *doxa*. Arendt's formulation in "Philosophy and Politics" stands squarely opposed to Strauss's conception of the goal of classical political philosophy and political philosophy as such. The point for Strauss is precisely to transcend the realm of plurality and conflicting opinion, to move dialectically to a comprehensive standpoint far removed from the "it appears to me" of the citizen. Describing the character of Socratic philosophy and dialectics in *Natural Right and History*, Strauss writes:

> Philosophy consists, therefore, in the ascent from opinions to knowledge or to the truth, in an ascent that may be said to be guided by opinions. It is this ascent which Socrates had primarily in mind when he called philosophy "dialectics." Dialectics is the art of conversation or of friendly dispute. The friendly dispute which leads toward the truth is made possible or necessary by the fact that opinions about what things are, or what some very important groups of things are, contradict one another. Recognizing the contradiction, one is forced to go beyond opinions toward the consistent view of the nature of the thing [for example, justice, piety, wisdom, virtue] concerned. That consistent view makes visible the relative truth of the contradictory opinions; the consistent view proves to be the comprehensive or total view. The opinions are thus seen to be fragments of the truth, soiled fragments of the pure truth.[44]

While, on this account, the *doxai* have not been "destroyed," it is clear that the mere fact of their plurality limits their value to raw material for the philosopher. For Strauss, the aim of Socrates is to ascend from the many (*doxai*) to the one (truth), while remaining conscious of the limits of human knowledge. Nothing could be further from Arendt's Socrates, who, as a "citizen among citizens," has as his goal the *improvement* of *doxa*, one opinion at a time.[45] This improvement takes place through dialectic, through "talking something through."

Strauss's formulation of Socrates' project is echoed in his definition of the nature and goal of political philosophy in "What Is Political Philosophy?" (1954–55). The opening of this essay finds Strauss at his most Platonic: the conception of political philosophy he offers is structured entirely upon the distinction between knowledge (*episteme*) and opinion. Philosophy is defined as the "quest for universal wisdom, for knowledge of the whole." *Political* philosophy—a discipline Strauss believes was founded by Socrates—is a "branch" of philosophy proper. Thus, in a well-known passage, Strauss writes:

> Political philosophy will then be the attempt to replace opinion about the nature of political things by knowledge of the nature of political things. Political things are by their nature subject to approval and disapproval, to choice and rejection, to praise and blame. It is of their essence not to be neutral but to raise a claim to men's obedience, allegiance, decision or judgment. One does not understand them as what they are, as political things, if one does not take seriously their explicit or implicit claim to be judged in terms of goodness or badness, of justice or injustice, i.e., if one does not measure them by some standard of goodness and justice. *To judge soundly one must know the true standards.* If political philosophy wishes to do justice to its subject matter, it must strive for genuine knowledge of these standards. Political philosophy is the attempt to truly know the nature of political things and the right, or good, political order.[46]

Political philosophy, then, is "the conscious, coherent, and relentless effort to replace opinions about political fundamentals by knowledge regarding them."[47] This definition of political philosophy assimilates the Socratic position to Plato's, and it is motivated by the demand that there be *some* way of rationally adjudicating the fundamental questions and controversies of political life (for example, what is the best regime?, who shall rule?, etc.). The political philosopher, as the classics conceived him, was the "teacher of legislators." But, even more important for Strauss, the political philosopher is the one whose knowledge of political things places him in a privileged position of judgment: "The umpire par excellence is the political philosopher. He tries to settle those political controversies that are both of paramount and permanent importance."[48]

The political philosopher is suited to this task because only he, as opposed to the politician, "political thinker," or intellectual, is neither partisan nor constrained by the "here and now."[49] His inquiry into the "What is?" questions (what is justice, piety, virtue, etc.) directs him toward knowledge of the good life and the good society; it enables him to address what Strauss calls the "essentially contro-

PHILOSOPHER VERSUS CITIZEN

versial" meaning of the common good in a comprehensive, rather than partial or partisan, fashion.[50]

Based as it is on a sense that the West has become "uncertain of its purpose" and mired in relativism, Strauss's conception of political philosophy is a self-conscious response to Max Weber's value pluralism and the historicism of Martin Heidegger's fundamental ontology.[51] Weber's denial that reason can find solutions to value conflicts occasions Strauss's most polemical and intemperate prose.[52] Strauss does not dogmatically assert that reason *can* indeed solve such conflicts. Rather, his primary intent is to question the dogma that, given the plurality of values, goods, and "ultimate commitments," reason is unable to aid us in ranking or choosing among the "warring gods" of politics, philosophy, or art (or nationalism, socialism, or liberalism, for that matter). Similarly, his critique of historicism, particularly the "radical historicism" of Heidegger, is motivated by what he sees as its rejection of the question of the good society and its insistence that all answers to this question are historically conditioned (indeed, the question itself is seen as a function of one particular fateful historical dispensation).[53] Strauss sees Weber's contempt for an overarching, adjudicative reason as matched by Heidegger's contempt for such "permanencies" as the distinction between the noble and the base. It is this contempt that, in Strauss's view, led directly to Heidegger's affiliation with National Socialism in 1933.[54]

This is the context in which we must understand Strauss's "necessary and tentative or experimental" return to the possibility opened by classical political philosophy.[55] "Social science positivism" and "historicism" both deny that there is any way out of the cave.[56] As symptoms of the "crisis in authority" referred to by Arendt, they both assert that "man cannot understand himself in light of the whole, in the light of his origin or end."[57] The "end of philosophy" trumpeted by Derrida and Rorty was, for Strauss, already fully perceived by Weber and Heidegger. Strauss's response was, apparently, to uphold philosophy's traditional ambition to view things *sub specie aeternitatis*, to rise from convention to nature and thus to gain a comprehensive grasp of the whole.[58] This response flows not from any simple nostalgia for the ancients, nor from a misplaced faith that they possess the answers to contemporary political problems.[59] Rather, it should be viewed as a conscious rebellion against the (historicist/relativist) spirit of the times.

169

The contrast with Arendt, both in terms of diagnosis and pre-scription, is manifest. For Arendt, the crisis in authority—the "death of God"—meant that one could no longer even gesture to-ward the realm of essence or nature Strauss wanted to pursue with his Socratic "What is?" questions. Glossing Nietzsche's aphorisms in *The Gay Science* and *The Twilight of the Idols* in her Introduction to *The Life of the Mind*, Arendt writes:

> What has come to an end is the basic distinction between the sensory and the supersensory, together with the notion, at least as old as Par-menides, that whatever is not given to the senses—God or Being or the First Principles and Causes (*archai*) or the Ideas—is more real, more truthful, more meaningful than what appears, that it is not just *beyond* sense perception but *above* the world of the senses. What is "dead" is not only the localization of such "eternal truths" but also the distinction itself.[60]

Arendt goes on to describe the *opportunity* presented by the de-mise of metaphysics and philosophy: "It would permit us to look on the past with new eyes, unburdened and unguided by any tradi-tions. . . ."[61] This sense of opportunity echoes her appreciation, given some twenty years earlier (in a lecture to the American Politi-cal Science Association), of Heidegger's contribution to the study of politics. Praising his concept of historicity (*Geschichlichkeit*) because it led Heidegger to reject the Platonic/Hegelian assumption that *theoria* occupies a standpoint from which the whole can be grasped, Arendt notes the revolutionary implications of this concept for philosophy and (ultimately) the study of politics. For with this notion "the philosopher left behind him the claim to being 'wise' and knowing eternal standards for the perishable affairs of the City of man," a claim that had force so long as the philosopher, unlike the citizen, was understood to dwell "in the proximity of the Absolute."[62]

Indeed, with Heidegger philosophy can rightly claim to have "left the arrogance of all Absolutes behind." The realm of human af-fairs no longer appears as an object fit for philosophical comprehen-sion and domination. Heidegger's "rejection of the claim to wis-dom" thus in principle opens the way to "a reexamination of the whole realm of politics in light of elementary human experiences *within this realm itself*, and demands implicitly concepts and judgments which have their roots in altogether different kinds of human experience."[63]

Of course, from Strauss's standpoint, Heideggerian historicity hardly facilitates a return to basic political problems and phenomena; rather, it is responsible for creating (in Strauss's striking image) a kind of "artificial pit" beneath the cave of human affairs.[64] Like other, less radical forms, Heidegger's historicism casts the "natural horizon of human thought" into oblivion by denying "the permanence of fundamental problems."[65] The "tentative" and "experimental" return to classical political thought is necessary as a means to recovering this "natural horizon": the world of the political association, of commonsense insights into political life. Not Heidegger, but the classical political philosophers return us "to the things themselves."[66] The return to the cave, to the world of the commonsense understanding of political things, is the necessary prelude to the ascent to truth. The world of commonsense experience, of "authoritative opinions," can serve as the basis for this ascent because it, unlike scientific or historical knowledge, reflects a "natural articulation" of the whole, albeit in clouded, fragmentary form.[67]

Arendt's and Strauss's vastly different responses to the provocation of Heidegger seem to trace an abyss between the two thinkers. On the one hand we have Arendt, the phenomenologist of the public realm, wary of the appeal to extrapolitical foundations or absolutes, anxious to abandon what she views as a distorting philosophical standpoint; on the other, Strauss, with his unyielding desire to reopen the possibility of philosophical wisdom of the "human things." From Arendt's point of view, Strauss's quest for the "true standards" cannot help but appear authoritarian in the worst, Platonist sense. And while Strauss might respond that his interpretation of Plato's ideas in the *Republic* expressly questions the Arendtian supposition that they were intended to provide genuinely applicable "yardsticks" for the realm of human affairs (Strauss calls the interpretation of the ideas as metaphysical certainties "incredible, not to say . . . fantastic"[68]), the authoritarian charge retains some plausibility.

As Arendt argues in "What Is Authority?," Aristotle's abandonment of the ideas did not prevent his political philosophy from being essentially authoritarian, centering as it did on the "natural" hierarchy of age in order to split ostensibly equal citizens along generational lines—as teachers and taught, rulers and ruled. This educational metaphor, which Arendt sees as both antidemocratic and antipolitical, is at the heart of Strauss's own view of political philosophy, statesmanship, and politics rightly construed (namely, as an "education in virtue" carried out differently by different regimes).[69] For Strauss, as opposed to Arendt, Socrates is emphatically a *teacher*, not a "citizen-philosopher,"[70] and a teacher who knows the first political lesson, namely, that philosophers must address different *types* of people differently.[71] Moreover, Strauss's Socrates (a very Platonic Socrates), "converses only with people who are not common people, who in one way or other belong to an elite. . . ."[72] Philosophical wisdom contributes to the gentleman's education in virtue. The gentlemen, in turn, will help sustain a suitable civic virtue for the hoi polloi.[73]

Strauss is vehement in his insistence that the virtue of the philosopher is qualitatively different, and higher, than that of the "gentleman." Likewise, he insists that the virtue of the gentleman is of a different order than the (merely political) virtue of the average citizen.[74] This leads him to stress the "fundamental disproportion between philosophy and the city" and to declare that "the philosophers and the nonphilosophers cannot have genuinely common deliberations."[75] When we combine this denial of the very possibility of an egalitarian public sphere with his insistence that "political life derives its dignity from something which transcends political life" (whether philosophy, faith, or natural right),[76] we seem to have all the evidence we need to convict Strauss of being "authoritarian" precisely in Arendt's sense.

There is, however, another Strauss, a more genuinely Socratic Strauss, a Strauss oddly akin to Arendt. This is the skeptical Strauss, the Strauss who insists that genuine philosophy demands a Socratic awareness that one does not know; that "human wisdom is knowledge of ignorance"; that there is no knowledge of the whole, but only partial knowledge of the parts; that, as a result, there can be "no unqualified transcending, even by the wisest man as such, of the sphere of opinion."[77] This Strauss does not offer philosophy as a form of foundationalism, but rather as the severest challenge to authority in *all* its forms.[78] The "discovery of nature" may be the work of philosophy, but "nature" turns out to be (at least in moral and political affairs) no more than a kind of "regulative ideal," a symbol not of ready-to-hand yardsticks or banisters, but of the desire to avoid the identification of the moral with the conventional, an identification that historicism (badly or superficially understood) facilitates.[79]

This Strauss is an enemy of all dogmatism, of all moral-political positions that base themselves on a secure possession of truth. Strauss identifies such certainty with "political idealism," that is, with movements which attempt to use theory as a blueprint for political practice, social reform, or societal transformation. Like Arendt—indeed, like Burke, Oakeshott, or even Lyotard—Strauss wants to alert us to the dangers of positing what Heidegger would call a "technical" relation between theory and practice.[80] Unlike them, he sees the warning against the deduction of just political action from theoretical premises as most forcefully articulated by Plato's *Republic*. The argument of the *Republic* is precisely one designed to make us realize a fully just polity is impossible to attain; hence, it liberates us "from the charms of what we would now call political idealism."[81]

In rejecting both conventionalism and an activist "theoreticism," Strauss wants to open up a space for judgment—a space he sees endangered by both historicism and "idealist" or ideological thinking. His fear is the same as we find in Arendt: judgment has become increasingly "automatic," the mere reflection of social norms and conventions, the unthinking application of customary rules. Like her, Strauss wants to reclaim judgment's specific autonomy. Their primary difference in this regard concerns less their aim than their diagnoses of the chief threats to judgment as an independent or autonomous faculty. For Arendt, the threat comes from rule-bound morality and social convention; for Strauss, the danger resides less in the identification of morality with rules than with the historicist relativization of moral codes. The point is that neither Arendt nor Strauss sees any advantage in cultivating an unthinking relationship to rule-bound morality or an uncritical patriotism. If their experience in Germany taught them anything, it was a deep suspicion of the morality of "my station and its duties."

Thinking—whether Socratic in Arendt's sense or philosophical in Strauss's—is thus absolutely essential for the liberation of judgment. But thinking, as both Arendt and Strauss emphasize, is dissolvent in character: the Socratic dialogues are aporetic, and lead to no firm ground. The essential difference between Strauss and Arendt concerns their attitudes toward the political implications of

173

such thinking in the public sphere. For Arendt, as we have seen, the potentially nihilistic consequences are offset by the value of the "stop and think," of the throwing out of gear of everyday moral evaluations and conclusions. For Strauss, the situation is more complicated. Setting aside the issue of the ordinary individual's capacity for thoughtfulness, he worries about the conclusions such an individual might draw from a dissolvent or endlessly critical rationality.[82] A thinking that takes place in the agora, which is truly open to everyone, will have a corrupting effect on those whose character is insufficiently virtuous to withstand the disorientation caused by Socratic negativity.

This, it seems to me, is Strauss's primary response to the Arendtian attempt to harmonize philosophy and politics through the figure of Socrates. His preference for the Socrates of the *Republic* and the *Gorgias* over the philosopher-citizen of the *Apology* flows from this fear. His intense concern with the relation of philosophy to poetry and rhetoric mirrors his conviction that philosophical insight will not draw the truth out of the citizen's *doxa*, but rather be transformed into the most dangerous form of untruth. It is no exaggeration to say, in this regard, that the prospect of an Arendtian Socrates fills him with horror: no good can come from the attempt to make the *demos* philosophical. The very project is an oxymoron.[83] Judgment must be liberated (from the *doxa* of historicism/relativism), but, in the case of the average citizen, it can never do without leading strings. Here Strauss stands not only against Arendt, but also against Kant. His distrust of the many makes him confine genuinely independent judgment to the few, while hoping for a more edifying (if not necessarily more truthful) *doxa* for the many.[84] Socratic in thinking and his moral ambitions, Strauss remains resolutely Platonist in his politics. The *demos* is, by nature, a beast immune to the "charms of philosophy."[85]

FROM ALIENATED CITIZENSHIP TO
RADICALLY ESTRANGED THEORY

Arendt's turn to Socrates in "Philosophy and Politics" and "Thinking and Moral Considerations" does not alter her fundamental conviction that active citizenship is the best bar against political evil. In making this judgment she sides with Machiavelli, chastizing philosophy (as did Callicles) for its "unmanly" withdrawal from the world. Yet both "Philosophy and Politics" and "Thinking and Moral Considerations" provide eloquent testimony of her awareness of the potentially grave deficits of all forms of (merely) civic virtue. Independent thinking for oneself—*Selbstdenken*—turns out to be not merely a supplement to political virtue, but its very basis.[86]

The "ordinary thinking" performed by Socrates in the agora for the benefit of his fellow citizens is to be distinguished from purely philosophical thought, whose withdrawal from the world is not temporary, but enforced. Arendt had the greatest respect for such "extraordinary thinking"—as her tribute to Heidegger on the occasion of his eightieth birthday attests.[87] But she also viewed such thought as unworldly in the extreme, since its pursuit of invisibles is predicated upon a radical devaluation of the world of appearances. Extraordinary thinking—the thinking of a Plato or Heidegger—bespeaks an ascetic form of *worldlessness*. And worldlessness, as Arendt reminds us, "is always a form of barbarism."[88]

Arendt turns to the figure of Socrates in order to find a way to make thinking worldly; to demonstrate how the capacity for thought is, in fact, crucial for both conscience and the activity of judgment. As Strauss's deprecating comments on the picture of Socrates as "philosopher-citizen" make clear, he has little patience for making philosophy serve politics in this way.[89] Yes, the philosopher must concern himself with politics, but only to insure that philosophy itself will not be banished or destroyed, reduced to ideology or propaganda.[90] Arendt's claim that the life of the citizen, of political action, is the highest form of existence is, from Strauss's point of view, palpably absurd: "Political life derives its dignity from something that transcends political life," namely, the contemplative life, the life of the philosopher.[91]

Only the philosophical life can genuinely achieve the aim of the political association, happiness. Hence, the highest subject of political philosophy is not, as Arendt thinks, the meaning or existential significance of political action; it is, rather, the philosophic life itself.[92] Existence is redeemed not through words and deeds in the public realm, but through the pursuit of understanding.[93] For Arendt's "love of the world" Strauss substitutes the love of wisdom. The world can be loved, if it can be loved at all, only insofar as it makes philosophy possible. We see how Arendt's and Strauss's opposing loyalties reflect deeper existential commitments. Arendt's

Socratic republicanism is built upon a Nietzschean affirmation of the world, while Strauss's classical rationalism betrays a (characteristically philosophical) devaluation of existence.[94] For Strauss, only the "understanding of understanding" can, after Auschwitz, reconcile us to the world and the human condition:

> We have no other comfort than that inherent in this activity. . . . This experience is entirely independent of whether what we understand primarily is pleasing or displeasing, fair or ugly. It leads us to realize that all evils are in a sense necessary if there is to be understanding. It enables us to accept all evils which befall us and which may break our hearts in the spirit of good citizens of the City of God. By becoming aware of the dignity of the human mind, we realize the true ground of the dignity of man, and therewith the goodness of the world . . . which is the home of man because it is the home of the mind of man.[95]

This pronounced difference in existential attitudes helps us appreciate the competing ideals of Arendt and Strauss in terms less artificial than an Aristotelian ranking of ways of life or *bioi*. Yet the juxtaposition of Arendt's affirmation of contingency with Strauss's philosophical effort to recognize necessity in the great "world drama" (Kant) returns us to the very dichotomy which, in their better moments, Arendt and Strauss help us to overcome.[96] The final choice they present us is not between a Socratic form of citizenship and a philosophical (skeptical or chastened) view of politics, but rather between the worldliness of the *bios politikos* and the contemplative stance of the *bios theoretikos*. In the end, Arendt urges us to become manly citizens, while Strauss would seduce us to philosophy. The terms set by the *Gorgias*, and by Callicles in particular, return in all their Procrustean violence.

I would suggest that we work very hard to resist reading Arendt and Strauss in these restrictive and mutually exclusive terms. Rather than view their partisanship for politics or philosophy as expressions of an "eternal" or necessary conflict, we should try to focus on the critical motivation behind their work. Even this, however, is easier said than done. In an intellectual world where a broadly contextualist or hermeneutic view of political theory is dominant—where John Rawls turns out to be just as historicist as Michael Walzer or Richard Rorty—Arendt and Strauss appear as either indefensibly metaphysical or hyper-nostalgic. Their lack of grounding in the "overlapping consensus" of liberal society makes their criticisms seem at once all-inclusive and shrill, and as such a theoretical *cul de sac*. They have too much "critical distance." Thus, Charles Larmore claims that the peculiar emptiness of Strauss's positive political ideal flows from the fact that he "stood back from so much that he had nothing left to go on."[97] In a similar vein George Kateb writes that Arendt's "spiritual distance" from America led her to distort, exaggerate, and caricature representative democracy.[98]

The liberal's skeptical view of Strauss and Arendt is legitimate so long as we view them as passionate spokespersons for the ideals of philosophy or a new version of civic republicanism. What Kateb calls their "questionable influence" flows from a shared perfectionist conviction that there is, in fact, a best life, whether this be the life of the philosopher or the heroic political actor.

There is, however, another way of viewing what Arendt and Strauss are up to, a perspective on their work enabled by their reflections on the episodic convergence of philosophy and politics. What these moments testify to is the *positive* value of alienated (or philosophical) citizenship; a citizenship that is morally suspicious of strongly held public purposes and the energies they enlist; a citizenship that is repelled by what Strauss calls the "selfishness" of patriotic republicanism.[99] Arendt and Strauss agree that "philosophical" citizens will always be in the minority. Nevertheless, it seems clear that such citizens are of greater political and moral value than either Arendt's heroic political actor or Strauss's philosophical tutor of gentlemen. We can, at least, read the "Socratic" Arendt and the "skeptical" Strauss as offering us this lesson against themselves.

Such citizens possess not only the ability to see the truth in their fellow citizen's *doxa* (what Arendt calls the capacity for representative thought) but, more importantly, the ability to imaginatively dissolve such *doxa* in "emergency situations." In other words, the ideal of Socratic citizenship cannot be reduced to the merely immanent probing of opinion. It entails the ability to relativize or transcend "the tradition of a particular community, the consensus of a particular culture."[100] It must possess the capacity to rise from the "we"— not to an Archimedean standpoint, but to the standpoint of a conscientious, nondogmatic "I."

This is, of course, Socrates' central lesson, as articulated in the *Gorgias*: "It would be better for me that my lyre or a chorus I directed should be out of tune and that a multitude of men should disagree with me than that I, being one, should be out of harmony

177

with myself and contradict me" (482c). This is the perspective of a genuinely secular conscience, a perspective discovered by Socrates and one that he tried to develop in his fellow citizens. We can view Arendt's and Strauss's broad critical projects as supports for such conscientious citizenship insofar as they strengthen our capacity to relativize the standpoint of the "we." Such a capacity is one that even "we liberals" cannot do without.

It is, of course, more than a little misleading to present *either* Arendt or Strauss as individualist champions of independent, secular conscience.[101] On the other hand, what does Arendt's assertion that thinking underlies conscience and liberates the faculty of judgment mean?[102] What is the goal of Strauss's prolonged, yet "tentative and experimental," attempt to revive the standard of "natural right" in the face of historicism and conventionalism? Viewed from a certain angle, Arendt's and Strauss's projects are valuable precisely for the *distance* they help the thinking citizen cultivate—a distance that the current consensus on the immanent nature of social and political criticism all but obliterates.[103]

This is not to say that critical distance is without its risks. As Michael Walzer reminds us, ". . . undercommitment to one's own society makes, or can make, for overcommitment to some theoretical or practical other."[104] The extreme distance that characterizes Arendt's and Strauss's critical perspectives on liberal democracy ultimately commits them to such "others"—to an agonistic "politics for the sake of politics" in the case of Arendt, and to a classical preference for an aristocracy of wisdom and virtue in the case of Strauss.

But if the pursuit of their "alien" ideals of the citizen and the philosopher do little to "strengthen modern democracy by their challenge," Arendt and Strauss can certainly be said to enhance our ability to dissolve the *doxa* of the day.[105] They may not provide the service of the maieutic Socrates, but they do offer something like the "paralysis" induced by Socrates in his capacity as "electric ray." Their work is no guide to practice, but rather the (necessarily disorienting) revelation of our unthought assumptions, the limits of the horizon that shapes our thinking about politics, morality, and political action.

Arendt and Strauss, I would argue, are radically estranged theorists, theorists whose work reflects the consciousness of the exile rather than that of the "connected" critic. Their work has the extraordinary capacity to take us out of the "cave" of liberal democracy. The mistake of Arendtians and Straussians is to assume that either guides us into the light. They do not. We cannot expect from Arendt and Strauss a "comprehensive perspective" on the "fundamental problems" of political life. All we are entitled to expect from them, as political philosophers, is the illumination of these problems from a radically novel perspective.

Political philosophy, as practiced by Arendt and Strauss, is precisely *not* "social criticism" as Walzer has defined it. It provides no guide to reform phrased in terms of an "actually existing moral world." Nor is it, to use Rawls's phrase, the articulation of "basic intuitive ideas and principles" implicit in a particular tradition.[106] It is, rather, the persistent attempt to remind ourselves of the finitude of *our* horizon, the localness of our "intuitive ideas and principles," the parochial nature of the "end of history" or ideology. As such, political philosophy does not provide the "saving power" of the Socratic "stop and think"—it does not rescue us in "emergency situations." What it does do is confront the liberal citizen with the question—the *Socratic* question—of what is the political? With the engagement of *this* question (an engagement Arendt and Strauss facilitate) the gap between the philosopher and the citizen begins to close.

Totalitarianism, Modernity, and the Tradition

INTRODUCTION

To what extent does Hannah Arendt view totalitarianism as a distinctively *modern* phenomenon, one that reveals essential aspects of our time? What is the connection between her conception of totalitarianism and the phenomenology of human activities laid out in *The Human Condition?* Finally, what is the link between the critique of the Western tradition of political philosophy she mounts in that book and her view of the "essence" of totalitarianism? Does Arendt believe that totalitarianism, most often regarded as the nihilistic negation of our tradition, is, in fact, a partial product of that tradition?[1] If so, what possible (and plausible) connection can there be between Plato and Aristotle (on the one hand) and Hitler and Stalin (on the other)?

These are, obviously, large, complex, and controversial questions. I can't pretend to offer adequate answers to them in the compass of a single chapter. Instead, I propose to sketch brief responses to the first two, so that I might devote the bulk of this chapter to the third—the question of a possible link between the "great tradition" of Western political thought and totalitarianism. I choose to focus on *this* question out of a desire to clarify some suggestions I made in my book *Arendt and Heidegger: The Fate of the Political.*

My focus is, admittedly, the result of an anxiety. I fear that readers of my interpretation of Arendt's thought might come away with the impression that she saw some mysterious inner logic working itself out in the course of the sequence from Plato to Marx, a nihilistic logic that led to the "devaluation of the highest values" and (thence) to the horrors of the twentieth century. So viewed, Arendt could be clumped in with Nietzsche, Heidegger, and other invertors of the Hegelian metanarrative of historical progress (for example, Horkheimer and Adorno, Leo Strauss and Eric Voegelin).[2]

To see Arendt's views on totalitarianism, modernity, and the tradition as fitting snugly within the confines of this genre of *Geistesge-*

schichte is to do her a great disservice. Throughout her work, from *The Origins of Totalitarianism* to *The Life of the Mind*, she is at war with all Hegelian-type teleologies, whether of progress or doom. Moreover, she was extremely skeptical of all causal explanations of totalitarianism, explanations which isolated one or several determining factors that allegedly "produced" totalitarianism.[3] Thus, she hardly thought that totalitarianism was, in any significant sense, the "result" of what Plato or Aristotle, Machiavelli or Hobbes, Nietzsche or Heidegger wrote, or of the "dialectic of enlightenment" (her distance from Strauss and the Frankfurt School on this issue is vast).[4] She frequently expressed more than mild contempt for the methodological idealism and historicist determinism underlying such approaches.[5]

But neither did she think that elements which truly were crucial "conditions of possibility" for the advent of totalitarianism—racism, imperialism, the decline of the nation-state, antisemitism—caused it to occur as a kind of logical consequence. Totalitarianism remained for her a monstrous, unprecedented event, one that "exploded our traditional categories of political thought (totalitarian domination is unlike all forms of tyranny and despotism we know of) and the standards of our moral judgment (totalitarian crimes are very inadequately described as 'murder' and totalitarian criminals can hardly be punished as 'murderers')."[6] Its chief characteristic was "a horrible originality which no farfetched historical parallels can alleviate."[7] To view totalitarianism as the predictable outcome of any configuration of causal forces perpetuates the denial of human freedom, which Arendt identifies as the *sine qua non* of totalitarian ideology and action.[8]

However, these caveats notwithstanding, Arendt *did* see a connection (albeit not a causal one) between totalitarianism and the tradition, just as she saw a connection between totalitarianism and the spirit of the modern age. We must try to make sense of these connections even as we avoid turning Arendt into something she was not, namely, a philosophical idealist *à la* Heidegger.

TOTALITARIANISM AND MODERNITY

What, then, made totalitarianism an essentially *modern* phenomenon in Arendt's view? First and foremost, one cannot exaggerate the strength of her conviction that totalitarianism was something radically novel, a new form of political regime that could not be grasped by the traditional categories of tyranny, dictatorship, or authoritarianism.[9] Hence her quest to understand the "essence" or nature of totalitarianism as a form of government, rather than as an updated (peculiarly German or Russian) version of despotism. As she insists in *The Origins of Totalitarianism* and the essays "On the Nature of Totalitarianism" and "Ideology and Terror," total domination is qualitatively different from tyrannical domination; rule by terror is different in nature from rule based on fear.[10]

Fear serves the tyrant's interest by radically isolating his subjects, exposing them to an overwhelming anxiety born of loneliness. Rule by fear makes a "desert" of the public realm, a desert in which isolated individuals despair of concerted action and resistance, experiencing daily their impotence and helplessness.[11] Yet action is still possible here as strategic reaction: complete obedience and the avoidance of all "questionable" activities provides the principle of survival. Thus, in tyrannies fear is a "principle of action" in Montesquieu's sense, just as virtue is the principle animating republics and honor that of monarchies.[12]

Rule by terror, however, goes much further. It is not satisfied with exploiting the human experience of radical loneliness and the impotence it creates. Nor is it satisfied with banishing plural individuals from the public sphere. Rather, rule by terror aims at eliminating the incalculable from human existence: it seeks to expunge not merely *public* freedom, but freedom as such.[13] It does this by systematically destroying the legal boundaries that separate public from private, thereby destroying the space required for individuality as well as for action. Rule by terror reveals not merely the *impotence* of men, but their sheer *superfluousness*.[14]

Arendt believed that in totalitarianism she had discovered a regime whose principle (in Montesquieu's sense) was terror. She did not deny that other regime forms have used terror in the past; none, however, made it an organizing principle, a *raison d'être*.[15] Totalitarianism is radically novel because terror "is the very essence of such a government." It is a form of regime that aims at eliminating the incalculable by remaking reality in accordance with the logic of its ruling ideology.[16]

Totalitarian regimes use terror to execute what their ideologies assume are the judgments of Nature or History. They do this, however, only *after* they have eliminated all genuine or potential political opposition. Terror is "deployed as an incomparable instrument of acceleration," as a way of speeding up the allegedly unquestionable "laws of motion" of Nature or History. "Decadent and dying classes," "inferior races," individuals who are "unfit to live": from the totalitarian point of view, all are destined for the ash heap of history. The purpose of terror is to carry out the death sentence of Nature or History with greater dispatch, to facilitate the removal of obstacles to this destiny and thus make mankind a "walking embodiment" of the laws of motion of Nature or History.[17]

Yet even this formulation is misleading, as it encourages us to think of terror in traditional terms, as merely a (deplorable) *means* of political power. According to Arendt, we will be incapable of understanding totalitarianism as a political phenomenon so long as we attempt to fit it within such a utilitarian framework. For terror to be a means, an instrument, it must serve the perpetrator's interest. Yet what interest is there in maintaining an elaborate and costly apparatus of terror such as the Nazi concentration camp system when the regime's very survival depends upon getting the most out of its dwindling resources?[18]

In this and other respects, it is not really the case that "the means has become the end." In Arendt's view, this formulation is "only a confession, disguised as a paradox, that the category of means and ends no longer work; *that terror is apparently without an end.*"[19] Terror is the *essence* of the totalitarian form of government because it stands as a kind of end in itself. Its meaning cannot be grasped in strategic or utilitarian terms, in terms of *raison d'état* or the maintenance of power.[20] To say, as Arendt does, that terror is an "incomparable instrument" is to say that millions were sacrificed—and even the regime, the party, and, ultimately, the nation itself—for the sake of an *idea* of reality as an endlessly destructive process. Terror not only accelerates the "laws of motion" of History or Nature, it expresses their innermost murderous essence. It is the "means" by which a recalcitrant reality is made to conform to the axiomatic logic of a single idea (human history as the history of class struggle; the natural process as the evolution and perfection of the species).[21]

Arendt is adamant that totalitarian terror explodes "the very alternative upon which all definitions of the essence of governments have been based in political philosophy, that is the alternative between lawful and lawless government, between arbitrary and legitimate power."[22] If, as Arendt writes, "lawfulness is the essence of nontyrannical government and lawlessness is the essence of tyranny," then totalitarianism confronts political theory with the conundrum of a regime whose essence is terror guided by "law."[23]

What needs to be stressed here is how, in Arendt's view, totalitarian terror is neither arbitrary nor self-serving. It is *not* tyrannical illegitimacy blown up to gigantic proportions.[24] On the contrary, she insists that totalitarian regimes are characterized by a strict and unvarying adherence to the "laws" of Nature or History that allegedly stand above positive laws. Indeed,

> it is the monstrous, yet seemingly unanswerable claim of totalitarian rule that, far from being "lawless," it goes to the sources of authority from which positive laws received their ultimate legitimation, that far from being arbitrary it is more obedient to these suprahuman forces than any government ever was before, and that far from wielding its power in the interest of one man, it is quite prepared to sacrifice everybody's vital immediate interests to the execution of what it assumes to be the law of History or the law of Nature.[25]

The surface impression of tyrannical lawlessness given by these regimes' contempt for positive law (including their own constitutions) is belied by a restless activism that has only one purpose: accelerating "the laws of motion" that will ultimately produce a new and beautified species, a world without class divisions or inferior races.[26] Far from being lawless, totalitarianism is distinguished by a peculiar and intense *lawfulness*. This lawfulness "pretends to have found a way to establish the rule of justice on earth—something which the legality of positive law could never attain."[27]

As a regime whose goal is the fabrication of a "perfected" mankind through the terroristic execution of such "laws," totalitarianism is unprecedented and unquestionably modern. But it is modern in a deeper sense in that it gives exaggerated expression to what Arendt considers to be the defining spirit of the age, namely, a hubristic belief in the limitless nature of human power. For Arendt, the modern age is one of boundless self-assertion growing out of a resentment of the human condition, a resentment of all the limits that define human existence (mortality, labor and natural necessity, earth-boundedness, etc.). Unwilling to accept what he hasn't made himself, modern man transforms reality by means of modern science and technology, making it over in the hope of creating a totally humanized world in which he can (finally) be at home. What Arendt calls "the modern triumph of *home faber*" in *The Human Condition* thus gives birth to the modernist credo that "everything is possible"—that there are no limits to humanity's capacity to mimic and exploit natural processes, and thus no limits to the reshaping of reality which we might accomplish. It is this hubris—the hubris of *homo faber*, of "everything is possible"—which finds expression in the totalitarian project of "fabricating mankind." This project consists in the violent reshaping of available human material so that, in the end, neither classes, races, or individuals exist, but only specimens of the (perfected) species.[28] In such a world, the incalculable truly has been eliminated.

One of the oddities of totalitarianism is that it couples this distinctively modern hubris with an equally modern determinism. As Margaret Canovan points out, Arendt thought that modern man was tempted to "purchase unlimited power at the cost of siding with inhuman forces and giving necessity a helping hand."[29] Totalitarian regimes demonstrate what happens when human beings surrender, without reservation, to this temptation. Submission to a racist "law of nature" (with its imperative of genocide) or historical "laws of motion" (which predict not only the extinction of capitalism but also all class enemies of the proletariat) create a feeling of power in the totalitarian leader and follower. Each feels themselves to be an instrument of suprahuman necessity, a necessity manifest in the historical laws of motion and the destruction they wreak.[30]

Arendt, then, sees totalitarian regimes as animated by a ruthless desire to remove all the obstacles which the "human artifice"—the civilized world of relatively permanent political and social structures—puts in the way of the forces of Nature or History. Hence the defining role of terror in totalitarian regimes. For it is terror which "razes the boundaries of man-made law" and makes it possible for "the force of nature or of history to race freely through mankind, unhindered by any spontaneous human action."[31] Only through the systematic elimination of legally and institutionally articulated spaces of freedom can a totalitarian regime destroy the capacity for action implicit in the simple fact of human plurality. Indeed, in Arendt's analysis, human plurality and freedom are the primary phenomena which must be overcome if "mankind" (understood as

185

"One Man of gigantic dimensions") is to be created.[32] Only then can reality be brought into line with the logic of a single idea.[33]

This is the goal of total domination: the complete organization of the "infinite plurality and differentiation of human beings as if all of humanity were just one individual."[34] As such total domination was achieved only in the concentration and extermination camps, for it was here, under "scientifically controlled conditions," that experiments aimed at the utter elimination of spontaneity and freedom from human existence were able to take place.[35]

In the camps human beings were reduced by terror into mere specimens of the human animal. Human personality was transformed into a "mere thing," into something *less* than animal, "an always constant collection of reactions and reflexes."[36] Totally conditioned by terror, shorn of their uniqueness and spontaneity, the inmates were the barely living proof that *human nature can be transformed through the application of human power.*[37] This is why Arendt refers to the camps as "the true central institution of totalitarian organizational power" and as "laboratories in which the fundamental belief of totalitarianism that everything is possible is being verified."[38]

Arendt's analysis of the three-step process necessary for making total domination a reality is well known but little appreciated.[39] Suffice it to note here that this process—the destruction of the *juridical person* through the deprivation of rights and citizenship, followed by the destruction of the *moral person* through the creation of conditions in which conscience can no longer function, culminating in the destruction of *individuality* performed by the camps themselves—is eminently repeatable, and in itself constitutes a system for establishing the "absolute superfluousness" of men. It is a process limited to no particular group (ethnic, religious, or political), but rather a moving and expansive apparatus which establishes that *all* human beings are, in principle, superfluous. This, in Arendt's view, is the *differentia specifica* of totalitarian power, which aims not at "despotic rule over men," but rather at "a system in which men are superfluous," replaced by as many bundles of conditioned reflexes as necessary.[40]

Thus, in the perfect totalitarian society (for which the camps provide the paradigm), terror binds individuals so tightly together that "all channels of communication" disappear and neither spontaneity nor individuality have space for expression. Frozen by terror, human beings are pliable raw material, incapable of offering resistance to the laws of motion of Nature or History as these "rage through mankind," performing their never-ending task of violently shaping human beings into their final, radically de-individualized, form. As Arendt writes in "Mankind and Terror," the ultimate political goal of totalitarianism was "to form and maintain a society, whether dominated by a particular race or one in which classes and nations no longer exist, in which every individual would be nothing other than a specimen of the species."[41] In other words, the "perfection" of the species mankind entails the destruction of humanity, both as a concept and as the phenomenological reality of unique individuals.

TOTALITARIANISM AND *THE HUMAN CONDITION*

It is in Arendt's reflections on the "perfected" totalitarian regime— on the regime in which totalitarian logic is carried through to the end and the goal of total domination achieved—that we see the clearest links to the phenomenology of human activities presented in *The Human Condition*. For if totalitarianism displayed, in exaggerated form, how modern extremist aspiration ("everything is possible") could lead to a radical destruction of freedom, then one central purpose of *The Human Condition* is to remind us that freedom's preservation demands a relatively stable human artifice of the sort totalitarianism makes impossible. Totalitarianism taught Arendt how absolutely indispensable such a realm of stability was, and how destructive the principle of unlimited dynamism (instantiated in the restless activism of the totalitarian movements themselves) could be.

The Human Condition turns from the danger of totalitarian dynamism to consider other "world destroying" forces that the modern age has unleashed. Among these are the tremendous growth in the forces of production and consumption brought about by the rise of capitalism. This growth, together with the hegemony of the economic concerns it creates, threatens to swallow up all other relatively autonomous spheres of human activity. Thus, it too fosters the eradication of human plurality, freedom, and uniqueness. Arendt is deeply convinced that only within the protective confines of such a relatively stable artifice can human plurality be preserved

from the automatism that characterizes the life of subsistence, biological reproduction, and the endless cycle of production and consumption. Only within the framework of artificial laws and institutions is the automatism of nature kept at bay, and the realms of
freedom and necessity kept distinct.

The image of fragile "islands of freedom" surrounded by a sea of
automatic, natural processes is a recurrent one in Arendt.[42] Both
totalitarianism and modern technological capitalism, with its transformation of man into the *animal laborans*, do their utmost to swamp
this artifice in processes of destruction or reproduction. Arendt reminds us of the differences between action, work, and labor in order
to underline just how dangerous it is to forget that an individual's
life is human to the extent that it has the possibility of a limited
transcendence of natural or pseudo-natural processes. In Arendt's
view, action—speech and deeds in the public realm—is the vehicle
by which we achieve this limited transcendence and (thereby) a
unique identity. To be deprived of this opportunity—an opportunity provided by an intact public realm—is to be deprived of the
chance of living a fully human life.[43] If the goal of totalitarianism
is to reduce human beings to mere examples of the species, technological capitalism has a parallel, if immeasurably less horrible,
logic. Both are insults to the human status in that they strive to
replace human plurality and spontaneity with a kind of oneness
(whether of the species or of the "household" blown up to national
proportions[44]), while moving us ever closer to rhythms of nature
and necessity.

Arendt's indictment of the "laboring society" in *The Human Condition* seems to place her in the company of such totalizing critics of
capitalist modernity as Herbert Marcuse. Consider, for example, the
following passage from the last part of *The Human Condition*:

> . . . even now, laboring is too lofty, too ambitious a word for what we are
> doing, or think we are doing, in the world we have come to live in. The
> last stage of the laboring society, the society of jobholders, demands of
> its members a sheer automatic functioning, as though individual life had
> actually been submerged in the over-all life process of the species and
> the only active decision still required of the individual were to let go, so
> to speak, to abandon his individuality, the still individually sensed pain
> and trouble of living, and acquiesce in a dazed, "tranquillized," func-
> tional type of behavior. . . . It is quite conceivable that the modern age—

which began with such an unprecedented and promising outburst of human activity—may end in the deadliest, most sterile passivity history has ever known.[45]

The echoes of Nietzsche, Weber, and Heidegger here are almost overwhelming, as is the temptation to describe what Arendt is talking about as a kind of "soft" totalitarianism. For what, finally, is the difference between the real thing and its capitalist, technological shadow if the result is the same: the "destruction of the common world," the eradication of freedom understood as speech and deeds in the public realm, and the ultimate assimilation of human beings to nature and necessity? Add to this the aforementioned emphasis on "resentment of the human condition" common to both the modern and totalitarian projects, and it is easy to accuse Arendt of diminishing, rather than enhancing, our understanding of modernity and totalitarianism's place within it.

Of course, Arendt herself would have repudiated any such conflation. She was far too aware of the "horrible originality" of totalitarianism to read it back into some broader, world-historical movement. Here we confront the irreducible difference between her approach and that of her teacher, Heidegger, whose own brand of *Seinsgeschichte* encouraged such conflation in pupils such as Marcuse. What links totalitarianism and capitalist, technological modernity in Arendt's view is nothing on the morphological level. If totalitarian domination is to be radically distinguished from tyranny and authoritarianism, it is, needless to say, altogether different in structure and movement from society as "national household." The sole link between them (aside from the hubris which drives both[46]) is that each represents a threat to the continuing reality of the human artifice and, thus, to freedom.

For Arendt, totalitarianism put human nature at stake. The totalitarian project was nothing less than the radical denaturing and deindividualization of human beings in order to produce a new and supremely pliable animal species, mankind.[47] Compared to this denaturing, even the most economically integrated, politically docile "national household" represents an extremely limited loss: the diminishment of public spirit and the capacity for political action. From the perspective of Arendt's quasi-Aristotelian ranking of the *bioi*, such a loss is still great, since it undermines the very thing which, in her view, makes life worth living.[48] It does not, however, come close to approximating the "hell on earth" established by totalitarian regimes and their never-ending reign of terror. It is one thing to be rendered relatively "worldless" by political or economic forces, quite another to be subject to the "law of killing" which Arendt saw as the core of totalitarianism.[49]

  Contra Marcuse, Horkheimer and Adorno, and some postmodernists, then, totalitarianism is not a trope for the modern age, nor the culmination of an epoch that was always already nihilistic. Totalitarianism was, in Arendt's view, a distinctly pathological form of modern politics; a pathology of modernity that illuminates modernity, but that cannot, in the end, be identified with it (even if, as George Kateb notes, Arendt sees the story of modern Europe as a story of pathologies, with Nazi and Stalinist totalitarianism as "the climactic pathology").[50] Despite the harshness of her critique of the modern age in *The Human Condition*, and despite her conviction that the rootlessness of the modern masses provided the soil for totalitarianism to take root, there is no inner link between the "worldlessness" of the modern age and the "essence" of totalitarianism, namely, terror.

  The most we can say is that, for Arendt, the modern age creates unprecedented alienation and loneliness; that the experience of radical loneliness or uprootedness deprives people not only of a "place in the world," but their sense of identity and their feeling for the world (their "common sense"); that, bereft of the sense that relates him to the world and to others, the modern individual is all too likely to turn an ideology which, with impeccable logic, explains the past, present, and future by deductions from a single premise (for example, the history of the world is the history of class struggle).[51] Having lost contact with his fellow men and the reality around him (a contact underwritten by a stable and vibrant public realm), the modern individual loses the capacity for both thought and experience.[52] Hence his susceptibility to totalitarian fictions. It is in this sense that totalitarianism can be said to base itself on the worldlessness inherent in loneliness, on "the experience of not belonging to the world at all, which is among the most radical and desperate experiences of man."[53]

  The reflections on the "worldlessness" of the modern masses in *The Origins of Totalitarianism* obviously prepare the way for the phenomenology of action and the public realm in *The Human Condition*. Arendt moves from the most pathological expression of worldlessness—intense loneliness and the embrace of totalitarian fiction—to a description of how political action on the public stage endows the world with meaning *and* offers the individual the chance to achieve both recognition and identity through the creation of a public self.[54] What matters most to her in *The Origins of Totalitarianism* are the pathological political possibilities opened up by the loss of a tangible, worldly reality. What drives her phenomenological descriptions in *The Human Condition* is the desire to show how a strong sense of the public world manifests itself in political action and the stories, judgments, and understanding such action inspires.[55]

A common fear, then, links *The Origins of Totalitarianism* to *The Human Condition*. Both texts locate the most basic threat to our political health in the loss of a sense of the public world, a public reality, among vast numbers of people. As long as we fail to confront the implications of this loss of a "common sense" we will fail to understand why racism, imperialism, antisemitism and totalitarianism had such enormous appeal in the late modern age, and why they encountered such minimal resistance. We will be unable to understand the peculiar mix of gullibility and cynicism that characterized European society between the wars, and that characterizes our own contemporary political culture.[56] Finally, we will be unable to "think what we are doing" as we make politics, the public sphere, and the claims of justice ever more subservient to the demands of the market, technology, and the "national" (now international) household.

TOTALITARIANISM AND THE TRADITION

The *Origins of Totalitarianism* is notable for its lack of attention to affiliations between totalitarian ideologies and canonical sources. In part, this had to do with Arendt's contempt for the "gutter-born ideology" that was National Socialism, with its "crack-pot" ideas cobbled together from the most dubious of sources. Thus, in the Preface to the first edition of the book, Arendt writes that a "subterranean stream of Western history has finally come to the surface and usurped the dignity of our tradition."[57] If an intellectual of the first rank like Heidegger supported the Nazis, it was only his fantasy of what the movement represented, and not any intrinsic depth of the ideology, that accounted for the attraction.[58] Yet when she contemplated the case of Stalinism, things were not so easy.

191

Here totalitarianism could claim a distinguished intellectual pedigree, one grounded in the towering work of Karl Marx and embodying some of the most cherished moral aspirations of European modernity. Moreover, although intellectually revolutionary, Marxism "was unquestionably a product of the mainstream Western tradition of political thought."[59] Contemplating the implications of this fact in the 1950s led Arendt to the conclusion that "to accuse Marx of totalitarianism amounts to accusing the Western tradition itself of necessarily [!] ending in the monstrosity of this novel form of government."[60] Thoughts along these lines led her to dwell increasingly upon the problem of "the missing link between the unprecedentedness of our present situation and certain commonly accepted traditional categories of political thought."[61]

Arendt never wrote the book on "Totalitarian Elements in Marxism" she suggested to the Guggenheim Foundation in 1952, in the proposal for which the last statement is to be found. Yet her detective work expanded, leading her to a rereading of the canon from Plato to Marx. The results of this rereading can be found in the essays that make up *Between Past and Future* and, of course, in *The Human Condition* itself. In turning to these texts, I want to restate Arendt's question: what are the links between "certain commonly accepted traditional categories of political thought" and totalitarianism?

Answering this question is easier if we, like Arendt, begin with Marx. At the center of Marx's thought, from the "Economic and Philosophical Manuscripts" of 1844 through the *Grundrisse* and *Capital*, is the notion that man creates himself though labor. As Arendt emphasizes in *The Human Condition*, Marx utterly conflates labor (the endless cycle of production and consumption required for the maintenance of human life) with work (the creation of lasting artifacts which add to the "thing-world," which stands between man and nature).[62] In viewing labor as the vehicle for the historical self-creation of mankind (the means by which we realize our "species-essence"—*Gattungswesen*), Marx makes human emancipation dependent upon the evolution of man's "metabolism with nature," blurring the all-important line between the man-made realm of freedom (the political realm) and the nature-determined realm of necessity (the "household" or economic sphere).

Even more telling for Arendt is the way Marx frames action—*praxis*—as a form of work or fabrication. While for the greater part

192

of the life of the species history has been something that happens to man, the advent of capitalism (with its tremendous increase in social forces of production and the means to dominate nature) allegedly makes possible political action that will hasten the next phase in social evolution (as predicted by the Marxian science of political economy). As a *political* movement, then, communism is presented by Marx as realizing the possibility of *making* history with will and intention. It is this identification of *action* with *work* and the making of history which Arendt saw as *the* crucial link between Marx's theory and totalitarian practice: "Marxism could be developed into a totalitarian ideology because of its perversion, or misunderstanding, of political action as the making of history."[63]

As Arendt notes in a number of places, all processes of making or fabrication are inherently violent, the creation of the envisaged end-product demanding the violent working over of raw materials by the producer.[64] In her view, it is a relatively short conceptual step from Marx's notion of revolutionary *praxis* as the making of history to the totalitarian project of fabricating mankind. Not only are both processes necessarily violent—"you can't make an omelet without breaking eggs"—they both aim at the eradication of the basic human condition of plurality (which, for Arendt, is the ground of all genuine political action[65]). Whether in the seemingly benign formula of Marx (the overcoming of class division leading to the withering away of the state and the flowering of a truly general will) or totalitarianism, the fabrication of the "end" of history demands the "violent molding of plural men to a single purpose."[66] Both Marx and totalitarianism view human plurality (and the myriad purposes, interests, and perspectives which derive from it) as the chief obstacle to the eventual realization of the (predetermined) *telos* of history. Hence their shared "misunderstanding" of action as work, a "misunderstanding" that facilitates acceptance of the idea that individuals, classes, and other groups must be sacrificed for the good of the species.[67]

The "work model of action" is often viewed as an isolated conceptualization peculiar to Marx and Marxist thought.[68] Arendt doesn't see it that way. In her view, Marx's "mistake" has a long and impressive history in Western thought, one that reaches back to the political theories of Plato and Aristotle. For it is in Plato and Aristotle that we find the first, founding examples of what Arendt calls the "traditional substitution of making for acting."[69] And it is this transposition which has the greatest impact on the concepts of action, freedom, and judgment within the Western tradition of political philosophy.

In the chapter devoted to action in *The Human Condition*, Arendt stresses how action performed in the public sphere, in the context of human plurality, is never sovereign, never in control of its range of effects or its ultimate meaning. Unlike fabrication, action does not shape material in order to bring about a preconceived end; rather, action is a kind of insertion into the human world, an insertion that is immediately caught up in what Arendt calls "the web of human affairs."[70] This web, born of plurality, is what renders the effects of action boundless and creates the impression of futility, at least when we judge action simply according to its success or failure. The truth is that political action rarely if ever achieves its goal. Moreover, "because the actor always moves among and in relation to other acting beings, he is never merely a 'doer' but always and at the same time a sufferer. To do and to suffer are like opposite sides of the same coin, and the story that an act starts is composed of its consequent deeds and sufferings."[71]

Action's futility, boundlessness, and uncertainty of outcome account for what Arendt calls "the frailty of human affairs." This frailty can be offset somewhat by the creation of relatively permanent laws and institutions which provide boundaries and shape for the public sphere, the arena of action.[72] Yet so long as human plurality is respected (through the political form of equal citizenship characteristic of democracies or free republics), this frailty and its frustrations cannot be eliminated. It is for this reason that "Plato thought that human affairs (*ta ton anthropon pragmata*), the outcome of action (*praxis*), should not be treated with great seriousness. . . ."[73] Insofar as he and Aristotle *do* take politics seriously, they focus on lawmaking and city building in their political philosophies, promoting these activities to the highest rank of political life, since here men "act like craftsmen: the result of their action is a tangible product, and its process has a clearly recognizable end."[74] As Arendt observes, "It is as though [Plato and Aristotle] had said that if men only renounce their capacity for action, with its futility, boundlessness, and uncertainty of outcome, there could be a remedy for the frailty of human affairs."[75]

Plato and Aristotle's desire to think action as a kind of making— to "rephrase" political action so that it appeared as unaffected by the fact of human plurality as the activity of fabrication—does not exhaust itself in their choice of political phenomena worthy of study. On the contrary, it led them to create an optic on political life in which the freedom, meaning and goal of action were reinterpreted so that the "unsettling" effects of human plurality (and democratic or republican citizenship) might be contained, if not outright eliminated. Both Plato and Aristotle make the concept of rule central to their political philosophies; both attempt to introduce something akin to the concept of authority into Greek thinking about politics; and both try to "naturalize" these innovations (less than palatable, from an Athenian democratic perspective) by relying heavily upon the supposed analogy between just political action and expert craftsmanship.[76]

It is in Plato's political dialogues (the *Republic*, *Statesman*, and the *Laws*) that this analogy receives its most systematic and authoritative articulation. Plato justified the separation of knowing from doing, and the identification of knowledge with command and action with obedience, by appealing to the expert knowledge of the physician or carpenter (or, in the *Statesman*, the expert "weaver"). If political judgment was acknowledged to be a kind of expert knowledge or *techne*, rather than a generalizable capacity of deliberating citizens, then the argument against the debilitating effects of plurality was all but won.[77] Just rulers would be a knowledge elite, unified not merely by prudence or statesmanship, but by their acquaintance with moral truth, the natural order culminating in the vision of the Good.[78] Their subjects would be similarly unified in their obedient execution of the commands issued by what Arendt calls Plato's "tyranny of reason."[79]

The "expert knowledge" argument is made more persuasive by Plato's utilization of an analogy drawn from the productive arts. Just as the craftsman envisages his end-product as an ideal before the actual process of fabrication, so the Platonic political actor oriented his action in light of the ideal standards provided by the forms of justice, the good, etc. The Platonic ruler is a "political artist of character," sculpting the plastic material of his subjects into an ordered and unified whole, all in accordance with the original, ideal model.[80]

Plato's reinterpretation of his doctrine of ideas to provide a set of "unwavering, 'absolute' standards for political and moral behavior and judgment in the same sense that the 'idea' of a bed in general is the standard for the making and judging the fitness of all particular beds" not only imports the metaphorics of making into the realm of action (the plural, political realm); it also sets the pattern for the Western idea of authority and legitimacy.[81] According to Arendt, it is the distinguishing characteristic of all genuinely authoritarian government (as opposed to tyranny) that its source of authority is always "a force external and superior to its own power; it is always this source, this external source which transcends the political realm, from which the authorities derive their 'authority,' that is, their legitimacy, and against which their power can be checked."[82]

Plato's interpretation of action as making and his authoritarian appeal to transcendent standards thus crucially depend on one another. Together, they provide a way out of the "frailty of human affairs" and the "futility, boundlessness, and uncertainty of outcome" which characterize political action. With the substitution of making for acting, politics is "degraded" into a "means to obtain an allegedly 'higher' end."[83] This instrumentalization of action is the inevitable outcome of its assimilation to making, since "the process of making is itself entirely determined by the categories of means and end."[84] A "technical" relation is thereby set up between theory and practice, first principles and action.[85] With this configuration (and its implied overcoming of the fact of human plurality) it becomes possible to escape the philosopher's sense that the freedom manifest in initiatory action is, in fact, a kind of bondage, dragging the agent down into a web of unintended consequences from which he cannot escape.

The genius of Plato—and the reason why his interpretation of action along "productionist" lines could become authoritative for an entire tradition—is that his "substitution of making for acting" made it possible to see the political actor not only as relatively sovereign, but as limited only by the availability of adequate means to realize his preconceived ends. From Plato and Aristotle to Machiavelli and Hobbes, and thence to Marx and Weber, the means/end category reigns supreme in Western political thought. Indeed, as Arendt notes, the persistence and success of the transformation of action into a mode of making is "easily attested by the whole terminology of political theory and political thought, which indeed makes it almost impossible to discuss these matters without using the category of means and ends and thinking in terms of instrumentality."[86] From our perspective, the problem of political action simply *is* the problem of means and ends; the nature of freedom is indissolubly associated with notions of mastery and control; and political judgment is viewed as the privileged possession of experts, moral or otherwise. The reality of human plurality—the very ground of political freedom, action, and the public realm, in Arendt's view—has been eviscerated.

What does all this have to do with totalitarianism? It is certainly not the case that Arendt wants to accuse Plato of being a totalitarian *avant la lettre*, in the manner of Karl Popper or Andre Glucksmann.[87] While her essay "What Is Authority?" makes a strong case for viewing Plato as the originator of a particular tradition of authoritarianism, her entire analysis is framed by a strict set of distinctions between authoritarianism, tyranny, and totalitarianism.[88] Rather, the paradigmatic importance of Plato resides in his influence upon a tradition of political thought which is deeply suspicious of the idea that human freedom manifested itself in spontaneous, unruly action in the public realm. From the standpoint of the tradition, the freedom of political action (the human ability to *begin*—but not control—radically new sequences of events) was merely a phantom; the possibility that freedom and nonsovereignty coincided a patent absurdity. Plato's instrumentalization of action enables the interpretation of freedom as sovereignty or control to become regnant in the Western tradition of political thought. Moreover, his appeal to transcendent standards repudiated any charge of arbitrariness on the part of the sovereign political actor. The latter's actions embodied not the human capacity to initiate a radically new beginning; rather, they manifested the human capacity to *correspond* to a larger necessity or order of being.[89]

When we note how, after Plato, "the concept of action was interpreted in terms of making and fabrication;" how the political realm came to be seen as a means to "obtain an allegedly higher end;" and how the phenomenon of human plurality is consistently effaced by the appeal to the metaphorics of making and the fiction of some sovereign agent who embodies the general interest (the philosopher-kings, Hobbes's sovereign representative, Rousseau's general will, Hegel's rational state, Marx's proletariat, etc.), we are forced to conclude that totalitarianism represents not the negation of the tradition, but a radicalization of some of its most cherished and foundational tropes.

The will to efface plurality, to overcome the "haphazardness" of spontaneity, to identify freedom with control, judgment with *episteme*, and legitimacy with obedience to a "higher law" are all distinguishing characteristics of the Western tradition of political thought (as Arendt understands it) and totalitarianism.[90] The totalitarian project of fabricating mankind, of "producing" the species through the execution of the law of Nature or the law of History, is unthinkable outside the metaphorics Plato installs at the root of our tradition. The antipolitics of the "state as artwork" find their most radical formulation in the totalitarian project of a violent, endless working-over of the "plastic material" of humanity itself.[91]

It is, of course, a long way from a regime based on correspondence to a metaphysical Truth to a regime that views Truth, like reality itself, as something to be fabricated; from a regime that bases itself on reason to a regime that appeals to the logic of an ideology or myth.[92] Similarly, it is a long way from Platonic restraint (manifest in the conclusion to Book IX of the *Republic* [592c], where the goal of actualizing the ideally just polity in this world is explicitly dismissed as a *political* project) to the modernist/totalitarian credo that "everything is possible."[93] Yet Arendt's ruminations on totalitarianism's effacement of human plurality, spontaneity, and freedom in the name of a kitsch aestheticism ("beautifying" the species by getting rid of the ugly, inferior, or historically anachronistic) and a "higher" law led her inexorably to the reexamination of the fundamental categories of Western political thought. In the course of this reexamination she discovered what Philippe Lacoue-Labarthe has called the "nonpolitical essence of the political" in the West, namely, an interpretation of acting as making guided by an ideal of political community that is at war with the human condition of plurality.[94]

BETWEEN FEAR AND TERROR

None of the reflections I have described above undermined Arendt's basic conviction (expressed most vividly in her essay "Ideology and Terror") that totalitarianism was a radically novel form of government. Unlike authoritarian, tyrannical, or despotic regimes, totalitarianism relied fundamentally on terror—not only as a means, but as a kind of end in itself.[95] It hoped to achieve what no form of government had ever dreamt of attempting: the complete elimination of the very space between individuals and (thus) their capacity for independent action. The goal, in other words, was not simply the monopolization of public power (as in tyranny or one-party dictatorship[96]), but the actual creation of "One Man of gigantic dimensions," of a world without plurality and the differences of perspective born of it.[97] This radical and terroristic elimination of all spontaneous freedom from the world (undertaken in the name of making mankind the "walking embodiment" of the law of Nature or History) is what distinguishes totalitarianism from all other regimes, past and present.

But despite this irreducible gap between the tradition (and the authoritarian and quasi-authoritarian forms of government it tends to endorse), on the one hand, and totalitarian regimes, on the other, the fact remains that Arendt devoted great theoretical energy and ingenuity to the task of tracing totalitarian impulses back to the spirit of modernity and the core of the tradition. We should view this theoretical labor, enormous in its ambition if finally one-sided in its insight, as part of the salutary project of reminding us that (in Arendt's words) the "crisis of our century" was, in fact, "no mere threat from the outside."[98]

But why one-sided? First because Arendt's engagement with the tradition is highly selective. Intent on drawing out the way the Platonic metaphorics of making echo and re-echo in our tradition of political thought, she devotes little attention to the liberal tradition and the theory of rights which animates it. The rights-based individualism of *that* tradition (the Levelers, Locke, Kant, Thoreau, Emerson, and Mill) is, of course, the greatest bar to the limitless instrumentalization of politics and the tendency to treat human beings as material in need of (publicly imposed) form. It matters not whether the formative project is Platonic soulcraft, Aristotelian habituation to virtue, civic republican inculcation of virtue, or the totalitarian sculpting of a "perfected" body politic. Rights-based individualism stands as the obvious and most successful response to any politics, theoretical or practical, which desires to overcome plurality and the "frailty of human affairs."

Why didn't Arendt recognize the obvious? In part out of ignorance (she is at her weakest and most spare in her readings of liberal theorists), in part out of prejudice (she tended to conflate liberalism with "the bourgeoisie" and bourgeois hypocrisy, as did many a Weimar intellectual). Her blindness, however, is mainly a function of a persistent theme of her political thought, one that is first

199

articulated in *The Origins of Totalitarianism*. This is her emphasis on the pervasive experience of loneliness (or worldlessness) encountered by the "superfluous masses" created by the modern age.

Convinced that capitalist expropriation, the dissolution of a stable class structure, and the decline of the nation-state (to say nothing of modern science's release of pseudo-natural forces in the human artifice) all fostered the experience of worldlessness and a corresponding sense of meaninglessness, Arendt focused on the one activity she thought could make us worldly once again. That activity was, of course, political action, by which Arendt meant the sharing of words and deeds on a public stage, the experience of acting together with peers in the founding and preservation of a space for freedom.

For Arendt, political action was not simply a sad necessity forced upon responsible individuals if they wanted to avoid disasters such as totalitarianism; it was, rather, the thing that made life worth living, the thing that bestowed meaning, identity, and coherence to an individual's life.[99] In political action, the worldly activity par excellence, we realize our humanity. No other activity has the same capacity to create meaning—to endow the human artifice with meaning—and no other activity provides the kind of happiness found in the "joy in action."[100]

The "politics of meaning" sketched out (negatively) in Arendt's analysis of the preconditions of totalitarianism and (positively) in her mature theory of political action is what has made her such an attractive theorist to so many different contemporary political sensibilities. The disenchantment of communitarians, feminists, "deliberative democrats," and postmodernists not only with liberal politics but with liberal theory attests to a shared desire for a vision of politics which, while not perfectionist, does far more than merely "avoid the worst" (to use Judith Shklar's phrase).[101] While these groups hardly share Arendt's relative unconcern with the topic of justice, they do share her sense that the reality of the public realm has been seriously, if not fatally, undermined.

It is tempting to dismiss Arendt's focus on the public realm as a space of meaning creation (and her critique of the modern age as responsible for the "loss" or "destruction" of this space) as hopelessly romantic. But before we do so, we should remember the original experience upon which Hannah Arendt built her political thought. This experience was not that of peers "acting together, acting in concert," as in the Greek *polis*; it was, rather, the experience of terror under totalitarianism. Arendt's virtually life-long focus on the public sphere and the life of action grew out of her encounter with this radical negation of public reality and human freedom. Her interest in the "positive" freedom of political action (as opposed to the "negative" freedom of civil rights) arose from a context in which totalitarian political forces had little trouble overwhelming the protective boundaries of positive law and enlisting "rootless" and "homeless" masses in their cause.[102]

I want to suggest that it makes a difference—perhaps all the difference—if one builds one's political theory on the experience of terror and loneliness or the experience of fear and cruelty. The enormous gap between Arendt's political theory and Judith Shklar's influential "liberalism of fear" can be explained in a number of ways, but in the final analysis it is the difference between totalitarian terror and the fear characteristic of tyrannical government that tells the tale.

What is this difference? What does it signify? In answering these questions, it is helpful to turn to a passage in Arendt's essay "On the Nature of Totalitarianism." She writes:

> As long as totalitarian rule has not conquered the whole earth and, with the iron band of terror, melded all individual men into one mankind, terror in its double function as the essence of the government and the principle—not of action, but of motion—cannot be fully realized. To add to this a principle of action, such as fear, would be contradictory. For even fear is still (according to Montesquieu) a principle of action and as such unpredictable in its consequences. Fear is always connected with isolation—which can be either its result or its origin—and the concomitant experiences of impotence and helplessness. The space freedom needs for its realization is transformed into a desert when the arbitrariness of tyrants destroys the boundaries of laws that hedge in and guarantee to each the realm of freedom. Fear is the principle of human movements in this desert of neighborlessness and loneliness; as such, however, it is still a principle which guides the actions of individual men, who therefore retain a minimal, fearful contact with other men. The desert in which these individual, fearfully atomized men move retains an image, though a distorted one, of that space which human freedom needs.[103]

This remarkable passage concludes a lengthy analysis of Montesquieu's discussion (in *The Spirit of the Laws*, Book III) of the principles of action animating different forms of government. Arendt focuses on his insight that fear is the principle of tyranny, just as virtue is the principle of republics or distinction that of monarchy. Her point vis-à-vis Montesquieu (and his disciple, Shklar) is that there is something worse than fear, and something worse than cruelty. However dehumanizing cruelty and the fear it inspires are, they are not, finally, the "worst thing we do to each other."[104] The worst thing, the true *summum malum* according to Arendt, is the totalitarian attempt to deprive human beings not only of their freedom and dignity, but of their *world*. In the passage above, Arendt is saying that even the subjects of a tyrannical regime still have a world, a simulacrum of the space for freedom. Insofar as they have a world—insofar as something stands between them and natural or pseudo-natural forces—they retain something of their humanity.

It is because totalitarian terror effectively levels the protective walls of the human artifice, exposing human beings to the violence of naturelike forces, that it can be said to qualitatively exceed the kinds of degradation Shklar discusses. To lose the world is to become a member of an animal species, whereas to live in fear is to be consigned to a degraded humanity. If cruelty is, as Shklar maintains, the center of a secular notion of evil, totalitarian terror is, in fact, a form of *radical* evil.

From Arendt's perspective, Shklar's insistence that we "put cruelty first" on the list of vices we (as good liberals) must combat remains at the level of "ordinary vices" (such as betrayal, hypocrisy, and misanthropy). Shklar's liberalism of fear begins, in other words, within a recognizable, if deeply flawed and often revolting, moral world; its hope is to lessen the amount of cruelty and fear human beings must face. In contrast, to begin, as Arendt did, with the experience of totalitarian terror is to enter a world in which "all our categories of thought and standards for judgment seem to explode in our hands the instant we try to apply them."[105] The ordinary vices, and the abuses they prompt, are not at the heart of totalitarianism: they do not even begin to make sense of the radical evil committed by such regimes.

This Arendtian point is confirmed, to a degree, by the pathetic inadequacy of viewing the totalitarian attempt to "fabricate mankind" as merely an "abuse of public power" or as Machiavellian *raison d'état* run amock. This qualitative gap between totalitarian evil and "ordinary" cruelty is why Arendt turned toward action in the public world rather than a consideration of liberal constitutionalism and civil rights after *The Origins of Totalitarianism.*[106] The specter of radical worldlessness and the negation of spontaneity—of a literal dehumanization—moved her attention away from legal structures and procedural mechanisms to the activity which, in her eyes, embodied and preserved our humanity. She moved, in short, from a phenomenology of terror and worldlessness to a phenomenology of worldly freedom, from negation to affirmation. No doubt this accounts for the "inspirational" character of her political thought. Yet, as I've tried to suggest, this inspiration comes at a heavy price.

If Arendt's attempt to link totalitarianism to the spirit of the modern age and the roots of the tradition sometimes strains credulity, we must remember her original goal of converting trauma into understanding in *The Origins of Totalitarianism. That* aim remained unfulfilled, in her view, so long as political theorists failed to confront the massive potential for evil lurking in the various formative projects of the tradition and the modern assimilation of human beings to natural and pseudo-natural processes. Rights, positive law, constitutional frameworks—all contribute mightily to containing the tendency to treat human beings as raw material. Yet, from Arendt's perspective, liberalism fails to imagine or comprehend the worst, and therefore fails to see that the preservation of rights and procedural safeguards ultimately depends on worldliness.[107] This, at any rate, is the fundamental and shaping conviction behind her political thought, and the reason why it will always remain, for better or worse, beyond the pale of a more sober liberalism.

CHAPTER NINE

Arendt and Socrates

> For philosophy, you know Socrates, is a pretty
> thing if you engage in it moderately in your youth;
> but if you continue in it longer than you should, it
> is the ruin of any man. For if a man is exceptionally
> gifted and yet pursues philosophy far on in life, he
> must prove entirely unacquainted with all the
> accomplishments requisite for a gentleman and a
> man of distinction. Such men know nothing of the
> laws in their cities, or of the language they should
> use in their business associations both public and
> private with other men, or of human pleasures and
> appetites, and in a word they are completely
> without experience of men's characters. And so
> when they enter upon any activity public or private
> they appear ridiculous, just as public men, I
> suppose, appear ridiculous when they take part
> in your discussions and arguments.
> (*Callicles in Plato's* Gorgias *[484d]*)

THERE CAN (alas) be little doubt that Hannah Arendt largely shared
the judgment of Callicles on the dangers of philosophy. *The Human
Condition*, Arendt's greatest statement on the nature and existential
significance of political action, is framed in terms of an exclusive and
highly partisan contrast between the *bios theoretikos* and the *bios politikos*. Rightly understood, the political life aims at earthly immortality through the performance of great deeds in the public realm,
while the philosophical life is founded upon the motionless contemplation of the eternal, which transcends the fleeting realm of human
affairs. From the point of view of the political actor, the philosophical life can only appear as "ridiculous and unmanly" (to again cite
Callicles), a retreat from everything that makes life worth living in
a tragically configured world. From the point of view of the philosopher, the life of action is nothing more than "vanity and vainglory."[1]

In Arendt's telling, the gap between these two ways of life becomes an abyss after the trial and condemnation of Socrates. Responding to this event, philosophy takes its revenge on politics, with Plato founding a tradition of political thought in which the standpoint and values of the contemplative man reign supreme. Arendt's enemy in *The Human Condition* is the sustained and systematic devaluation of the political life and the public realm we find in the Western philosophical tradition, a tradition which (in her view) never outgrew its original Platonic prejudices.[2] The enormous theoretical labor undertaken in *The Human Condition* aims at restoring action to its rightful place in the hierarchy of human activities, at overcoming the disdain for the political life which characterizes not only the contemplative tradition, but also the modern age because of its "activist" glorification of work and labor.

Arendt's greatest and most characteristic work thus wars on philosophy. It also wars on solitude and non-agonistic forms of individualism. Yet there are important moments in her *oeuvre* where she suggests the possibility of a rapprochement between the life of action and the life of the mind. I want to focus on one of these, the essay "Philosophy and Politics," written in 1954 but unpublished by Arendt in her lifetime (it appeared in *Social Research* in 1990, in a version edited by Jerome Kohn). This essay contains an astonishingly original and extremely sympathetic interpretation of Socrates' philosophical activity, an interpretation at odds with her published comments on Socratic moral individualism (in the essay "Civil Disobedience") and the nature of Socratic thinking (in the essay "Thinking and Moral Considerations" and *The Life of the Mind*).

My aim is twofold. First, I want to underline how untypical Arendt's portrait of Socrates (and the suggestion of a reconciliation between philosophy and politics) is in relation to her published work. My second (and more involved) aim is to point out the cost—to Socrates, to moral individualism, and to philosophy—which this reconciliation demands. It is my contention that, even at her most seemingly Socratic, Arendt remains fundamentally un- (even anti-) Socratic. In "Philosophy and Politics" she subordinates Socrates to the task of making Athenian democracy more beautiful, the task Pericles urged upon his fellow citizens in his famous "Funeral Oration." Arendt reconciles philosophy and politics through a novel interpretation of Socrates, but this interpretation hinges on putting his philosophical activity in the service of a Periclean (that is to say, manly and civic-minded) aestheticism. Placed within these limits, the urgency of the Socratic demand for moral integrity is lost, as is the force of his relentless negativity (the essence of Socratic intellectual integrity). This is not to say that I prefer the civic republican Arendt to the more philosophy-friendly Arendt of "Philosophy and Politics." I do, however, want to raise the question what is left of Socrates (and philosophy) once we have made him, as Arendt does in her essay, the servant of the "common sense" of citizens.

. . . . .

In her various textual encounters with the figure of Socrates, Arendt emphasizes the three similes for his philosophical activity found in the Platonic dialogues. The first, familiar to all readers of the *Apology*, is Socrates as gadfly, a persistent irritant whose questioning and reproaches aim at preventing the citizens of Athens from sleeping till the end of their days, from living and acting without genuine moral reflection or self-examination (30d). The second, from the *Theaetetus*, is Socrates as midwife, whose dissolution of the prejudices and prejudgments of his interlocutors helps them toward the revelation of their own thoughts. The third simile, from the *Meno*, is Socrates as "electric ray," a stinging fish who paralyzes and numbs all whom it comes in contact with. Through his questioning, Socrates infects his listeners with his own perplexities, interrupting their everyday activities and paralyzing them with thought. Once drawn into the dissolvent current of thought, his conversational partners can no longer mechanically apply general rules of conduct to particular cases, as they typically do in ordinary life.[3] To ask not whether something is an instance of x, but what x itself is, is to dissolve the taken-for-granted ground of action.

In "Philosophy and Politics" it is the second simile—Socrates as midwife—which Arendt emphasizes, to the virtual exclusion of the other two. According to Arendt, Socrates practiced the art of midwifery in order "to help others give birth to what they themselves thought anyhow, to find the truth in their *doxa*."[4] This enigmatic statement requires some unpacking. Arendt wants to underline that for Socrates (unlike Plato) there was no opposition between truth and opinion: whatever truth was available to human beings was necessarily part of the world of appearances and of speech.[5] Dialectic (*dialegesthai*) as practiced by Socrates was *not* what it became for

Plato, namely, a specifically philosophical form of speech, one defined by its opposition to persuasion (*peithein*) and rhetoric. Rather, Socratic dialectic was a "talking something through with somebody," a conversation among friends which aimed at elucidating the truth of an individual's *doxa* or perspective on the world: "To Socrates, as to his fellow citizens, *doxa* was the formulation in speech of what *dokei moi*, that is, of what appears to me."[6]

But "what appears to me" is not what is given, unthinkingly, to an individual in the largely reflexive attitude of everyday life. *Doxa* cannot be reduced to shadows on the wall of the cave nor to what the "they" think. Nor does its lack of universal validity render it arbitrary or merely idiosyncratic. Rather, we tend, in everyday life, to be radically unaware of our own *doxa*, our own perspective on the common world. It needs to be worked on, drawn out of us, in the painful manner the midwife simile implies. To be delivered of one's own doxa is to made aware of oneself as an individual member of the community possessed of a unique perspective, *not* as an adherent to some creed or ideology shared with the group.

Thus, one's *doxa* is by no means a matter of course, and the specific truth of one's *doxa* even less so. If, as Arendt asserts, "every man has his own *doxa*, his own opening to the world," then the revelation of its specific truth can be brought about only by a questioning which makes sure of "the other's position in the common world."[7] This is where Socratic cross-examination comes in. It ascertains the other's position in the world through questioning, and then draws out the truth of his particular perspective by forcing him to give a consistent account of otherwise half-formed or barely articulate views. One's *doxa* is the result of this process, a process few perform unless relentlessly prodded by the Socratic midwife. Thus, the last thing Socratic dialectic aims at is the destruction of opinion. Socrates himself is neither the teacher of an absolute truth nor the practitioner of a relentlessly dissolvent rationality. He is, rather, a "citizen among citizens," one whose philosophical activity is motivated by the desire to "make the city more truthful by delivering each of the citizens of their truths."[8] *Unlike* Plato, Socrates "did not want to educate the citizens so much as he wanted to improve their *doxai*, which constituted *the political life in which he too took part*."[9]

But this motivation itself stands in need of explanation. *Why* devote one's life, as Socrates did, to the task of improving the *doxai* of one's fellow citizens? Arendt's emphasis on Socrates' maieutic function displaces his moral passion—his stress on care for one's soul and avoiding injustice—rendering the drive behind his philosophical activity opaque. To some degree, this opacity is dissolved when we recall that her goal in "Philosophy and Politics" is to show how Socrates reconciled the demands of these two apparently exclusive activities. Thus, according to Arendt, Socrates' philosophical activity grows out of a profoundly political concern, namely, the imperative of containing the more Hobbesian tendencies of Greek agonistic individualism. Where the "fiercely agonal spirit" animates political life (to use her formulation from *The Human Condition*), with every citizen in competition with every other to prove himself "the best of all," there the preservation of the community is continually threatened. Socratic dialectic serves to beautify the world, to make citizens more fully aware of its richness and variety; but it also serves to make those who were previously competitors into conversational partners, into friends who gain an increased appreciation of what they have in common as they talk things through outside the press of daily business.

The other side of Socrates' maieutic activity, then, was making citizens aware of what they shared—the world of their particular city or culture, the thing which formed the basis of their individual *doxa*. Arendt's surprising contention in "Philosophy and Politics" is that not even the Greeks (not even the Athenians!) possessed a robust sense of the public world. The Athenians needed Socrates, needed *philosophy*, because "the commonness of the political world was constituted only by the walls of the city and the boundaries of its laws, [and] was not seen or experienced in the relationships between the citizens, not in the world which lay *between* them, common to them all, even though opening up in a different way to each man."[10] By talking through something shared, citizens not only came to grasp the truth in each others' opinion, they also came to be more aware of the implications of their political equality and of the world which this equality created. Thus, Socratic dialectic aims "at making friends of Athens's citizenry," and "community is what friendship achieves."[11] Dialectic is the "dialogue between friends," the thing which (in principle if not in practice) can keep the *polis* from tearing itself apart through agonal excess.

Arendt's formulation of the nature and goal of Socratic dialectic is remarkable, and for a number of reasons. Not only does she unexpectedly reconcile philosophy with politics; she also presents an image of Socrates found nowhere else in her writings. In her essay "Civil Disobedience" (1970) she brands Socratic conscientiousness and care for one's soul as "unpolitical," arguing that his moral rigor is based, ultimately, not on any care for the world, but on self-interest. The Socratic idea of conscience (articulated in the famous passage from the *Gorgias* [482c] on the supreme value of self-agreement, of being able to live with oneself) is presented as the sponsor of a radical withdrawal from the world, the responsibilities of citizenship, and the joys of acting with others. From the standpoint of the conscientious individual, such withdrawal minimizes the possibility of committing acts that jeopardize one's inner harmony, one's continued ability to live with oneself, particularly in moments of thoughtful solitude.[12] Arendt would have us believe that the Socratic idea of moral integrity thus reduces to a kind of selfishness, the result of valuing of our inner harmony above our worldly responsibilities. Socrates loves his soul more than his city, a ranking Arendt considers almost sinful.

Things get a bit better in "Thinking and Moral Considerations" (1971). Continuing to mull over the "extraordinary shallowness" of Adolf Eichmann and his "curious, quite authentic inability to think," Arendt asks "Is our ability to judge, to tell right from wrong, beautiful from ugly, dependent upon our faculty of thought? Do the inability to think and a disastrous failure of what we commonly call conscience coincide?"[13] Her answer is a qualified yes, since she thinks that thoughtlessness and stupidity (in the Kantian sense of an inability to judge) have played a far greater role than wickedness in promoting political evil (the pursuit of evil *as policy*) in the twentieth century. To paraphrase one of her earlier formulations: the unthinking everyman has been the great criminal of the twentieth century.

If this is the case, then Arendt's usual emphasis upon the cultivation of such civic virtues as participation and public-spiritedness needs to be supplemented.[14] The "classic virtues of civic behavior," it turns out, are no substitute for individual moral reflection or the prohibitions of conscience. Thus, it is not entirely surprising when Arendt turns to Socrates as a model in this essay, describing him as "someone who did think without becoming a philosopher, a citizen among citizens, doing nothing, claiming nothing that, in his view, every citizen should do and had a right to claim"—namely, thinking and demanding that others think.[15]

As in "Philosophy and Politics," the Socrates of "Thinking and Moral Considerations" is portrayed as a citizen first and foremost. He is far indeed from the race of what Arendt disparagingly referred to as "professional thinkers." However, a subtle transformation has occurred in her portrait of the "political" Socrates. He is still a "midwife," an individual possessed of "the expert knowledge of delivering others of their thoughts," of making them see "the implications of their opinions."[16] But the nature of his midwifery has changed. Just as one of the Greek midwife's primary functions was to decide whether the child she helped deliver was fit to live, so Socratic midwifery consisted not simply in eliciting thoughts and opinions, but in deciding whether they amounted to anything more than a mere "windegg." If not, the bearer of these thoughts must be cleansed. And here Arendt makes a sweeping and surprising claim:

> . . . looking at the Socratic dialogues, there is nobody among Socrates' interlocutors who ever brought forth a thought that was no windegg. He rather did what Plato, certainly thinking of Socrates, said of the sophists: he purged people of their "opinions," that is, of those unexamined prejudgments which prevent thinking by suggesting that we know where we not only don't know but cannot know, helping them, as Plato remarks, to get rid of what was bad in them, their opinions, without however making them good, giving them truth.[17]

This powerful and approving characterization of Socratic negativity is followed by an even more surprising (and again approving) account of how Socrates, once having aroused his conversational partners, *paralyzes* them as acting beings by awakening in them the "wind of thought." This wind sets all that had seemed stable in motion—all the concepts, standards, and rules that man as an acting being takes, and must take, for granted. Once roused from slumber by the "gadfly" Socrates, the partner in dialogue finds himself subject to a twofold paralysis. The activity of thinking *interrupts* all other activities, and its primary effect is to create perplexity where there had once been (apparently) firm ground, thus rendering the resumption of action uncertain. Thus, Socrates' dialogical partners may find themselves not only purged of worthless opinions, but unable to act at all.[18]

The point Arendt wishes to make about Socratic thinking is that it is a "dangerous and resultless enterprise," one which has "a destructive, undermining effect on all established criteria, values, [and] measurements for good and evil. . . ."[19] To genuinely experience the unraveling power of thought is to risk not only inactivity, but cynicism and even nihilism. And yet, despite this risk, despite this danger, Arendt presents the paralysis of thought as of urgent political and moral consequence because it *slows people down*. It loosens the grip of "whatever the prescribed rules of conduct may be at a given time in a given society"; it is "equally dangerous to all creeds and, by itself, does not bring forth any new creed."[20] Dissolving the solidity of social codes and creedal beliefs—our most frequently appealed to grounds for action—thinking inhibits the average citizen's coordination with or unreflective endorsement of official injustice, of evil as policy.

This is a breathtaking moment in Arendt's thought, one in which the scale of values which governs her life-long defense of the *bios politikos* is temporarily inverted.[21] Thinking, the experience of the dialogue of me with myself (as Plato describes it), turns out to be the experiential ground of conscience and it prohibitions. These in turn form the inner core of the morality of abstention, a morality based on the avoidance of injustice rather than the cultivation of positive virtues. Socratic negativity—the dissolvent quality of thinking— thus finds its moral fulfillment in the conscientious avoidance of injustice. According to Arendt, the lesson of Socrates is that where thinking is absent (whether due to unquestioning commitment or everyday thoughtlessness), there can be no effective conscience, no active faculty that makes clear the simple virtue of nonparticipation in moments of widespread, but unrecognized, moral corruption (such as imperial Athens or inter-war Europe).

Bearing this in mind, it must be said that the conclusion of "Thinking and Moral Considerations" restores the familiar balance of Arendt's thought by limiting the political importance of thinking's negativity to those "rare moments when the chips are down," when acting in public with others has become either impossible or suicidal. Thinking's ability to slow people down, to withdraw them from the world of action, is politically significant *only* when "everybody is swept away unthinkingly by what everybody else believes in." Arendt writes as if such moments of self-loss are extraordinarily rare, rather than the all-too-familiar norm of political life (here she could have learned from the Heidegger of *Being and Time* or the

Mill of *On Liberty*, both of whom lay bare the essentially mimetic character of social life). She is willing to entertain an individualist ethos of nonparticipation in "emergency situations" only because such circumstances warrant what is, in effect, a kind of moral *sauve qui peut*. Otherwise, even in this most uncharacteristic of her texts, she remains steadfastly committed to the idea that political evil is best avoided through active citizenship.

. . . . .

Arendt's unexpected appreciation of the political and moral importance of Socratic negativity in "Thinking and Moral Considerations" points back to her consideration of the maieutic Socrates in "Philosophy and Politics." It forces us to see the earlier text, exceptional as it is, as less in the service of moral individualism and the virtue of saying no than as the expression of a peculiar (public and politically grounded) perspectivism. The key contrast here is between her early and late descriptions of the nature of Socratic midwifery. In "Thinking and Moral Considerations" the primary effect of Socrates' maieutic activity is purgative, destructive of *doxa*. In "Philosophy and Politics" Socrates is presented as acting on the assumption that every *doxa*, as a distinct opening to the world, is no mere "windegg," but an offspring worth preserving, the locus of a particular and valuable truth. In cultivating the partial truths given through individual perspectives on the shared world, the Socrates of "Philosophy and Politics" reveals a human world characterized by the absence of any *absolute* truth, yet one that is made beautiful by the availability of innumerable openings upon it. Truth for mortals, in other words, inheres in the plurality of perspectives, which endow the shared world with a fullness of presence found nowhere else, a fullness that always exceeds the powers of any (singular) representation.

The Socrates Arendt presents in "Philosophy and Politics" can scarcely be said to be in the service of either a civic republican or communitarian agenda (at least as these terms are ordinarily understood). But, despite his loving attention to the uniqueness of every individual's *doxa*, Socrates cannot really be said to be performing in the service of an individualist conception of moral or intellectual integrity either. As with Nietzsche, the overarching criterion is aesthetic rather than moral. What matters in Arendt's rendition of Socratic dialectic is the richness of the phenomenal world revealed through the conversation among friends. The (more obviously moral) effect of limiting or restraining the agonal spirit is distinctly secondary. So, we are left with the question of what cause, precisely, the Socratic midwifery of "Philosophy and Politics" serves.

Here it helps to turn to Arendt's essay "The Crisis in Culture," which contains a remarkable discussion of the Greek idea of culture (a word, of course, of Roman origin). Arendt turns to Pericles' "Funeral Oration" to reveal the Greek sense of what they did *not* have a name for. Offering a free translation of Thucydides' original, Arendt quotes Pericles as "saying something like this: 'We love beauty within the limits of political judgment, and we philosophize without the barbarian vice of effeminacy.'"[22] She offers this translation while discussing how, for the Greeks, the love of beauty and wisdom was active in nature. Thus, Pericles' statement—made in the course of describing the source of Athens' beauty, uniqueness, and glory to his fellow citizens—celebrates the Athenians' love of beauty (*ta kalon*) and wisdom (*sophia*), while simultaneously articulating their fear of these activities taken to extremes. From "doing beauty," Arendt tells us, they feared over-refinement and an "indiscriminate sensitivity which did not know how to choose."[23] Lack of a discriminating faculty of taste leaves those sensitive to beauty in a state of perpetual ravishment. Worse, the unrestricted love of wisdom fosters a lack of virility and, with it, inactivity. Athens is great, Pericles says, because the Athenians subject their love of beauty and wisdom to the demands of the public world: "Here each individual is interested not only in his own affairs, but in the affairs of the state as well . . . we do not say that a man who takes no interest in politics is a man who minds his own business; we say that he has no business here at all."[24] Athens' greatness demands that her citizens love their city more than their souls, but also more than beauty or wisdom. That, at least, is the Periclean understanding, and it is one that Arendt affirms.

We are back, then, with Callicles. However, the Pericles of the "Funeral Oration" offers us an aestheticized (and hence more edifying) Callicles, one whose main objection to the life of the mind is not that it is "ungentlemanly" or lacking in distinction, but that it threatens Athens' unique and unsurpassable beauty (a beauty created and preserved by great and memorable deeds). The love of wisdom, then, must be subjected to the love of beauty, but to the love of *Athens'* beauty. This is the paramount criterion, and Pericles appeals to it, rather than to concern for individual welfare, in urging his fellow citizens to carry on the struggle against their enemies:

> I could tell you a long story (and you know it as well as I do) about what is to be gained by beating the enemy back. What I would prefer is that you should fix your eyes every day on the greatness of Athens as she really is, and should fall in love with her. When you realize her great-ness, then reflect that what made her great was men with a spirit of adventure, men who knew their duty, men who were ashamed to fall below a certain standard. . . . It is for you to try to be like them.[25]

To be ravished daily by the beauty of the city is, evidently, to "love beauty within the limits of political judgment."

What does this Periclean aestheticism—the appeal to the beauty of Athens—have to do with the Socrates whom Arendt presents in "Philosophy and Politics"? When we read Arendt's characterization of Socrates' activity in this essay, we see that she downplays Socratic negativity so that his "midwifery" can be enlisted in the cause of making Athens, the most beautiful *polis*, ever more beautiful, ever more lovely. In other words, she accepts the canons of Periclean "taste" and tailors her portrait of Socrates to conform to them. The result is a Socrates who serves his fellow citizens not by disabusing them of their dogmatic conceptions of the good life, or by question-ing the worth of a life lived for the glory of Athens, but rather by eliciting the truth of their diverse and unique *doxai*. The maieutic practice of *this* Socrates has no purgative effect: his function is rather to multiply and sharpen individual perspectives on Athens the beau-tiful, thereby making her beauty that much richer and more varied. If the "Funeral Oration" presents a city whose beauty was created and sustained by great deeds, then "Philosophy and Politics" pre-sents this beauty as finding daily and unexpected expression in the opinions and experience of its individual citizens. Socratic mid-wifery thus complements Periclean monumentalism by drawing out a complex web of perspective and perception, humanizing through talk a terrible beauty, one built on power and a terrifying dynamism. When Pericles says, "Mighty indeed are the marks and monuments of our empire which we have left. Future ages will won-der at us, as the present age wonders at us now," we become fully aware of the magnitude of the task Arendt has imposed on her "maieutic" Socrates.[26]

Yet, while great, the task of humanizing a beauty held to be worth more than life itself is nothing compared to the more genuinely Socratic task of trying to get individual citizens to care about their souls and the avoidance of injustice. In "Philosophy and Politics" Arendt reconciles the life of the mind with the life of the citizen, but only by making the former the (strangely devoted) servant of the latter, or of what she calls "common sense." Even if we understand this term in its distinctively Arendtian sense (as denoting the individual's feeling for a common or shared world) we still have a drastic inversion of the Socratic mission as articulated in the *Apology*, a mission that Arendt herself clearly recognized and paid tribute to in "Thinking and Moral Considerations." Thus, neither the "gadfly" nor the "electric ray" make much of an appearance in "Philosophy and Politics." Purging people of opinions, slowing them down, making them realize that they do not know what they think they know: none of these activities plays any real role in the *polis*-enhancing version of Socratic dialectic Arendt virtually invents in this essay.

The most we can say is that the Socrates of "Philosophy and Politics" indirectly serves moral forces by helping his fellow citizens avoid the nastier excesses of agonistic individualism. To the Periclean virtues of restless activity and striving for greatness, Arendt's Socrates adds an appreciation of the others' standpoint, of talk for talk's sake, and the value of thoughtful solitude.[27] But there is nothing here of the transvaluation of values that led Mill to praise, and Nietzsche to bemoan, Socrates' appearance on the world stage. With Socrates—with philosophy—it became possible to question the standpoint of the *polis* from what we would today call a secular moral perspective. It became possible to distinguish individual moral integrity from the duties and obligations of the citizen, and to see the former as setting the standard by which all strictly political obligations should be assessed. Socrates thus provided the means for cutting through the moral confusion introduced by the Periclean rhetoric of cultural greatness and the realist rhetoric of power, necessity and political survival so memorably captured in the Melian dialogue. Socrates made it possible, in other words, to see loving one's soul more than one's city as *the* precondition for creating *doxai* that are morally valuable, that do not simply reflect the beauty of the political association but hold it instead to a higher (but nonetheless human or humane) standard.

. . . . .

Even if Arendt's 1954 attempt at reconciling philosophy and politics falls short, offering us only a civic form of individualism rather than an authentically moral one, we are still left with a paradox. For it cannot be said that she remained blind to the central purpose of Socratic dialectic: philosophical conversation as a disabusing activity, a purging of opinions which served the ultimate goal of avoiding injustice. In both "Personal Responsibility Under Dictatorship" (1964) and "Thinking and Moral Considerations," she gives eloquent and powerful testimony to the way thinking—which necessarily begins with the purging of prejudgments—can save us from the worst by liberating our faculty of judgment from the narrow confines of preconceived categories and social habit. Why then does she limit the moral and political relevance of thinking (as dissolvent, action-impeding activity) to "emergency situations"? Why can't she bring herself to acknowledge that Socrates—the gadfly and electric ray—plays a far more important and potentially transformative role on Western conceptions of citizenship and moral agency than the one she allots him as the discoverer of a secular form of conscience? Why is Arendt finally unable to make room for either philosophy or an authentic moral individualism in her vision of politics?

A full answer to these questions would involve recapitulating the central arguments of both *The Origins of Totalitarianism* and *The Human Condition*—something I cannot do here. But I would like to conclude by offering some suggestions about the sources of her inhibitions on these questions.

First, there is Arendt's fear that individualism and subjectivism go hand in hand—a conclusion she seems to have arrived at from personal experience, her study of Rahel Varnhagen's diaries, analysis of Romanticism and the French Revolution, and (of course) her critical encounter with Heidegger's "solipsistic" early philosophy. The aggressive indictment of Socratic conscience found in "Civil Disobedience" makes sense only when we take into account Arendt's fear that the goal of comfortably "living together with oneself" uses up all of one's energy, producing a "good man," perhaps, but a deficient citizen. It is as though she thought that Socrates' appeal to the self and its inner dialogue somehow corrupted the very moral energies it mobilized. Her profound ambivalence on this score, manifest in her now damning, now approving invocations of the formula from the *Gorgias* ("it would be better for me . . . that multitudes of men should disagree with me than that I, being one, should be out of harmony with myself and contradict me"), betrays her inability to conceive a self that is not a trap, that is not founded upon a narcissistic retreat from the world into the enjoyment of conflicting emotions and inner tensions. She knows that Socrates is not the grandfather of Rousseau and Romanticism, and yet she can't help claiming that he is somehow responsible for them, for underwriting "world alienation."

Secondly, there is her Nietzschean suspicion that philosophy itself is profoundly antipolitical, a form of life built upon *ressentiment* and the spirit of revenge. The main story she tells in "Philosophy and Politics" concerns not the Socratic reconciliation of these two activities, but Plato's revenge on the *polis* for killing Socrates and endangering his memory. In Arendt's view, Plato's "tyranny of truth" in the *Republic* was motivated by the fear that democratic *polis* life, with its low estimate of the "good for nothing" *sophos*, would invariably deprive the philosopher of the remembrance he so richly deserved: "The same *polis* . . . which guaranteed its inhabitants an immortality and stability which they never could hope for without it, was a threat and a danger to the immortality of the philosopher."[28] The war on *doxa* and the *Republic*'s call for philosophical rulership are Plato's attempt to imagine political conditions suitable to the flourishing of the philosophical form of life, the *bios theoretikos*.

Arendt follows Nietzsche's argument that "every animal—therefore the *bête philosophe*, too—instinctively strives for an optimum of favorable conditions under which it can expend all its strength and achieve a maximal feeling of power. . . ." very closely here, just as she does in *The Human Condition*.[29] The tension between philosophy and politics brought to the fore by Plato and inscribed in our tradition of political philosophy is not reducible to the opposed tonalities of thinking vs. acting. Rather, it is about two opposed forms of life—the life of the citizen and the life of the philosopher—whose maximal conditions of existence are utterly incompatible, and which are (as a result) engaged in an endless struggle for domination over each other. Hence, philosophy and politics *might* have been reconciled, as Arendt suggests, in a Socratic practice that deferred to *polis* life, but this reconciliation was necessarily fleeting. It was bound to fall apart the moment practically oriented citizens expressed their impatience with what they saw as meddling by "good for nothing" *sophos* in the realm of human affairs. Arendt takes up this struggle between the two forms of life in her own writings because she was convinced that philosophers have been unopposed in their libels on the life of action for far too long. Thus, her portrait of a "civic" Socrates can be seen as her revenge on Plato's revenge, and as such akin to Nietzsche's "inverted Platonism."

Third, there is her strange insistence that the world can be beautified through political action, through great words and deeds, even though this may mean relegating "care for one's soul" and the avoidance of injustice to the rank of "ridiculous and unmanly" pursuits. As an individual, Arendt witnessed the worst the pursuit of politics had to offer. As a political theorist, she did more than anyone else to understand the peculiar nature of political evil in the twentieth century. Yet in *The Human Condition* and, indeed, in "Philosophy and Politics," she seems driven by the need to theorize *genuine* political action as an activity capable of restoring luster to a world made unimaginably ugly. It is as if the experience of totalitarianism had made an innocent love of the world, a simple affirmation of existence, impossible. One had, somehow, to actively restore the worldly beauty totalitarianism had rendered a distant and unreal memory. Political action—the sharing of words and deeds in the public realm by diverse equals—is the avenue Arendt fixed upon as adequate to this task, and for reasons that will always remain at least partially obscure. Whether political action is even remotely capable of providing what she claims is, of course, an open question. But what the detached reader of her work is struck by is the sheer will with which she pursues this alternative, blind to the possibility that care for the world may take a variety of forms, and that the beauty or wonder of existence is something human beings can neither definitively destroy (except, perhaps, through nuclear annihilation) nor actively, willfully re-create.

Abbreviations

Arendt, *BPF*	Hannah Arendt, *Between Past and Future* (New York: Penguin Books, 1968)
Arendt, *EU*	Hannah Arendt, *Essays in Understanding, 1930–1954*, edited by Jerome Kohn (New York: Harcourt Brace & Company, 1994)
Arendt, *HC*	Hannah Arendt, *The Human Condition* (Chicago: University of Chicago Press, 1958)
Arendt, *IT*	Hannah Arendt, "Ideology and Terror," in *Totalitarianism: Part Three of the Origins of Totalitarianism* (New York: Harcourt Brace Jovanovich, 1968)
Arendt, *LM*	Hannah Arendt, *The Life of the Mind* (New York: Harcourt Brace Jovanovich, 1977)
Arendt, *MDT*	Hannah Arendt, *Men in Dark Times* (New York: Harcourt Brace Jovanovich, 1968)
Arendt, *MT*	Hannah Arendt, "Mankind and Terror," in *EU*
Arendt, *NT*	Hannah Arendt, "On the Nature of Totalitarianism: An Essay in Understanding," in Arendt, *EU*
Arendt, *OR*	Hannah Arendt, *On Revolution* (New York: Penguin Books, 1990)
Arendt, *OT*	Hannah Arendt, *The Origins of Totalitarianism* (New York: Harcourt, Brace, Jovanovich Publishers, 1973)
Arendt, *PP*	Hannah Arendt, "Philosophy and Politics," *Social Research* vol. 57, no. 1 (spring 1990)
Arendt, *TMC*	Hannah Arendt, "Thinking and Moral Considerations," in *Social Research: Fiftieth Anniversary Issue* (spring/summer 1984)
Levi, *Survival in Auschwitz*	Primo Levi, *Survival in Auschwitz* in *Survival in Auschwitz and The Reawakening: Two Memoirs* (New York: Summit Books, 1985)
Nietzsche, *BGE*	Friedrich Nietzsche, *Beyond Good and Evil*, translated by Walter Kaufmann (New York: Vintage Books, 1989)
Nietzsche, *GM*	Friedrich Nietzsche, *On the Genealogy of Morals*, translated by Walter Kaufmann (New York: Vintage Books, 1989).
Strauss, *CM*	Leo Strauss, *The City and Man* (Chicago: University of Chicago Press, 1978)
Strauss, *LAM*	Leo Strauss, *Liberalism, Ancient and Modern* (Chicago: University of Chicago Press, 1995)

Strauss, *NRH*   Leo Strauss, *Natural Right and History* (Chicago: University of Chicago Press, 1953)

Strauss, *RCPR*   Leo Strauss, *The Rebirth of Classical Political Rationalism*, edited by Thomas Pangle (Chicago: University of Chicago Press, 1989)

Strauss, *WIPP*   Leo Strauss, *What Is Political Philosophy? And Other Studies* (Chicago: University of Chicago Press, 1988)

Villa, *Arendt and*   Dana R. Villa, *Arendt and Heidegger: The Fate of the Po-
Heidegger*   litical* (Princeton: Princeton University Press, 1996)

Notes

INTRODUCTION

1. Readers seeking an overview are advised to consult George Kateb's *Hannah Arendt: Politics, Conscience, Evil* (Totowa, NJ: Rowman and Allanheld, 1983), or Margaret Canovan's *Hannah Arendt: A Reinterpretation of Her Political Thought* (New York: Cambridge University Press, 1992). A number of shorter introductions to Arendt's thought have recently appeared; in my opinion, Maurizio Passerin d'Entreves's *The Political Philosophy of Hannah Arendt* (New York: Routledge, 1994) is the best of them. Seyla Benhabib's *The Reluctant Modernism of Hannah Arendt* (Thousand Oaks: Sage Publications, 1996) provides a concise critical appropriation of Arendt for contemporary politics, as well as illuminating philosophical analysis. Richard Bernstein's *Hannah Arendt and the Jewish Question* (Cambridge, MA: MIT Press, 1997) focuses on Arendt's long and complex relation to Jewish politics. Finally, Elisabeth Young-Bruehl's biography, *Hannah Arendt: For Love of the World* (New Haven: Yale University Press, 1982) remains an invaluable source, unlikely to be surpassed.

2. Dana R. Villa, *Arendt and Heidegger: The Fate of the Political* (Princeton: Princeton University Press, 1996).

CHAPTER ONE
TERROR AND RADICAL EVIL

1. It would be wrong to include Vietnam in this list of near or attempted genocides. However, the assumption that American hands remain clean—that America has made no contributions to "industrial killing" in the twentieth century—is untenable. Given the moral presuppositions of constitutional democracy, the slaughter of innocents from the air during this immoral war remains a permanent stain.

2. See Hannah Arendt, *The Origins of Totalitarianism* (New York: Harcourt, Brace, Jovanovich Publishers, 1973), chapter 9.

3. Ibid., p. 459.

4. This interpretation is, of course, highly controversial. I deal with some of the moral and philosophical issues its raises in the third section of this chapter.

5. Arendt, *OT*, p. 459.

6. Ibid.

7. The so-called "information age" threatens to bear out Arendt's prognostications about a world in which human beings are reduced to the status of *animal laborans*, while the opportunities for labor become increasingly rare.

8. See George Kateb's essay "On Political Evil" in Kateb, *The Inner Ocean* (Ithaca: Cornell University Press, 1992).

9. An exception to this rule is Wolfgang Sofsky's masterful "thick description" of the concentration camp as a kind of self-enclosed society in which absolute power knew no constraints whatsoever. See Sofsky, *The Order of Terror: The Concentration Camp*, trans. William Templer (Princeton: Princeton University Press, 1997). For a sophisticated account of the dangers of applying a "rational actor" model to National Socialism, see Dan Diner's essay "Historical Understanding and Counterrationality: The *Judenrat* as Epistemological Vantage," in *Probing the Limits of Representation*, edited by Saul Friedlander (Cambridge, MA: Harvard University Press, 1992).

10. Arendt, *OT*, p. 440.

11. Ibid.

12. Ibid.

13. See especially Arendt's discussion of this point in "Ideology and Terror" in Arendt, *OT*.

14. Ibid., p. 456: "We have learned that the power of man is so great that he really can be what he wishes to be."

15. Hannah Arendt, *Essays in Understanding, 1930–1954*, edited by Jerome Kohn (New York: Harcourt Brace & Company, 1994), p. 298.

16. Ibid., p. 300. Cf. Arendt, *OT*, pp. 463–464.

17. Ibid., p. 301.

18. Ibid., pp. 302–303.

19. Arendt, *OT*, p. 443. Cf. Sofsky, p. 14.

20. Ibid., pp. 442, 452. Cf. Primo Levi, *Survival in Auschwitz* in *Survival in Auschwitz and The Reawakening: Two Memoirs* (New York: Summit Books, 1985), p. 90. With respect to Arendt's formulation, the inversion Heidegger's fundamental point in *Being and Time* concerning the "mineness" of one's death is of note.

21. Arendt, *EU*, p. 303.

22. Ibid., p. 305.

23. Ibid., p. 304.

24. Sofsky's analysis confirms Arendt's basic points. As he notes, the absolute power created in the concentration camps was "not bent on achieving blind obedience or discipline, but desires to generate a universe of total uncertainty, one in which submissiveness is no shield against even worse outcomes. It forces its victims together in an aggregate, a mass; it stirs up differences and erects a social structure marked by extreme con-

trasts. It uses various procedures for total control—not for the development of individual self-discipline, but as instruments of quotidian harass-
ment, of daily cruelty. Terror dissolves the link between transgression and
punitive sanction. It requires neither occasions nor reasons, and has no
interest in obligating itself by threat. Absolute power goes on a rampage
whenever it desires. It does not wish to limit freedom, but to destroy it"
(Sofsky, *The Order of Terror*, p. 17).

25. Ibid., p. 305.

26. Ibid., pp. 305–306.

27. Levi, *Survival in Auschwitz and The Reawakening*, p. 51.

28. Ibid., p. 55.

29. Such accounts are found in survivor narratives, such as Levi's, and
in analytic studies such as Sofsky's *The Order of Terror*.

30. Arendt, *OT*, p. 447.

31. Ibid.

32. Ibid. p. 448. In chapter 9 of *OT*, Arendt darkly observes that "the
best criterion by which to decide whether someone has been forced outside
the pale of law is to ask if he would benefit by committing a crime. If a small
burglary is likely to improve his legal position [by placing him within the
bounds of the criminal justice system], at least temporarily, one may be
sure he has been deprived of human rights" (Arendt, *OT*, p. 286).

33. Ibid., p. 438.

34. Ibid., p. 449.

35. Ibid., p. 451.

36. One needs to keep in mind the fact that, in *The Origins of Totalitarianism*, Arendt was providing a theoretical analysis of the constellation of
events that enabled the unprecedented to happen, and of the nature of
totalitarianism itself. The fact that there were obvious and important differences between the German and Soviet camp systems (the Soviets, for
example, never attempted to exterminate the children of an entire group)
does not render Arendt's theoretical aim incoherent—unless one is willing
to question the existence of totalitarianism as such, or the fact that Nazi
Germany was a totalitarian society.

37. Rousset, quoted in Arendt, *OT*, p. 451. Cf. Levi, *Survival in Auschwitz*, pp. 88–90.

38. Recounted in Tzvetan Todorov's *Facing the Extreme: Moral Life
in the Concentration Camps* (New York: Metropolitan Books, 1996), pp.
63–64.

39. Arendt, *OT*, p. 452.

40. See Istvan Deak's essay "Memories of Hell"in *The New York Review
of Books*, June 26, 1997.

41. Of course, the "conditions under which conscience ceases to be
adequate and to do good becomes utterly impossible" (*OT*, p. 452) are

extreme, and do not have any real parallel in life outside the camps. Arendt's point about totalitarianism is that it creates a society-wide threat or blackmail, designed to leave the individual with very little, if any, moral room for maneuver. The Soviet system under Stalin clearly exceeded Nazi Germany in this regard, creating an atmosphere of utter distrust, mendacity and suspicion in society at large. See, for example, Nadezhda Mandelstam's memoir, *Hope Against Hope*, tran. Max Hayward (New York: Atheneum, 1970).

42. Levi, *Survival in Auschwitz*, p. 98.

43. See Levi, *Survival in Auschwitz*, especially chapters 5 and 6, and Sofsky, *The Order of Terror*, parts IV and V.

44. Levi, *Survival in Auschwitz*, p. 90.

45. Arendt, *OT*, p. 455.

46. Rousset, quoted in Arendt, *OT*, p. 455.

47. Cf. Sofsky, *The Order of Terror*, p. 25.

48. Todorov, *Facing the Extreme*, pp. 32, 33, 39.

49. Ibid., p. 39.

50. Levi, *Survival in Auschwitz*, p. 87: ". . . the Lager was pre-eminently a gigantic biological and social experiment."

51. Arendt, *OT*, p. 459.

52. Arendt, *Essays in Understanding*, p. 408.

53. Montesquieu, quoted in Arendt, Ibid. See Montesquieu, *The Spirit of the Laws*, translated by Anne Cohler, Basia Miller, and Harold Stone (New York: Cambridge University Press, 1989), pp. xliv–xlv.

54. *Hannah Arendt–Karl Jaspers Correspondence 1926–1969*, edited by Lotte Kohler and Hans Saner (New York: Harcourt Brace Jovanovich, 1992), p. 166.

55. Arendt, *OT*, p. 457: "Totalitarianism strives not toward despotic rule over men, but toward a system in which men are superfluous. Total power can be achieved and safeguarded only in a world of conditioned reflexes, of marionettes without the slightest trace of spontaneity."

56. Ibid., p. 459.

57. *Arendt-Jaspers Correspondence*, p. 69.

58. In *OT*, Arendt cites Rousset: "Nothing is more terrible than these processions of human beings going like dummies to their death" (Arendt, *OT*, p. 455). In *Survival in Auschwitz*, Levi recounts being herded with his fellow slave-laborers into the roll-call square at Buna-Monowitz, to watch the execution of a *Haftlinge* who evidently helped blow up one of the crematoriums at Birkeneau. Just before the trapdoor on the scaffold opens, the condemned prisoner shouts *"Kamaraden, ich bin der Letz!"* (Comrades, I am the last one!). Levi recounts: "I wish I could say that from the midst of us, an abject flock, a voice rose, a murmur, a sign of assent. But nothing

happened. . . . the SS watch as we pass with indifferent eyes: their work is finished, and well finished. The Russians can come now: there are no longer any strong men among us, the last one is hanging above our heads. . . . To destroy a man is difficult, almost as difficult as to create one: it has not been easy, nor quick, but you Germans have succeeded. Here we are, docile under your gaze; from our side you have no more to fear; no acts of violence, no words of defiance, not even a look of judgment" (Levi, *Survival in Auschwitz*, pp. 149–150).

59. Margaret Canovan, *Hannah Arendt: A Reinterpretation of Her Political Thought* (New York: Cambridge University Press, 1992), p. 27.

60. See Tzvetan Todorov's *The Conquest of America* (New York: Harper and Row, 1984), especially pp. 127–167.

61. Arendt, *OT*, p. 297.

62. Ibid., p. 459.

63. Michael Ignatieff, "After the Holocaust: Reinventing Human Rights," lecture given at NYU, March 3, 1998.

64. Our predicament is precisely the opposite of the one Arendt faced when writing *The Origins of Totalitarianism*: we don't read the camps back into historical precedents (like slave labor); rather, we read everything back into the camps. Some of the less thoughtful responses to Serb atrocities in Bosnia illustrate this point.

CHAPTER TWO
CONSCIENCE, THE BANALITY OF EVIL, AND THE
IDEA OF A REPRESENTATIVE PERPETRATOR

1. Daniel Jonah Goldhagen, *Hitler's Willing Executioners: Ordinary Germans and the Holocaust* (New York: Vintage Books, 1997), p. 379.

2. Ibid., p. 406.

3. Ibid., p. 597, note 74.

4. Hannah Arendt, "Thinking and Moral Considerations," pp. 7, 36.

5. See Karl Jaspers's letter to Arendt from December 13, 1963, where he emphasizes this point, in *Hannah Arendt—Karl Jaspers Correspondence: 1926–1969*, edited by Lotte Kohler and Hans Saner (New York: Harcourt Brace Jovanovich Inc., 1992), p. 542. Of course, Arendt believed that there where others like Eichmann, but she did not elevate him to the symbolic status of the representative Nazi.

6. See Elisabeth Young-Bruehl, *Hannah Arendt: For Love of the World* (New Haven: Yale University Press, 1982), pp. 360–61.

7. See Zygmunt Bauman, *Modernity and the Holocaust* (Ithaca: Cornell University Press, 1989); also Max Horkheimer and Theodor Adorno, *Dialectic of Enlightenment* (New York: Seabury Press, 1972).

8. Hannah Arendt, *Eichmann in Jerusalem* (New York: Penguin Books, 1983), pp. 218, 288. It should be noted that the term "administrative massacres" makes its appearance in contradistinction to the "wild mass killings" conducted in the early part of the war by the *Einsatzgruppen* on the Eastern front. For the exchange with Scholem, see Hannah Arendt, *The Jew as Pariah*, edited by Ron H. Feldman (New York: Grove Press, 1978), pp. 250–51. I discuss Arendt's "change of mind" regarding the nature of (totalitarian) evil—her move from the notion of "radical" to "banal" evil—below.

9. Goldhagen, *Hitler's Willing Executioners*, p. 28.

10. See, for example, Hannah Arendt, "Approaches to the German Problem" and "Organized Guilt and Universal Responsibility," both in Arendt, *EU*.

11. Richard Wolin, "The Ambivalences of German-Jewish Identity: Hannah Arendt in Jerusalem," *History and Memory*, vol. 8, no. 2. (1996): 9–35.

12. Ibid., p. 27.

13. See, for example, Christian Bay's comment about "the Eichmann in us all" and Arendt's agitated response ("Oh no! There is none in you and none in me. . . . I always hated this notion of 'Eichmann in each one of us.' This is simply not true.") in Arendt, "On Hannah Arendt" in *Hannah Arendt: The Recovery of the Public World*, edited by Melvyn Hill (New York: St. Martin's Press, 1979), pp. 307–8. Cf. Arendt, *EJ*, pp. 278, 286, where Arendt strongly repudiates the "Eichmann in us all" idea.

14. Hannah Arendt, "Organized Guilt," in *EU*, p. 128.

15. Seyla Benhabib, "Identity, Perspective and Narrative in Hannah Arendt's *Eichmann in Jerusalem*," *History and Memory*, vol. 8, no. 2 (1996): 48–53.

16. There are problems with this proposed shift, not least of which is the fact that it doesn't jibe with what Arendt considered the "central moral, political and even legal" problems posed by the trial. Arendt's commentary on the notion of "crimes against humanity" occurs in her "Epilogue" and it is certainly the most abstractly legalistic discussion in the whole book, intended mainly to clarify some of the thornier jurisdictional issues raised by the event of the trial itself.

17. See Gershom Scholem, "An Exchange of Letters" in Arendt, *Jew as Pariah*, pp. 241–42; Walter Z. Laqueur, "A Reply to Hannah Arendt", ibid., p. 278; Seyla Benhabib, "Identity, Perspective, and Narrative," pp. 35–36; and Elisabeth Young-Bruehl, *Hannah Arendt*, pp. 339–40, 344.

18. Benhabib, "Identity, Perspective, Narrative," p. 35.

19. David Ben-Gurion, article in the *New York Times Magazine*, quoted in Young-Bruehl, *Hannah Arendt*, p. 341.

20. Arendt, *EJ*, p. 6.

21. The television documentary *The Trial of Adolf Eichmann* (PBS, April 30, 1997) provides ample confirmation that this was indeed the case.

22. Arendt, *EJ*, "Postscript," p. 298: ". . .the question of individual guilt or innocence, the act of meting out justice to both the defendant and the victim, are the only things at stake in a criminal court. . . . The present report deals with nothing but the extent to which the court in Jerusalem succeeded in fulfilling the demands of justice."

23. Ibid., p. 5. Cf. p. 6, where she characterizes the prosecution's case as "built on what the Jews had suffered, not on what Eichmann had done." For Arendt, such an approach not only failed to meet the demands of justice, it had the effect of putting history, rather than an individual, on trial, with the result that individual responsibility for deeds was obscured by categories like "the eternal anti-Semitism of the West" and "the fate of the Jews." See Arendt, *EJ*, pp. 18–19.

24. Ibid., p. 253. Cf. "Postscript,"in Arendt, *EJ*, p. 286: "I held and I hold that this trial had to take place in the interests of justice and nothing else."

25. As one assistant prosecutor puts the prosecution line in *The Trial of Adolf Eichmann*, Eichmann "held all the strings," including responsibility for the activities of the *Einsatzgruppen* and what happened in *all* the death camps. Arendt's analysis shows how grossly inflated this claim was given the evidence in the case and Eichmann's relatively limited authority.

26. See, in this regard, Arendt's comments in *EJ*, p. 285.

27. Arendt, *EJ*, p. 25.

28. Ibid.

29. Ibid., pp. 26–27.

30. Young-Bruehl, *Hannah Arendt*, p. 338. This concern is, in fact, explicitly raised as a general issue only in the "Postscript" to *EJ*.

31. Arendt, it must be said, chose to understand *Eichmann in Jerusalem* as a work of reportage pure and simple, and thus in some sense beyond argument for those who bothered to actually *read* it. Illuminating in this regard is a passage from a letter Arendt wrote to Mary McCarthy on October 3, 1963: "My basic notion of the 'ordinariness' of Eichmann is much less a notion than a faithful description of a phenomenon. I am sure there can be drawn many conclusions from this phenomenon and the most general I drew is indicated: 'banality of evil.' I may sometime want to write about this, and then I would write about the nature of evil, but it would have been entirely wrong of me to do it with the framework of the report." See *Between Friends: The Correspondence of Hannah Arendt and Mary McCarthy, 1949–1975*, edited by Carol Brightman (New York: Harcourt Brace and Company, 1995), p. 152.

32. This is how readers friendly to Arendt, like Baumann, as well as those who are harshly critical, like Goldhagen, tend to read her. In fact,

Arendt makes frequent and repeated reference to Eichmann's "zeal" in carrying out his murderous duties. See, for example, Arendt, *EJ*, pp. 24–25, 126–27, 147, 201.

33. Cf. Arendt, *OT*, p. 459: "Just as the victims in the death factories . . . are no longer human in the eyes of the executioners, so this newest species of criminals is beyond the pale even of solidarity in human sinfulness."

34. See Arendt, *EJ*, pp. 251–52.

35. Ibid., p. 21.

36. Ibid., p. 113.

37. Ibid., pp. 90–91.

38. Ibid., p. 93.

39. Ibid., p. 95.

40. Ibid., p. 96.

41. In this regard, Arendt cites the similar example of *Generalkommisar* Wilhelm Kube, who served in Occupied Russia and was enraged when German Jews who had won the Iron Cross in World War I arrived in the East for "special treatment."

42. Arendt, *EJ*, p. 114.

43. Ibid., p. 116.

44. Ibid., p. 131.

45. Ibid., p. 126.

46. Ibid., pp. 126, 18, 52, 98: ". . . the overwhelming majority of the German people believed in Hitler."

47. Ibid., p. 110.

48. Ibid., p. 125. One needs to bear in mind the large proportion of European nations that displayed enthusiasm at the prospect of becoming "clean of Jews."

49. Ibid., p. 21.

50. Ibid., p. 135.

51. Ibid., pp. 135–36.

52. Ibid., p. 136.

53. Ibid.

54. Ibid.

55. Ibid., pp. 136–37.

56. Ibid., p. 137.

57. Ibid., p. 146.

58. Ibid. Cf. Hannah Arendt, "Personal Responsibility Under Dictatorship," *The Listener*, August 6, 1964, p. 187.

59. Ibid., p. 186.

60. Ibid., pp. 185–86.

61. Arendt, *EJ*, p. 287.

62. Ibid., p. 52.

63. Ibid., p. 148.

64. Hence Emerson's dictum, "the law is but a memorandum." It is interesting to note, in this context, the contrast between Arendt's approach to Eichmann and that of Bauman to the "bureaucrats" among the perpetrators. While Arendt presents Eichmann in all his thoughtless banality, she does not present him as *essentially* a bureaucrat, nor does she try to explain his actions primarily in terms of bureaucratic rationality. For Arendt, Eichmann's "bureaucratic" conduct in solving the transport problem raised by the Final Solution is not the result of a narrow, technical horizon that made him utterly blind to what he was, in fact, doing. Rather, Eichmann knew where the deportations wound up, and the routinization of his conduct depended upon a prior moral approval of the end for which he was obliged to supply the (partial) means. In contrast, Bauman emphasizes how bureaucratic "remoteness" from the goals of action serves to enable modern forms of genocide. Such remoteness depends upon the substitution of "technical responsibility" for "moral responsibility," and the forgetting of the ultimate end which the functionary's limited means serve. See Bauman, "Uniqueness and Normality of the Holocaust" in *Modernity and the Holocaust*, especially pp. 101–2. For Arendt, Eichmann's "motivation" is moral-political: to execute the law. For Bauman, it is merely technical, the performance of his designated function within a gigantic bureaucratic apparatus.

65. Arendt, *EJ*, p. 288.
66. Ibid., pp. 52–53.
67. See Arendt, *EU*, pp. 315–16.
68. Ibid., p. 276.
69. Both Goldhagen and Wolin view *Eichmann in Jerusalem* as a direct continuation of *The Origins of Totalitarianism*, with Arendt using Eichmann as a confirmation of her previous theory (which does indeed hinge upon an analysis of the massification of European society). The reading I am suggesting here, and one confirmed by comments Arendt made to Jaspers and Mary McCarthy, is that confrontation with Eichmann in the flesh forced Arendt to rethink many of her previous assumptions about the role of ideology and the nature of evil.
70. Of course, this comes very close to Goldhagen's central argument. He repeatedly points out how the ordinary Germans among the perpetrators thought their actions were justifiable if not laudable. But Goldhagen's explanation has the curious effect of dissolving the moral puzzle and, indeed, the question of responsibility itself. For if antisemitism was as pervasive and as deeply rooted in Germany as he makes out, the choice of these "ordinary Germans" is entirely predictable, and without any moral curiosity whatever. Inhabiting a moral world importantly defined by what Goldhagen calls "a cognitive model of the evil Jew," ordinary Germans are presented to us as the objects of a culturally specific illusion. This illusion

leads them to commit morally heinous acts, but it also makes the possibility of their recognizing the true nature of their deeds exceedingly remote. In condemning "Hitler's willing executioners" as they are presented by Goldhagen, we find ourselves in a situation weirdly parallel to condemning a society that burnt witches at the stake: we find what *they* do morally reprehensible, and yet we cannot seriously expect them to see what they do as wrong, given their irrational yet deeply imbued "cognitive model" of the sources of evil. Goldhagen's account aims at laying bare ordinary German complicity and guilt in the Final Solution, but his social scientific psychology winds up making such perpetrators the unwitting instruments of a collective fantasy, one they are virtually powerless to escape. Arendt's emphasis in *Eichmann in Jerusalem* on the role of self-deception played in the case of Eichmann and millions of "ordinary Germans" avoids this determinism and allows her to preserve, in a far more convincing manner than Goldhagen, the idea of moral and criminal responsibility for the Holocaust. See also her Introduction to Bernd Naumann's *Auschwitz: A Report on the Proceedings Against Robert Karl Ludwig Mulka and Others Before the Court at Frankfurt* (New York: Frederick A. Praeger, Publishers, 1966), where she stresses the choice of camp personnel to be brutal, and not just for reasons of ideology or antisemitism.

71. One of the more egregious charges leveled against Arendt during the Eichmann controversy was that she substituted the "banal" Nazi for the "monstrous," fanatical, or sadistic Nazi—as if all Nazis had to conform to one type. In this regard, it should be noted that Arendt's account in *Eichmann in Jerusalem* hardly poses Eichmann as the paradigmatic Nazi. In recounting his activities, Arendt has ample opportunity to introduce us to a rogues' gallery of fanatical antisemites (like Julius Streicher and Heydrich), moral monsters (like Hitler), and sadists (encountered again and again among the "foot soldiers" of the Final Solution, particularly in the camps). Goldhagen's charge revives this canard, one that was demolished long ago by Arendt's Introduction to Bernd Naumann's *Auschwitz* (see note 70). See especially pp. xi–xvi, and p. xx: "What stands revealed at these trials [of Auschwitz personnel] is not only the complicated issue of personal responsibility [under dictatorship] but naked criminal guilt; and the faces of those who did their best, or rather their worst, to obey criminal orders are still very different from those who within a legally criminal system did not so much obey orders as do with their doomed victims what they pleased."

72. Arendt, "Personal Responsibility," pp. 186, 187.

73. Ibid., p. 205.

74. See Immanuel Kant, "What Is Enlightenment?" in *Kant's Political Writings*, edited by Hans Reiss (New York: Cambridge University Press, 1971), pp. 54–61.

75. Arendt, *EJ*, p. 287.

76. Gershom Scholem in Arendt, *The Jew as Pariah*, p. 245.

77. Ibid., pp. 250–51.

78. See Richard Bernstein, "Did Hannah Arendt Change Her Mind?: From Radical Evil to the Banality of Evil" in *Hannah Arendt: Twenty Years Later*, edited by Jerome Kohn and Larry May (Cambridge, MA: MIT Press, 1996); and Adi Ophir, "Between Eichmann and Kant: Thinking on Evil After Arendt," *History and Memory*, vol. 8, no. 2 (1996): 89–134.

79. This is Richard Bernstein's strategy in "Did Hannah Arendt Change Her Mind?"

80. Arendt, *Jew as Pariah*, p. 251.

81. Arendt, quoted in Young-Bruehl, *Hannah Arendt*, p. 371.

82. It is in this context that Arendt makes her private confession to Mary McCarthy that she wrote *Eichmann in Jerusalem* in a "curious state of euphoria. And that ever since I did it, I feel—after twenty years [since the war] light-hearted about the whole matter." See *Between Friends*, p. 168. The "light-heartedness" was, as Young-Bruehl remarks, a function of the Eichmann trial's releasing Arendt from "the idea that monsters and demons had engineered the murder of millions." See Young-Bruehl, *Hannah Arendt*, p. 367.

83. Arendt to Thompson, quoted by Jerome Kohn in his essay "Evil and Plurality: Hannah Arendt's Way to *The Life of the Mind*, I" in Kohn and May, eds., *Hannah Arendt: Twenty Years Later*, p. 155.

84. Arendt, "Nightmare and Flight" in *EU*, p. 134.

85. See Arendt, *OT*, chap. 12, sec. 3, especially pp. 458–59.

86. See chap. 1, "Terror and Radical Evil," in this volume. The criticism I make of Arendt here departs from the more sympathetic reading I give of her notion of radical evil in that essay.

87. See Villa, *Arendt and Heidegger: The Fate of the Political* (Princeton: Princeton University Press, 1996), chap. 3.

88. I deal with these issues at greater length in Chapter 1 of this book.

89. Arendt, *EJ*, p. 286.

90. Bauman's appropriation is a good example, since it serves the purpose of sociological generalization about the nature of modern society as such.

91. As Arendt notes with regard to German youth at the time of the Eichmann trial, "It is quite gratifying to feel guilty if you haven't done anything wrong: how noble! Whereas it is rather hard and certainly depressing to admit guilt and repent. The youth of Germany is surrounded, on all sides and in all walks of life, by men in positions of authority and in public office who are very guilty but who *feel* nothing of the sort" (*EJ*, p. 251).

92. Goldhagen, *Hitler's Willing Executioners*, pp. 28–34.

CHAPTER THREE
THE ANXIETY OF INFLUENCE: ON ARENDT'S
RELATIONSHIP TO HEIDEGGER

1. Elisabeth Young-Bruehl, *Hannah Arendt: For Love of the World* (New Haven: Yale University Press, 1982).

2. See Hannah Arendt/Martin Heidegger, *Briefe 1925 Bis 1975*, edited by Ursula Ludz (Frankfurt: Vittorio Klostermann, 1998). This chapter was written before the publication of these letters.

3. Elzbieta Ettinger, *Hannah Arendt/Martin Heidegger* (New Haven: Yale University Press, 1995), p. 78.

4. Richard Wolin, "Hannah and the Magician" in *The New Republic*, October 15, 1995, pp. 27–37.

5. Ibid., p. 34.

6. Hannah Arendt, "The Image of Hell" in Arendt, *EU*, p. 201.

7. Ibid.

8. Ibid., p. 202.

9. In a letter to her friend J. Glenn Gray toward the end of her life, Arendt characterizes Heidegger's pro-Nazi Rectoral Address of 1933 as less an authentic expression of National Socialist ideology than "a very unpleasant product of nationalism." See Young-Bruehl, *Hannah Arendt*, p. 443.

10. See Hans Sluga's essential work, *Heidegger's Crisis* (Cambridge, MA: Harvard University Press, 1993).

11. In this regard, it's helpful to remember Arendt's description (in *The Origins of Totalitarianism*) of the attraction of the pre- and intra-war intelligentsia to anti-bourgeois "mob movements" of one form or another. See Arendt, *OT*, pp. 326–40 (the section entitled "The Temporary Alliance Between the Mob and the Elite"). Young-Bruehl offers a penetrating analysis of how Arendt's description applies to Heidegger in *Hannah Arendt*, pp. 219–22. She concludes by noting "Hannah Arendt never claimed that those intellectuals who were, like Heidegger, enchanted by the mob should be absolved of responsibility for their own roles in the National Socialist revolution. But . . . she did not look on the European intellectual tradition as responsible for Nazism."

12. Hannah Arendt, "What Is Existential Philosophy?" in Arendt, *EU*, p. 177. The gist of Arendt's critique here is more appropriately aimed at the version of existentialism found in Sartre's *Being and Nothingness*.

13. Ibid., p. 178.

14. Ibid.

15. Ibid., pp. 171, 178.

16. Ibid., pp. 180–81.

17. Ibid., p. 181.

18. Ibid., p. 183.
19. Ibid.
20. Ibid., p. 187.
21. *Hannah Arendt–Karl Jaspers Correspondence: 1926–69*, ed. Lotte Kohler and Hans Saner, trans. Robert and Rita Kimber (New York: Harcourt Brace Jovanovich, 1992), p. 43.
22. Ibid.
23. Ibid., pp. 47–48. Jaspers replied: "I share your judgment of Heidegger—alas. My earlier remarks referred only to the correctness of the facts as you presented them" (p. 63).
24. Ibid., p. 142. It is interesting to place Arendt's judgment against the background of the history of Heidegger's personal and professional relationship with Husserl, as described by Hugo Ott in his book *Martin Heidegger: A Political Life* (New York: Basic Books, 1993), pp. 172–86. While Ott is, if anything, more severe in his judgment of Heidegger, his story reminds us that Heidegger had already "betrayed" his mentor on a strictly philosophical level before his ascension to the rectorship of Freiberg. Relations had been strained long before the "Jewish question" reared its ugly head in the form of the Reich Law of 1933 banning Jews from the teaching faculties of German universities.
25. In a letter to her husband Heinrich Blucher from December, 1949, Arendt recounts telling Jaspers about her relationship with Heidegger. Jaspers's statement to Arendt on this occasion ("Poor Heidegger, we sit here now, the two best friends he has in the world, and see right through him") nicely captures the mix of loyalty and intense skepticism which colored their relations with Heidegger. See Young-Bruehl, *Hannah Arendt*, p. 246.
26. Ibid., p. 603. See also Jaspers's postwar report to Allied authorities on Heidegger which, while recommending barring him from teaching, is extremely judicious in its view of his political engagement with the Nazis. The report is reprinted in Ott, *Martin Heidegger*, pp. 336–41.
27. See, for example, Arendt's September 29, 1947 letter to Jaspers, in which she expands on the dangers Heidegger's "lack of character" held for his own philosophical activity, threatening to distort and kitschify it: "He probably thought he could buy himself loose from the world [by retreating to his 'hut' at Totnauberg] . . . at the lowest possible price, fast-talking his way out of everything unpleasant, and do nothing but philosophize. And then, of course, this whole intricate and childish dishonesty has quickly crept into his philosophizing" (*Arendt-Jaspers Correspondence*, p. 143.)
28. See Young-Bruehl, *Hannah Arendt*, pp. 304–7.
29. Arendt, "Concern with Politics in Recent European Thought" in *EU*, p. 431.
30. Ibid., p. 430.

31. Ibid., p. 432.
32. Ibid.
33. Ibid., p. 433. Cf. Arendt's invocation of Heidegger's statement *"Das licht der offentlichkeit verdunkt alles"* in the Preface to Arendt, *Men in Dark Times* (New York: Harcourt, Brace, Jovanovich, 1968) (hereafter cited as *MDT*), p. x.
34. Ibid.
35. Ibid.
36. Ibid.
37. Ibid., p. 442.
38. Ibid., p. 441.
39. Ibid., p. 443.
40. Ibid., p. 444.
41. Ibid., p. 446.
42. Quoted in Ettinger, *Hannah Arendt/Martin Heidegger*, p. 114.
43. See Arendt's essay "What Is Freedom?" in Arendt, *Between Past and Future* (New York: Penguin, 1968).
44. See, in this regard, Heidegger's essays "The Age of the World Picture" and "The Question Concerning Technology," both in Heidegger, *The Question Concerning Technology and other Essays* (New York: Harper and Row, 1977). See also my *Arendt and Heidegger*, chap. 6.
45. See Arendt's Heidegger critique in Arendt, *The Life of the Mind* (New York: Harcourt, Brace, Jovanovich, 1978), vol. 2, chap. 15.
46. See Arendt, *The Human Condition* (Chicago: University of Chicago Press, 1958), chap. 6.
47. See Martin Heidegger, "Letter on Humanism" in Heidegger, *Basic Writings*, edited by David Farrel Krell (New York: Harper and Row, 1977).
48. See Arendt, *On Revolution* (New York: Penguin Books, 1990), p. 229: ". . . opinion and judgment obviously belong among the faculties of reason, but the point of the matter is that these two, politically most important, rational faculties have been almost entirely neglected by the tradition of political as well as philosophical thought."
49. It is hardly the case that Arendt denigrates such liberty, as her analyses of totalitarianism make clear. Her critical point, developed in *On Revolution*, is that being a "participant in government" and "public happiness" are the dimensions of freedom most cherished by those who have experienced them, but all to often seen as a needless burden by those who have not.
50. *Arendt—Jaspers Correspondence*, pp. 447, 453, and 457. Arendt recounts being snubbed by Fink during her visit in a letter dated August 6, 1961, in which she also tells Jaspers of Heidegger's failure to get in touch with her.
51. Young-Bruehl, *Hannah Arendt*, p. 442.

52. Ettinger, *Hannah Arendt–Martin Heidegger*, p. 10.
53. Wolin, "Hannah and the Magician," pp. 34–35.
54. Hannah Arendt, "Martin Heidegger at Eighty" in *Heidegger and Modern Philosophy*, edited by Michael Murray (New Haven: Yale University Press, 1978), p. 302.
55. See the text of Heidegger's interview with *Der Spiegel*, reprinted in *Martin Heidegger and National Socialism*, edited by Gunther Nesler and Emil Kettering (New York: Paragon House, 1990).
56. Rudiger Safranski, *Ein Meister aus Deutschland: Heidegger und seine Zeit* (Munich: Carl Hanser Verlag, 1994).
57. Arendt, "Martin Heidegger at Eighty," pp. 296–97.
58. Ibid., p. 299.
59. Ibid., p. 300.
60. Ibid., pp. 300–301.
61. Ibid., p. 301.
62. This paragraph outlines the argument Arendt makes in "Thinking and Moral Considerations."

CHAPTER FOUR
THINKING AND JUDGING

1. Hannah Arendt, "On Hannah Arendt," in Melvyn Hill, ed., *The Recovery of the Public World* (New York: St. Martin's Press, 1979), p. 308.
2. Ibid., pp. 304–5.
3. Hannah Arendt, "Thinking and Moral Considerations," in *Social Research*, vol. 51, nos. 1–2 (1984): 36.
4. Ibid., p. 8.
5. In *The Life of the Mind*, Arendt states that "the faculty of judging particulars (as brought to light by Kant), the ability to say 'this is wrong,' 'this is beautiful,'" and so on, is not the same as the faculty of thinking. Thinking deals with invisibles, with representations of things that are absent; judging always concern particulars and things close at hand. But the two are interrelated. . . ." See Hannah Arendt, *The Life of the Mind* (New York: Harcourt Brace Jovanovich, 1977), vol. 1, p. 193 (hereafter cited as *LM*). Cf. Arendt, *LM*, I, pp. 69, 70; and Arendt, "Thinking and Moral Considerations," p. 37.
6. See Arendt, "On Hannah Arendt," p. 305. For a very different account of the relation between thinking and acting in Arendt's political thought, see Leah Bradshaw, *Acting and Thinking: The Political Thought of Hannah Arendt* (Toronto: University of Toronto Press, 1989).
7. Hannah Arendt, "Ideology and Terror," in Arendt, *OT*.
8. I am guilty in this regard myself. See Villa, *Arendt and Heidegger*, chapter 3.

9. Richard Bernstein, "Judging—The Actor and the Spectator," in Bernstein, *Philosophical Profiles* (Philadelphia: University of Pennsylvania Press, 1986), p. 231.

10. Beiner, "Interpretive Essay," in Hannah Arendt, *Lectures on Kant's Political Philosophy* (Chicago: University of Chicago Press, 1982), p. 112.

11. Hannah Arendt, "Thinking and Moral Considerations," pp. 36–37.

12. Ibid., p. 37.

13. Ibid.

14. Arendt, "Thinking and Moral Considerations," p. 36.

15. Beiner, "Interpretive Essay" in Arendt, *Lectures on Kant's Political Philosophy*, p. 91.

16. Ibid.

17. Arendt, "The Crisis in Culture," in Hannah Arendt, *Between Past and Future* (New York: Penguin Books, 1968), pp. 221, 223–25. Hereafter cited as *BPF*.

18. See the Postscriptum to "Thinking," vol. 1 of *LM*, p. 216.

19. Arendt, *OT*, p. 469.

20. Ibid., pp. 470–71.

21. Ibid., p. 471.

22. Ibid., pp. 471–72.

23. Ibid.

24. Ibid., p. 473.

25. Ibid.

26. Plato, *Republic*, 493b–c.

27. Ibid., 464a–e.

28. Arendt, "What Is Authority?" in *BPF*, pp. 107–12.

29. Arendt, *HC*, pp. 225–27.

30. Ibid., p. 228.

31. Jean-Francois Lyotard, *Just Gaming*, trans. Wlad Godzich (Minneapolis: University of Minnesota Press, 1979), pp. 19–25.

32. As Arendt notes in her essay "What Is Authority?," the reduction of judgment to the activity of subsuming particulars under universals infects even Kant, who tends to view "determinant" judgment as more typical than the reflective mode (in which the universal is not given, but must be imagined or invented for the particular). See Arendt, *BPF*, p. 110–11. Cf. Arendt, *Lectures on Kant's Political Philosophy*, pp. 15, 61. For a general perspective on Kant's tendency to marginalize the role of judgment in moral matters, see Charles Larmore's *Patterns of Moral Complexity* (New York: Cambridge University Press, 1987), chap. 1.

33. The extent of Hobbes's "instrumentalist" approach to the political sphere is limited by his deep commitment to the right to life. See George Kateb's essay "The Liberal Contract" in his *The Inner Ocean* (Ithaca: Cor-

nell University Press, 1992). Plato of course views the subjects of the republic as "human material," to be sculpted (or discarded) by the political artist of character. Hegel famously noted in his *Lectures on the Philosophy of History* that "many an innocent flower" would be trampled as the Idea of freedom realized itself in history. That the proletarian revolution and the realization of human freedom would occur through violent means was, of course, a basic element of Marx's thought.

34. See Aristotle, *Politics*, bk. II, chap. 2 and bk. III, chap. 11. Cf. Arendt, "What Is Authority?" in *BPF*, pp. 116–19; and *Lectures on Kant's Political Philosophy*, p. 21.

35. Hannah Arendt, "Philosophy and Politics," *Social Research*, vol. 57, no. 1 (spring 1990): 73–74, 79 (hereafter *PP*).

36. Ibid., p. 75.

37. Ibid., p. 81.

38. Ibid. See the chapter "Arendt and Socrates" in this book.

39. Arendt, *On Revolution*, p. 229.

40. Arendt, "Truth and Politics" in *BPF*, pp. 240–41.

41. Ibid. p. 241.

42. Bernstein, "Judging—The Actor and the Spectator," p. 228.

43. Cf. Seyla Benhabib's essay, "Judgment and the Moral Foundations of Politics in Hannah Arendt's Thought" in Benhabib, *Situating the Self* (New York: Routledge, 1992); Albrecht Wellmer, "Hannah Arendt on Judgment: The Unwritten Doctrine of Reason," in Larry May and Jerome Kohn, editors, *Hannah Arendt: Twenty Years Later* (Cambridge: MIT Press, 1996); and Maurizio Passerin d'Entreves, *The Political Philosophy of Hannah Arendt* (New York: Routledge, 1994), chap. 3.

44. Arendt, "The Crisis in Culture," in *BPF*, pp. 221–22. Cf. Immanuel Kant, *The Critique of Judgment*, trans. Meredith (Oxford: Oxford University Press), p. 151; and Arendt's commentary in her *Lectures on Kant's Political Philosophy*, pp. 70–72.

45. Bernstein, "Judging—The Actor and the Spectator," p. 230.

46. See Seyla Benhabib, "Judgment and the Moral Foundations of Politics in Hannah Arendt's Thought," p. 121.

47. Bernstein, "Judging—The Actor and the Spectator," p. 233.

48. Ibid., p. 231.

49. To be fair, Bernstein points in the direction of "independent thought" or *Selbstdenken* in his essay, but tends to restrict its hermeneutical importance to thinking about Arendt's own activity as a writer and political thinker. See Bernstein, "Judging," p. 234.

50. In the former essay, Arendt emphasizes the difficulties confronting understanding and judgment in the wake of the "growth of meaninglessness" and "the loss of common sense"; in the latter essay she underlines the

"inability to judge" of mass man. See Arendt, *Essays in Understanding*, ed. Jerome Kohn (New York: Harcourt Brace Jovanovich, 1994), pp. 314–15; and Arendt, "The Crisis in Culture" in *BPF*, p. 199.

51. Ibid.

52. See Arendt's account of bourgeois hypocrisy and the reaction of the elite and the mob to it in *OT*, chaps. 5 and 10.

53. It is important to remember, in this regard, that Arendt wrote *HC*, her consideration of the *vita activa*, *not* in order to stimulate activism, but in order to help us "think what we are doing." See Arendt, *HC*, p. 5.

54. Arendt, *PP*, p. 81; "Thinking and Moral Considerations," p. 23; *Lectures on Kant's Political Philosophy*, pp. 37–39.

55. Arendt, "Thinking and Moral Considerations," p. 24.

56. Ibid., p. 25.

57. Arendt, comments at a 1973 conference sponsored by the American Society for Christian Ethics, cited in Elisabeth Young-Bruel, *Hannah Arendt: For Love of the World* (New Haven: Yale University Press, 1982), p. 452.

58. Arendt, "Thinking and Moral Considerations," p. 36.

59. Arendt, *Lectures on Kant's Political Philosophy*, pp. 38–39.

60. Immanuel Kant, cited by Arendt, Ibid., p. 43.

61. Ibid., pp. 42–43.

62. Ibid., p. 44. I disagree with those who view Arendt's notion of representative thinking as akin to empathy. See, for example, Lisa Disch, *Hannah Arendt and the Limits of Philosophy* (Ithaca: Cornell University Press, 1994).

63. Ibid., pp. 37–40.

64. I develop the affiliations between Arendt's theory of judgment and Nietzschean perspectivism in *Arendt and Heidegger*, chap. 3.

65. Friedrich Nietzsche, *On the Genealogy of Morals*, trans. Walter Kaufmann (New York: Vintage, 1989), III, 12.

66. Arendt, *Lectures on Kant's Political Philosophy*, p. 56.

67. Arendt, "Thinking and Moral Considerations," p. 36.

68. Arendt, *Lectures on Kant's Political Philosophy*, p. 65.

69. Arendt, "Thinking and Moral Considerations," p. 36.

70. Arendt, "Truth and Politics," in *BPF*, pp. 258, 264.

71. Hannah Arendt, *Eichmann in Jerusalem* (New York: Penguin Books, 1977), p. 252.

72. Arendt, "Thinking and Moral Considerations," p. 7.

73. Ibid., p. 13.

74. See Elisabeth Young-Bruehl's account of such reactions in her *Hannah Arendt: For Love of the World*, pp. 347–355.

75. Arendt, *Eichmann in Jerusalem*, pp. 25–26; 48–52.

76. It is important to note that, as a *judgment* of a particular, the "banal-

ity of evil" was not intended as a global redefinition of the *nature* of evil *tout court*. See chap. 2 of this book.

77. See Young-Bruehl, *Hannah Arendt*, pp. 347–48.

78. Arendt, "The Crisis in Culture" in *BPF*, p. 222.

79. "The Perversity of Brilliance" is the title of a review written by Norman Podhoretz. The Scholem quote is from an exchange of letters between him and Arendt included in Hannah Arendt, *The Jew as Pariah*, edited by Ron H. Feldman (New York: Grove Press, 1978, pp. 241, 245.

80. See my chapter "Conscience, the Banality of Evil, and the Idea of a Representative Perpetrator" in this volume.

81. Walter Benjamin, "Theses on the Philosophy of History" in *Illuminations*, edited by Hannah Arendt (New York: Schocken Books, 1968), p. 261.

CHAPTER FIVE
DEMOCRATIZING THE AGON: NIETZSCHE, ARENDT, AND THE
AGONISTIC TENDENCY IN RECENT POLITICAL THEORY

1. See Sheldon Wolin, "Fugitive Democracy," and Chantal Mouffe, "Democracy, Power, and the Political," both in *Democracy and Difference*, edited by Seyla Benhabib (Princeton: Princeton University Press, 1996); Bonnie Honig, *Political Theory and the Displacement of Politics* (Ithaca: Cornell University Press, 1993); and William E. Connolly, "A Critique of Pure Politics," *Philosophy and Social Criticism*, vol. 23, no. 5 (1998). I should note that Wolin is the most expressly critical of Arendt's agonism and Nietzsche's influence upon her, while the others tend to wish that she were more consistently Nietzschean. See Wolin's essay "Hannah Arendt: Democracy and the Political" in *Hannah Arendt: Critical Essays*, edited by Lewis P. Hinchman and Sandra K. Hinchman (Albany: State University of New York Press, 1994). However, as "Fugitive Democracy" and his essay "What Revolutionary Action Means Today" (in *Dimensions of Radical Democracy*, edited by Chantal Mouffe [New York: Verso, 1992]) demonstrate, Wolin's participatory stance is quite consistent with a democratized (anti-aristocratic) agonism.

2. See John Rawls, *Political Liberalism* (New York: Columbia University Press, 1993), and Charles Larmore, "Political Liberalism," in Larmore, *The Morals of Modernity* (New York: Cambridge University Press), 1996.

3. Michael Sandel, *Democracy's Discontent* (Cambridge, MA: Harvard University Press, 1996).

4. These are not Sandel's terms, but it is helpful to be reminded of the classical liberal divide so fiercely attacked by Rousseau and Marx. For a defense of political (Rawlsian) liberalism's continued insistence upon some form of this distinction, see Larmore's essay "Political Liberalism."

5. See Martin Jay's "Afterword" to *Hannah Arendt and the Meaning of Politics*, edited by Craig Calhoun and John McGowan (Minneapolis: University of Minnesota Press, 1997), p. 348.

6. See Richard Sennett, *The Fall of Public Man* (New York: W. W. Norton, 1992), and Michel Foucault, *The History of Sexuality*, vol. 1 (New York: Vintage, 1976).

7. I borrow the latter phrase from Seyla Benhabib. See her Introduction to *Democracy and Difference*, p. 9.

8. Of course, Nietzsche recognizes his own participation in the "will to truth" and the Socratic project, broadly conceived. The pertinent reflections are in *On the Genealogy of Morals*, essay III. For a sophisticated account of the seeming paradox, see Alexander Nehamas, *Nietzsche: Life as Literature* (Cambridge, MA: Harvard University Press, 1985).

9. Nietzsche, *On the Genealogy of Morals*, trans. Kaufmann, I, 10 (hereafter cited as *GM*).

10. Friedrich Nietzsche, *Beyond Good and Evil*, translated by Walter Kaufmann (New York: Vintage Books, 1989), pp. 115–16 (hereafter cited as *BGE*). Cf. Nietzsche, *GM*, I, 16.

11. Ibid., p. 113. This theme is central to both Hobbes and Kant, who both viewed political discord as arising from competitive "vainglory."

12. See Friedrich Nietzsche, *Twilight of the Idols*, translated R. J. Hollingdale (New York: Penguin Books, 1990), p. 133, "My conception of freedom"; also *BGE*, pp. 110–11 and 117–18; and *GM*, III, 14.

13. Nietzsche, *GM*, II, 12.

14. See the famous passage in Friedrich Nietzsche, *The Gay Science*, translated by Walter Kaufmann (New York: Random House, 1974), section 290, where he lays out his conception of self-fashioning.

15. Michel Foucault, *Discipline and Punish*, translated by Alan Sheridan (New York: Vintage Books, 1979).

16. John Stuart Mill, *On Liberty*, edited by David Spitz (New York: Norton, 1975), p. 59.

17. See Michel Foucault, "The Subject and Power," Afterword to Hubert Dreyfus and Paul Rabinow, *Michel Foucault: Beyond Structuralism and Hermeneutics* (Chicago: University Of Chicago Press, 1983).

18. See Benjamin Barber, *Strong Democracy* (Berkeley: University of California Press, 1984) for a defense of action as the central political problem.

19. Hannah Arendt, *Between Past and Future* (New York: Penguin, 1968), p. 151 (hereafter cited as *BPF*); *The Human Condition* (Chicago: University of Chicago Press, 1958), p. 177 (hereafter cited as *HC*); *On Revolution* (New York: Penguin Books, 1990), p. 21 (hereafter cited as *OR*). Cf. Nietzsche, "The Utility and Liability of History," pp. 90–91, 96–102.

20. Nietzsche, *GM*, I, 13.

21. Arendt, *OR*, pp. 30–31. Of course, Arendt follows the Greeks in viewing equality as a political status accorded to citizens, rather than as an attribute of human beings as such, or as a broader social ideal.

22. Arendt, *HC*, pp. 188–89.

23. Arendt, *OR*, p. 30.

24. Arendt, *HC*, pp. 17–18.

25. See Arendt, *OR*, chap. 6, and *BPF*, Preface.

26. Honig, *Political Theory and the Displacement of Politics*, p. 77. See also my essay "Postmodernism and the Public Sphere," *American Political Science Review*, 86, no. 3 (September 1992): 712–21.

27. Arendt, *HC*, p. 40.

28. See especially Arendt's discussions in "What Is Authority?" (in *BPF*) and *OR*, chap. 5. I discuss Arendt's antifoundationalism at length in Villa, *Arendt and Heidegger: the Fate of the Political* (Princeton: Princeton University Press, 1996).

29. Honig, *Political Theory and the Displacement of Politics*, p. 116. See also Chantal Mouffe, *The Return of the Political* (New York: Verso, 1993), p. 14

30. See Arendt, *HC*, pp. 57–58.

31. Wolin, "Hannah Arendt: Democracy and the Political," p. 290. Wolin specifically attacks Arendt's Nietzschean inheritance, viewing it as the source of her disdain for the "masses" and her aristocratic preference for a politics of "lofty ambition, glory, and honor" rather than one essentially concerned with questions of social justice.

32. Connolly, "A Critique of Pure Politics," p. 17.

33. This has been a frequent charge in the critical literature generated by Arendt. See, for example, Hanna Pitkin's essay "Justice: On Relating Public and Private," in Hinchman and Hinchman, eds., *Hannah Arendt: Critical Essays*.

34. Honig, *Political Theory and the Displacement of Politics*, pp. 118–23.

35. See Aristotle, *The Politics*, Bk. III, chaps. 6 and 7. See also George Kateb's discussion in his *Hannah Arendt: Politics, Conscience, Evil* (Totowa, NJ: Rowman and Allanheld, 1983), pp. 18–19.

36. One genuine problem with political liberalism is that it frames constitutional essentials or basic principles as beyond argument. There is an extremely broad sense in which this must be true (for example, the principle of equal rights under the law); however, the tendency of political liberals is to pack the maximum possible content under the rubric of "constitutional essentials." See, for example, Larmore's discussion in "Political Liberalism," pp. 135–36.

37. For reasons set out below, I think Honig's assertion that Arendt sets up a "public-private distinction that is beyond contestation" (*Political*

Theory and the Displacement of Politics, p. 119) misses the point of Arendt's insistence on the distinction.

38. Wolin, "Fugitive Democracy," pp. 37, 43.

39. Honig, *Political Theory and the Displacement of Politics,* pp. 85–86, 103. There is an uncontroversial sense in which Honig's interpretation is correct, for like Hobbes and the social contract tradition generally, Arendt sees agreement, rather than tradition, nature, or the Deity, setting the terms of political association. But Honig wants to go further than this, insisting that nothing but a *practice* or performative speech act underlies the establishment of an arena for agonistic *praxis.* Arendt's suspicions concerning the will in politics (and particularly Rousseau's formulation of its fundamental or grounding role), should make us somewhat skeptical of this reading. For her, promising creates a binding web of obligation, artificial but permanent, a worldly structure that stands independent of continued willing or nilling. See Arendt, *BPF,* pp.163–64.

40. See my chapter "Theatricality and the Public Realm" in this volume.

41. See Arendt, *HC,* pp. 55–77.

42. Arendt, *BPF,* p. 153.

43. Honig emphasizes action as a *performative* in Arendt, drawing on J. L. Austin's work to conceptualize speech that is also a deed. She ignores, however, the explicitly theatrical dimension of Arendt's theory of political action.

44. Wolin, "Hannah Arendt: Democracy and the Political," p. 303; Honig, *Political Theory and the Displacement of Politics,* pp. 77–84; Connolly, "A Critique of Pure Politics," *passim.* I should note that whereas Honig thinks Arendt celebrates a Nietzschean "multiple self," Connolly sees her denial of the body as placing her in the mainstream of Western philosophical thought.

45. Connolly, "A Critique of Pure Politics," p. 21. See also William E. Connolly, *The Ethos of Pluralization* (Minneapolis: University of Minnesota Press), 1995.

46. Rawls, *Political Liberalism,* pp. xxiv–xxvi.

47. Ibid., p. xxiv.

48. Honig proposes a similar strategy, arguing that the Nietzschean idea of the "subject as multiplicity" enables a democratization of the overman, in which the latter is seen not as a peculiar and rare subject or caste, but as a part of the self—indeed, of all selves. See Honig, *Political Theory and the Displacement of Politics,* p. 65.

49. Arendt, *HC,* p. 57 (my emphasis).

50. This, obviously, was the result of her experience and analysis of totalitarianism. See especially her essay "Ideology and Terror" included in Arendt, *OT.*

51. Arendt, *BPF,* p. 241.

52. Ibid., p. 242. Cf. pp. 219–22 and Arendt, *Lectures on Kant's Political Philosophy*, edited by Ronald Beiner (Chicago: University of Chicago Press, 1982).

53. Nietzsche, *GM*, III, 12.

54. See Wolin, "Fugitive Democracy," along with the essays in Sheldon Wolin, *The Presence of the Past: Essays on the State and Constitution* (Baltimore: The Johns Hopkins University Press, 1989).

55. Arendt, *Men in Dark Times* (New York: Harcourt Brace Jovanovich, 1968), p. 30.

CHAPTER SIX
THEATRICALITY AND THE PUBLIC REALM

1. Hannah Arendt, *The Human Condition* (Chicago: University of Chicago Press, 1958). (Hereafter cited as *HC*.)

2. Hannah Arendt, *OR*; Hannah Arendt, *Crises of the Republic*.

3. Maurizio Passerin d'Entreves, *The Political Philosophy of Hannah Arendt* (New York: Routledge, 1994), p. 84. I note a similar tension in my study of Arendt. See Villa, *Arendt and Heidegger*, pp. 54–55.

4. Ibid., p. 85.

5. Seyla Benhabib, "Models of Public Space: Hannah Arendt, the Liberal Tradition, and Jurgen Habermas," in Calhoun, ed., *Habermas and the Public Sphere* (Cambridge: MIT Press, 1992), pp. 77–78; Seyla Benhabib, *The Reluctant Modernism of Hannah Arendt* (Thousand Oaks: Sage Publications, Inc., 1996), p. 125. Benhabib also cites the passage from d'Entreves.

6. Benhabib, "Models of Public Space," p. 78.

7. Benhabib, *The Reluctant Modernism of Hannah Arendt*, p. 125.

8. Benhabib, "Models of Public Space," p. 78.

9. Ibid., p. 79.

10. Ibid., p. 95.

11. Ibid., p. 76.

12. I have attempted a similar project, albeit from a very different direction, in my essay "Postmodernism and the Public Sphere," *American Political Science Review* 86 (1992): 712–21.

13. Jurgen Habermas, *The Structural Transformation of the Public Realm*, translated by Thomas Berger (Cambridge: MIT Press, 1989), hereafter cited as *ST*; Richard Sennett, *The Fall of Public Man* (New York: W. W. Norton and Co., 1976).

14. See Jean Cohen and Andrew Arato, *Civil Society and Political Theory* (Cambridge: MIT Press, 1992), chap. 4.

15. Hannah Arendt, "On Violence" in *Crises of the Republic*, p. 143.

16. Hannah Arendt, "On Humanity in Dark Times" in Arendt, *MDT*, pp. 3–31.

17. Ibid., p. 8.

18. Ibid., p. 24.

19. Ibid., p. 30.

20. Arendt, *HC*, p. 50.

21. Ibid., p. 52.

22. Ibid.

23. Ibid., pp. 50–51. The phenomenon Arendt is tracing in these pages, and in *HC* generally, has much in common with the "subjectification of the real" addressed by Heidegger in such texts as his essay "The Age of the World Picture." For a discussion of this relation, see Villa, *Arendt and Heidegger*, especially chap. 6.

24. *HC*, p. 53.

25. See Arendt's discussion in her essay "The Crisis in Culture" in *BPF*.

26. This is an aspect of Arendt I did not see clearly enough when writing my study of the relation of her political theory to Heidegger's philosophy. It also makes me dubious of the definition of worldliness George Kateb gives in his fine study, *Hannah Arendt: Politics, Conscience, Evil*, p. 2, where he calls worldliness "a common commitment to the reality, beauty, and sufficiency of the culture or way of life that sustains political action, as well as a commitment to political action itself." By so framing worldliness as that which contributes to the sustenance of political action, Kateb overly restricts the resonance of Arendt's term.

27. Hannah Arendt, "Ideology and Terror" in Arendt, *OT*. As Benhabib notes, even under totalitarian regimes, it is a bit misleading to say that the public realm is destroyed, or that worldliness becomes impossible. More often than not, there is a kind of migration of the public sphere, and the creation of a kind of "underground" public. See Benhabib, *The Reluctant Modernism of Hannah Arendt*, pp. 69–75.

28. Arendt, *OR*, pp. 74–75, 269.

29. Arendt, *BPF*, p. 153.

30. See, for example, Hanna Pitkin, "Justice: On Relating the Public and the Private" in Hinchman and Hinchman, eds., *Hannah Arendt: Critical Essays*, p. 272.

31. See Arendt, *HC*, pp. 176–79.

32. Arendt, *OR*, pp. 98–109 (chap. 2, section 5).

33. Ibid., p. 101.

34. Ibid.

35. Ibid.

36. Ibid.

37. For Arendt, this politics has no built-in stopping point: everyone, including the original unmaskers, can be revealed as hypocrites. Hence the origin of revolutionary terror and the phenomenon of the revolution devouring its own children.

38. In her essay "Civil Disobedience" in *Crises in the Republic*, Arendt gives a reading of Socrates at odds with the one outlined here. The later essay presents Socratic moral integrity as a kind of self-interest, to be contrasted with the worldliness of Machiavelli's civic republicanism. Machiavelli's *cri de coeur*—"I love my city more than my soul"—obviously stands in stark opposition to the lesson Socrates was trying to teach his fellow Athenians. All the more reason, then, to be surprised by the use Arendt makes of this pair in attacking the emergent politics of authenticity in the French Revolution.

39. Arendt, *BPF*, pp. 152, 151.

40. Ibid., p.152.

41. Ibid.

42. Ibid.

43. Kateb, *Hannah Arendt*, p. 12.

44. See Villa, *Arendt and Heidegger*, pp. 90–92 for a discussion of this point.

45. It's fairly clear that Arendt is writing against the Rousseau, Schiller, Hegel, Marx sequence, which attempts to overcome the dichotomy of *homme* and *citoyen*.

46. Benhabib, *The Reluctant Modernism of Hannah Arendt*, pp. 126–27.

47. Ibid., pp. 125–26.

48. Ibid., p. 127.

49. See Jurgen Habermas, *The Philosophical Discourse of Modernity*, translated by Frederick Lawrence (Cambridge: MIT Press, 1987).

50. Ibid., p. 111.

51. Ibid., p. 127. As Benhabib puts it "Narrative action is ubiquitous, for it is the stuff out of which all human social life . . . is constituted." Benhabib draws this point out more fully in chapt. 4 of her book, pp. 107–13. Cf. her earlier discussion of the Arendtian idea of plurality in Benhabib, *Critique, Norm, and Utopia* (New York: Columbia University Press, 1986), p. 241ff.

52. Ibid., pp. 112–13.

53. Ibid., chap. 1, pp. 14–22.

54. Ibid., p. 145.

55. Ibid., p. 201.

56. Ibid., p. 200.

57. Habermas, *ST*, pp. 177–78.

58. Arendt, *HC*, pp. 38–49. See Hanna Fenichel Pitkin's skeptical treatment of this Arendtian theme in Pitkin, *The Attack of the Blob: Hannah Arendt's Concept of the Social* (Chicago: University of Chicago Press, 1998).

59. Habermas, *ST*, p. 28.

60. Ibid., p. 27.

61. Ibid., p. 29.

62. Ibid., pp. 54–56.

63. Ibid., pp. 90–101.

64. Habermas cites Guizot's classic formulation in this regard. See Habermas, ibid., p. 101.

65. Ibid., pp. 106–7. Of course, Habermas criticizes Kant for his limitation of the public sphere to those who are property owners, and turns to Hegel and Marx in order to draw out the "contradictions" of the bourgeois public sphere (see *ST*, pp. 110, 117–29). Nevertheless, his enthusiasm for the Kantian formulation of legitimation through a public test of universalization is unmistakable, and forms the basis for much of his subsequent work on a deliberative conception of democracy.

66. Ibid., pp. 132–40.

67. Ibid., p. 135.

68. Ibid., pp. 159–74.

69. Ibid., p. 162.

70. Ibid., p. 163.

71. Ibid. p. 164.

72. Ibid., p. 177.

73. Ibid., p. 178.

74. Ibid., pp. 195, 5–8.

75. Ibid., p. 221.

76. Ibid., p. 234.

77. See, especially, the critique of rhetoric in Plato's *Gorgias*, 459d–467a.

78. See Sennett, *Fall of Public Man*, pp. 31–32 for how he distinguishes his approach from Habermas's.

79. Ibid., p. 259.

80. Ibid.

81. Ibid.

82. Ibid., p. 107.

83. Ibid., pp. 109–10 (Sennett quoting Fielding).

84. Sennett cites, amusingly, a French pamphlet against floating a loan from 1758, in which the author's opponents are described as "Scaly monkeys, slaves of the dung hill on which they gibber" (p. 100).

85. Sennett contrasts this attitude with the "trial by character" evident in both sides of the Dreyfus Affair, paying particular attention to the rhetoric of Zola's *J'accuse* (pp. 240–51). He concludes: "Trial by character is the only way politics can proceed once the line between public and private has been erased" (p. 248). This is all the more relevant given the impeachment proceedings mounted against President Bill Clinton, in which "trial by character" becomes the excuse for what amounts to a procedural *coup d'état*.

86. Ibid., p. 264.
87. Ibid., pp. 40–41; 90–92.
88. Ibid., p. 82.
89. Ibid., p. 37.
90. Ibid., p.20.
91. Ibid., p. 25.
92. Ibid., p. 25.
93. Ibid., p. 237.
94. Ibid.
95. Ibid.
96. Ibid., p. 261.
97. See, in this regard, Arendt's essay "The Crisis in Culture" in *BPF*.
98. Charles Larmore, *The Morals of Modernity*, p. 12.
99. See Habermas, *ST*, pp. 234–35. For a sympathetic critique of this strand of Habermas's thinking see Thomas McCarthy's essay, "Practical Discourse: On the Relation of Morality to Politics" in Calhoun, ed., *Habermas and the Public Sphere*.

CHAPTER SEVEN
THE PHILOSOPHER VERSUS THE CITIZEN: ARENDT,
STRAUSS, AND SOCRATES

1. John Gunnell, *Political Theory: Tradition and Interpretation* (Cambridge, MA: Winthrop Publishers, 1979).
2. See Hannah Arendt, "Preface" and "Tradition and the Modern Age" in *BPF*; and Leo Strauss, *The City and Man* (Chicago: The University of Chicago Press, 1978) pp. 1–3 and *Natural Right and History* (Chicago: University of Chicago Press, 1953), pp. 3–6. These works hereafter cited as *CM* and *NRH*, respectively.
3. Hannah Arendt, *MDT*, pp. 201–6. Strauss, *CM*, p. 9.
4. Karl Lowith and Leo Strauss, "Correspondence Concerning Modernity," *Independent Journal of Philosophy* 4 (1983): 107–8 and 113. See also Leo Strauss, *Liberalism, Ancient and Modern* (Chicago: University of Chicago Press, 1995) pp. 19–20, 24 (hereafter cited as *LAM*).
5. See my essay "Socrates, Lessing and Thoreau: The Image of Alienated Citizenship in Hannah Arendt," in Austin Sarat and Dana Villa, eds., *Liberal Modernism and Democratic Individuality* (Princeton: Princeton University Press, 1996).
6. Margaret Canovan, *Hannah Arendt: A Reinterpretation of her Political Thought* (New York: Cambridge University Press, 1992), p. 257.
7. Much has been written about how Arendt gets the nature of the *polis* wrong, anachronistically positing a rigid divide between the realm of

freedom, the public space of the assembly, and that of necessity, the household. See, for example, Bernard Yack, *The Problems of a Political Animal* (Berkeley: University of California Press, 1993) pp. 11–13. I think such objections presume what they need to show, viz., that Arendt's "ideal type" was intended as a historical representation.

8. Hannah Arendt, *OR*, p. 31.
9. Arendt, *BPF*, pp. 51–52.
10. Arendt, *HC*, pp. 26–27.
11. Hannah Arendt, *PP*, 80.
12. Arendt, *HC*, p. 57.
13. Arendt, *PP*, p. 81.
14. Ibid., p. 82.
15. Ibid., p. 84.
16. Arendt, *PP*, p. 85.
17. Ibid., p. 86.
18. Hannah Arendt, "Thinking and Moral Considerations," in *Social Research: Fiftieth Anniversary Issue*, 1984, p. 8 (hereafter cited as *TMC*).
19. Arendt, "What Is Authority?" in *BPF*.
20. Arendt, *HC*, p. 222.
21. Arendt, *BPF*, p. 91.
22. Ibid., p. 92.
23. Ibid., p. 93.
24. Ibid.
25. Ibid., pp. 104–5.
26. Ibid., pp. 107–8.
27. Ibid., p. 97.
28. Ibid., p. 110.
29. Ibid. See also Arendt's comments on the Categorical Imperative in "On Humanity in Dark Times" in *MDT*, p. 27.
30. Arendt, *MDT*, p. 27.
31. Hannah Arendt, "Understanding and Politics" in *Partisan Review* 20 (1953): 379. Arendt tended to exaggerate the extent to which our tradition "lies in ruins," largely as a result of her reading of the significance of European fascism and totalitarianism. Not only did these regimes commit utterly novel crimes; in her view, they were made possible by the internal collapse of the West's most fundamental moral propositions.
32. Ibid., p. 391.
33. Hannah Arendt in *Hannah Arendt: The Recovery of the Public World*, ed. Melvin Hill (New York: St. Martin's Press, 1976), p. 315.
34. Arendt, *TMC*, p. 25; *Kant Lectures*, p. 38.
35. Ibid., p. 36.
36. Ibid., p. 37.
37. Ibid., p. 37.

38. See Margaret Canovan's *Hannah Arendt: A Reinterpretation of her Political Thought* for a presentation of Arendt's "new" republicanism.

39. Arendt, *TMC*, p. 25; *Lectures on Kant's Political Philosophy*, pp. 36–38.

40. Strauss, *CM*, pp. 20–21.

41. Arendt, *HC*, p. 20.

42. Strauss, *CM*, pp. 20, 29.

43. Ibid.

44. Strauss, *NRH*, p. 124.

45. Arendt, *PP*, p. 81.

46. Strauss, *What Is Political Philosophy? And Other Studies* (Chicago: University of Chicago Press, 1988) (hereafter *WIPP*), pp. 11–12 (my emphasis). Cf., however, the formulation Strauss gives in *NRH*, p. 162.

47. Ibid., p. 12.

48. Strauss, "On Classical Political Philosophy" in *WIPP*, pp. 84, 81.

49. Ibid., pp. 15–16.

50. Ibid., p. 17.

51. Strauss, *CM*, p. 3.

52. Ibid., p.23; also *NRH*, chapter 2.

53. Ibid., pp. 26–27.

54. Ibid., p. 27.

55. Strauss, *CM*, p. 11.

56. Strauss, *NRH*, p. 12.

57. Strauss, "An Introduction to Heideggerian Existentialism" in *The Rebirth of Classical Political Rationalism*, edited by Thomas Pangle (Chicago: University of Chicago Press, 1989), p. 37. Hereafter cited as *RCPR*.

58. This is a standard view of Strauss. See, e.g., Charles Larmore's description of Strauss's project, "The Secret Philosophy of Leo Strauss," in his *The Morals of Modernity* (New York: Cambridge University Press, 1996), p. 66, where he writes of Strauss's "metaphysical conception of reason."

59. See Strauss, *CM*, p. 11: "We cannot reasonably expect that a fresh understanding of classical political philosophy will supply us with recipes for today's use."

60. Arendt, *LM*, p. 10.

61. Ibid. Cf. Strauss, *CM*, p. 9.

62. Hannah Arendt, "The Concern for Politics in Recent European Philosophical Thought," in *EU*, pp. 432–33.

63. Ibid.

64. Leo Strauss, *Persecution and the Art of Writing* (Glencoe, IL: The Free Press, 1952), pp. 155–56. See Jurgen Gebhardt's discussion in his "Leo Strauss: The Quest for Truth" in *Hannah Arendt and Leo Strauss: German Emigres and American Political Thought after World War II*, edited by Peter G. Kielmansegg, Horst Mewes, and Elisabeth Glaser-Schmidt (New York: Cambridge University Press, 1995), pp. 101–2.

65. Strauss, "On Collingwood's Philosophy of History," quoted by Gebhardt, in *Hannah Arendt and Leo Strauss*, ed. Kielmansegg, et al., p. 100.

66. Strauss, *CM*, pp. 11-12.

67. Strauss, *NRH*, p. 124.

68. Strauss, *CM*, pp. 119-20; *NRH*, pp. 122-23. See Thomas Pangle's remarks on Strauss's "new interpretation of the Ideas" in his Introduction to Leo Strauss, *Studies in Platonic Political Philosophy* (Chicago: University of Chicago Press, 1983), pp. 2-5. Emphasizing Strauss's incredulity at the notion that the ideas are "self-subsisting, being at home as it were in an entirely different place from human beings" (*CM*, p. 119), Pangle argues that Strauss nevertheless took the doctrine of ideas seriously "insofar as it appears to provide a sound way of conceiving our experience of the nature of things." So viewed, the doctrine of ideas is merely the extension of the logic of the "class character" presumed by Socrates' "What is . . . .?" questions. It expresses the attempt of Socratic dialectic to "ascend from the many local and temporary particulars to their universal and lasting (transhistorical, though not necessarily eternal) class characteristics . . . ." (p. 3).

69. Strauss, *WIPP*, p. 34. Here Strauss defines "regime" in terms of the dominance of one particular kind of character (e.g., democratic, aristocratic, tyrannical, etc.) and describes classical political philosophy as the quest for the best regime. The notion of political society as a school is readily apparent in "Liberal Education and Responsibility" in *LAM* (pp. 20-21) and in his essays on Aristotle and Plato in *CM* (see especially pp. 25-27; 33-34; 38-41). See also Strauss, *NRH*, pp. 153-56. Cf. Arendt, "What Is Authority?" in *BPF*, pp. 116-19.

70. Strauss, *RCPR*, pp. 139; 150-54.

71. Strauss, *RCPR*, p. 152; *CM*, p. 54.

72. Strauss, *RCPR*, p. 154; *LAM* pp. 6-7; *Studies in Platonic Political Philosophy*, p. 47; *CM*, p. 54.

73. Strauss, *RCPR*, p. 163. For the relation between civic and genuine (philosophical) virtue, see p. 133. See also *CM*, pp. 25-28, and *NRH*, pp. 138-43. For the relation between the virtue of the "gentleman" and that of the "vulgar," see *LAM*, pp. 11-14, 16.

74. Strauss, *LAM*, p. 13-14. See also the discussion of "citizen morality" in *NRH*, pp. 149, 151.

75. Ibid. See Ronald Beiner's discussion in his "Hannah Arendt and Leo Strauss: The Uncommenced Dialogue," *Political Theory* 18, no. 2 (1990): 247-49.

76. Strauss, *RCPR*, pp. 161-62.

77. Strauss, *CM*, p. 20. Cf. *WIPP*, p. 11. See Steven Smith's essay, "*Destruktion* or Recovery? Leo Strauss's Critique of Heidegger," *Review of*

Metaphysics 51, no. 2 (1997): 345–77. Smith makes a powerful argument for what I call the "skeptical" Strauss.

78. Strauss, *NRH*, pp. 270, 278; Cf. *LAM*, p. 14.

79. See Strauss, *NRH*, pp. 284–85, where he warns of the possibility, indeed likelihood, of the "natural-right teacher" identifying natural right "with those notions of justice that are cherished by his own society." Cf. the more "pious" statements found in the Introduction to the same work, particularly p. 5: "The contemporary rejection of natural right leads to nihilism—nay, it is identical with nihilism." With regard to historicism's encouragement of the reduction of morality to convention, see *WIPP*, p. 71.

80. Strauss, *LAM*, p. 20.

81. Strauss, *RCPR*, pp. 160, 162; *CM*, p. 121.

82. Strauss, *NRH*, p. 124.

83. In his chapter on Strauss in *The Anatomy of Antiliberalism* (Cambridge, MA: Harvard University Press, 1993), Stephen Holmes presses the gap between the Nietzschean truths "philosophers" (in Strauss's sense) are able to ingest and the metaphysical noble lies the masses require if order is to be maintained. I think Holmes goes too far in his characterization of Strauss's motivation for maintaining the classical distinction between the philosophical few and the unphilosophical many. Nevertheless, there is more than a grain of truth to Holmes's focus on Strauss's worry about "harmful truths" and his Platonic desire to foster "beneficial lies," that is, to bolster the metaphysical dimension of popular political culture.

84. Strauss, *RCPR*, p. 171; *CM*, pp. 54–55; *NRH*, pp. 1–2; *LAM*, pp. 16–17. See Holmes's discussion, pp. 63–66; also Kateb's remarks in *Hannah Arendt and Leo Strauss*, ed. Kielmansegg, et al., p. 41. Cf. Arendt, *Kant Lectures*, pp. 35–36.

85. Strauss, *NRH*, p. 143; *CM*, p. 37.

86. Arendt, *PP*, pp. 86–89. See also her essay on Lessing, "On Humanity in Dark Times" in *MDT*, especially pp. 7–11, which frames such thinking in a more explicitly worldly form.

87. Hannah Arendt, "Martin Heidegger at Eighty," in Murray, ed., *Heidegger and Modern Philosophy*.

88. Arendt, *MDT*, p. 13.

89. Strauss, *RCPR*, pp. 150–53.

90. Ibid., p. 133: "Philosophy is primarily political philosophy because philosophy is the ascent from the most obvious, the most massive, the most urgent, to what is highest in dignity. Philosophy is primarily political philosophy because political philosophy is required for protecting the inner sanctum of philosophy."

91. Ibid., p. 161; *LAM*, p. 13; *CM*, pp. 28–29: *NRH*, p. 151.

92. Strauss, *RCPR*, p. 60.

93. Compare, in this regard, the closing of Arendt's *On Revolution* with Strauss's characterization of the theme of political philosophy in "On Classical Political Philosophy" in *RCPR*.

94. See George Kateb's and Robert Pippin's comments in the Roundtable Discussion in *Hannah Arendt and Leo Strauss*, ed. Kielmansegg, et al., pp. 166–68.

95. Strauss, *LAM*, p. 8. Cf. Arendt, *Lectures on Kant's Political Philosophy*, pp. 22–25.

96. It is interesting to note, in this regard, that Arendt conceived *The Human Condition* as a *criticism* of the traditional dichotomy between the *vita activa* and the *vita contemplativa*. See Jerome Kohn's essay "Evil and Plurality" in *Hannah Arendt: Twenty Years Later*, ed. Kohn and May, p. 176, note 26.

97. Charles Larmore, "The Secret Philosophy of Leo Strauss," in *The Morals of Modernity*, p. 66.

98. George Kateb, "The Questionable Influence of Hannah Arendt and Leo Strauss," in *Hannah Arendt and Leo Strauss*, ed. Kielmansegg, et al., p. 33.

99. Strauss, *WIPP*, p. 47.

100. The quoted phrase is from Richard Rorty, "The Priority of Democracy to Philosophy," in his *Objectivism, Relativism, and Truth* (New York: Cambridge University Press, 1991), p. 176.

101. See, for example, Strauss, *NRH*, pp. 125–30.

102. Arendt, *TMC*, p. 13.

103. I am thinking especially of the work of Walzer and Rorty.

104. Michael Walzer, *Interpretation and Social Criticism* (Cambridge, MA: Harvard University Press, 1987), p. 60.

105. Kateb in *Hannah Arendt and Leo Strauss*, ed. Kielmannsegg, et al., p. 43.

106. John Rawls, "Justice as Fairness: Political, Not Metaphysical," *Philosophy & Public Affairs* 14, no. 3 (summer 1985): 230.

CHAPTER EIGHT
TOTALITARIANISM, MODERNITY, AND THE TRADITION

1. See, for example, Stuart Hampshire's characterization of the Nazi regime in his *Innocence and Experience* (Cambridge, MA: Harvard University Press, 1989), pp. 66–72.

2. This is precisely what John Gunnell has done in his stimulating study, *Political Theory: Tradition and Interpretation* (Cambridge, MA: Winthrop Publishers, 1979).

3. See Elisabeth Young-Bruehl, *Hannah Arendt: For Love of the World* (New Haven: Yale University Press, 1983) pp. 200–203 for a good discussion of Arendt's general approach to totalitarianism as a phenomenon, one that emphasized understanding rather than causal explanation.

4. In a note to her essay "Martin Heidegger at Eighty" in *Heidegger and Modern Philosophy*, edited by Michael Murray (New Haven: Yale University Press, 1978), Arendt writes "We are still surrounded by intellectuals and so-called scholars, not only in Germany, who, instead of speaking of Hitler, Auschwitz, genocide, and 'extermination' as a policy of permanent depopulation, prefer, according to their inspiration and taste, to refer to Plato, Luther, Hegel, Nietzsche, or to Heidegger, Junger, or Stefan George, in order to dress up the horrible gutter-born phenomenon with the language of the humanities and the history of ideas" (p. 302).

5. See, for example, Arendt's remarks in the lecture "Concern with Politics in Recent European Thought" in *EU*, p. 431, or those in her tribute to Heidegger in "Martin Heidegger at Eighty" in *Heidegger and Modern Philosophy*, p. 302.

6. Arendt, "A Reply to Eric Voegelin" in *EU*, p. 405.

7. Hannah Arendt, "Understanding and Politics" in *EU*, p. 309.

8. See the second sentence of Arendt's "The Nature of Totalitarianism": "Totalitarianism is the most radical denial of human freedom" (p. 328).

9. Hannah Arendt, "What Is Authority?" in Arendt, *BPF*, pp. 95–97. See also Arendt, "Ideology and Terror: A Form of Government" (hereafter cited as *IT*) in *Totalitarianism: Part Three of the Origins of Totalitarianism* (New York: Harcourt Brace Jovanovich, 1968), p. 159; and Arendt, "On the Nature of Totalitarianism: An Essay in Understanding" (hereafter cited as *NT*) in Arendt, *EU*, p. 331.

10. Arendt, *NT*, pp. 339, 353. Cf. Arendt, *IT*, p. 172.

11. Arendt, *NT*, pp. 336–37.

12. Ibid., p. 330.

13. Arendt, *OT*, p. 456; *MT*, p. 304; *NT*, pp. 328, 342.

14. Arendt, *OT*, p. 457.

15. Arendt, *MT*, pp. 297–98; also *NT*, p. 345.

16. Arendt, *MT*, p. 305.

17. Arendt, *IT*, p. 163. Cf. Arendt, *NT*, p. 341.

18. See Arendt, *Eichmann in Jerusalem*, pp. 163–219.

19. Arendt, *MT*, p. 302.

20. Arendt, *OT*, pp. 439–41.

21. Arendt, *OT*, p. 471.

22. Arendt, *IT*, p. 159.

23. Arendt, *IT*, p. 162. Needless to say, the very notion of lawfulness is altered when totalitarianism shifts the focus away from positive law (under-

NOTES TO PAGES 184–188

stood as the relatively permanent yet mutable framework which "translates" universal principles for particular men in particular societies) to the "laws of motion" of Nature or History. As Arendt puts it in *NT*, "The very term 'law' has changed its meaning; from denoting the framework of stability within which human actions were supposed to, and were permitted to, take place, it has become the very expression of these motions themselves" (p. 341).

24. Arendt, *NT*, p. 353.

25. Ibid., p. 159.

26. Arendt, *NT*, pp. 341–43. See also Arendt, "Mankind and Terror" (hereafter cited as *MT*) in *EU*, p. 306. I should note that Arendt's emphasis tends to shift depending on context: when assessing totalitarianism's relation to structures of positive law, she stresses its lawlessness (see, for example, Arendt, *MT*, p. 300); when analyzing the source of its restless activism, she emphasizes its adherence to natural or historical "laws of movement" (see, for example, Arendt, *NT*, p. 340).

27. Arendt, *IT*, p. 160.

28. Ibid., p. 163.

29. Margaret Canovan, *Hannah Arendt: A Reinterpretation of her Political Thought* (New York: Cambridge University Press, 1992), p. 13.

30. Arendt, *NT*, p. 357: "If it were true that there are eternal laws ruling supreme over all things human and demanding of each human being only total conformity, then freedom would be only a mockery, some snare luring one away from the right path; then homelessness would be only a fantasy, an imagined thing, which could be cured by the decision to conform to some recognizable universal law."

31. Arendt, *IT*, p. 163. Cf. Arendt, *NT*, pp. 342–44. For terror as the essence of totalitarianism, see also Arendt, *MT*, pp. 302–5.

32. Arendt, *IT*, p. 164.

33. Arendt, *OT*, p. 469.

34. Ibid., p. 438.

35. Ibid.

36. Arendt, *MT*, p. 304.

37. Arendt, *OT*, p. 455.

38. Ibid. pp. 438, 437.

39. Ibid., pp. 447–57. I discuss this process in detail in my chapter "Terror and Radical Evil" in this volume.

40. Arendt, *OT*, p. 457.

41. Arendt, *MT*, pp. 305–6.

42. See, for example, Arendt's essay "What Is Freedom?" in Arendt, *BPF*, p. 168.

43. See Arendt, *HC*, p. 176.

44. Ibid., pp. 38–46.

45. Ibid., p. 322.

46. See Nietzsche, *GM*, essay III, section 9.

47. In "Understanding and Politics" Arendt writes of the totalitarian attempt "to rob man of his nature under the pretext of changing it." (*EU*, p. 316.)

48. See, in this regard, Arendt's invocation of the choral ode from Sophocles's *Oedipus at Colonus* at the end of *On Revolution*. In her translation: "Not to be born prevails over all meaning uttered in words; by far the best in life, once it has appeared, is to go as swiftly as possible whence it came." As George Kateb points out in his *Hannah Arendt: Politics, Conscience, Evil*, the only thing that redeems life from this tragic wisdom is, in her view, the possibility of political action and freedom (p. 1).

49. Arendt, *MT*, pp. 299, 306.

50. Kateb, *Hannah Arendt*, p. 66.

51. Arendt, *IT*, pp. 173–75.

52. Ibid., p. 172.

53. Ibid., p. 173.

54. See especially Hannah Arendt, *HC*, pp. 175–99 and my discussion in *Arendt and Heidegger* (Princeton: Princeton University Press, 1996), pp. 90–99.

55. See Seyla Benhabib, *The Reluctant Modernism of Hannah Arendt* (Thousand Oaks: Sage Publications, Inc., 1996), for a good discussion of what she calls "the narrative structuration of action" in Arendt.

56. See, in this regard, Arendt's contention in the essay "Understanding and Politics" that stupidity (understood as the inability to think and to judge) has, with the death of common sense (the *sensus communis*, our "feeling for the world") become our shared destiny. See Arendt, *EU*, p. 314.

57. Arendt, *OT*, p. ix. Cf. the Preface to Part One, "Antisemitism," p. xv.

58. Arendt, "The Image of Hell" in *EU*, pp. 201–2. As Arendt says in her interview with Gunter Gaus: "No one ever blamed someone if he 'coordinated' [with the regime] because he had to take care of his wife or child. The worst thing was that some people really believed in Nazism! For a short time, many for a very short time. But that means that they made up ideas about Hitler, in part terrifically interesting things! Completely fantastic and interesting and complicated things! Things far above the ordinary level! I found that grotesque. Today I would say that they were trapped by their own ideas. That is what happened" ("What Remains? The Language Remains" in *EU*, p. 11). It seems clear that Heidegger was one of the people Arendt was thinking of when she made this statement.

59. Canovan, *Hannah Arendt: A Reinterpretation*, p. 64.

60. Arendt, draft of "Karl Marx and the Tradition of Western Political Thought," quoted in Canovan, *Hannah Arendt*, p. 64. This was a lecture Arendt delivered at Princeton in 1953.

61. Arendt, "Project: Totalitarian Elements in Marxism" (Guggenheim book proposal), quoted in Canovan, *Hannah Arendt*, p. 64.

62. Arendt, *HC*, pp. 94–101.

63. Arendt, "The Ex-Communists," in *EU*, p. 396.

64. See, for example, Arendt, "What Is Authority?" in *BPF*, p. 111.

65. Arendt, *HC*, pp. 50–53.

66. Canovan, *Hannah Arendt*, p. 73.

67. Arendt, *NT*, p. 355

68. See, for example, the treatments given it by Jurgen Habermas in *Theory and Practice* (Boston: Beacon Press, 1973), and Seyla Benhabib in *Critique, Norm, and Utopia* (New York: Columbia University Press, 1987).

69. Arendt, *HC*, pp. 220–30.

70. As Arendt puts it: "Action, as distinguished from fabrication, is never possible in isolation; to be isolated is to be deprived of the capacity to act. Action and speech need the surrounding presence of others no less than fabrication needs the surrounding presence of nature for material, and of a world in which to place the finished product. Fabrication is surrounded by and in constant contact with the world: action and speech are surrounded by and in contact with the web of the acts and words of other men" (*HC*, p. 188).

71. Arendt, *HC*, p. 190.

72. Arendt, *IT*, p. 163; also *NT*, p. 343.

73. Arendt, *HC*, p. 185. Cf. Arendt's citation of Pascal's famous description of Plato and Aristotle as "amusing themselves" when they turned to consider the "madhouse" of human affairs (in Arendt, *Lectures on Kant's Political Philosophy*, edited by Ronald Beiner [Chicago: The University of Chicago Press, 1982], p. 22).

74. Arendt, *HC*, pp. 185, 195.

75. Ibid., p. 195.

76. Ibid., pp. 225–30. Cf. Arendt, "What Is Authority?" in *BPF*, pp. 104–15. While Aristotle hardly relies on the craftsmanship analogy to anything like the degree that Plato does, and while he emphatically distinguishes between *praxis* and *poiesis*, *phronesis* and *techne* in the *Nicomachean Ethics*, Arendt still regards him as succumbing to desire to interpret action as a kind of making. I have tried to reconstruct Arendt's argument against Aristotle in chapter 2 of *Arendt and Heidegger*.

77. This is made clear by the alternatives posed in the dialogue *Protagoras* between Socrates' "art of measurement" and Protagoras' allegory of democratic education and judgment.

78. See the famous allegory of the Cave in Plato, *Republic*, Book VII.

79. The *leitmotif* of unity is one that runs throughout the *Republic*, and takes a variety of forms, from the communism of the Guardians to what

Eric Voegelin has called "the somatic unity of the polis." See especially Plato, *Republic*, 423–24, 432a.

80. See Plato, *Republic*, 472c; 484d; and (especially) 500d.

81. Arendt, "What Is Authority?," p. 110. Cf. Arendt, *HC*, pp. 225–26.

82. Arendt, "What Is Authority?" in *BPF*, p. 97.

83. Arendt, *HC*, p. 229.

84. Ibid. p. 143.

85. See Martin Heidegger, "Letter on Humanism," in Heidegger, *Basic Writings*, edited by David Farrell Krell (New York: Harper and Row, 1977), pp. 193–94 for a discussion of the "technical relation" set up between thinking and acting in Plato and Aristotle. See also my discussion, *Arendt and Heidegger*, pp. 227–28.

86. Arendt, *HC*, p. 229.

87. See vol. 1 of Popper's *The Open Society and Its Enemies* (Princeton: Princeton University Press, 1960) and Andre Glucksmann, *The Master Thinkers* (New York: Harper and Row, 1980).

88. Arendt, "What Is Authority?" in *BPF*, pp. 95–100.

89. This reading of the tradition—and Plato's role in it—obviously has the closest affinities with Heidegger's metahistory of philosophy. It is interesting to note, in this regard, that Arendt specifically cites Heidegger's great essay *Platon's Lehre von der Wahrheit*, with its contrast between correctness (*orthotes*) and discovery or unconcealedness (*Unverborgenheit*). See Arendt, "What Is Authority?," note 16 (p. 291).

90. See Arendt's comments on the supposedly "scientific" character of totalitarian ideology in *IT*, pp. 166–72. For similar conclusions reached from a perspective not very friendly to Arendt, see Isaiah Berlin, "The Pursuit of an Ideal," in Berlin, *The Crooked Timber of Humanity* (New York: Vintage Books, 1992).

91. One of the primary differences between the totalitarian project of fabricating mankind and more traditional teleologies is precisely the ongoing, literally end-less quality of the former. So long as it exists, totalitarianism must manifest the law of motion of Nature or History, i.e., it must keep itself in motion and find ever new groups to eliminate. Otherwise, the motion of Nature or History (the locus of the totalitarian sense of reality as the hidden movement behind appearances) comes to an end, which would be an insupportable contradiction for the totalitarian mind. See Arendt, *IT*, p. 162, and *NT*, p. 341.

92. Arendt, *NT*, p. 354.

93. See Leo Strauss, *The City and Man* (Chicago: The University of Chicago Press, 1963), p. 127.

94. See Philippe Lacoue-Labarthe, *Heidegger, Art, and Politics*, translated by Chris Turner (New York: Blackwell, 1990), p. 77.

95. Arendt, *MT*, p. 306.

96. Ibid., p. 298.

97. Arendt, *IT*, p. 163. Cf Arendt, *HC*, p. 58.

98. Arendt, *IT*, p. 158.

99. See Arendt's discussion of the meaning creative capacity of political action in *HC*, pp. 175–88. It is precisely this capacity that separates action, in Arendt's mind, from both work and labor.

100. See Arendt, *OR*.

101. See Judith Shklar, "The Liberalism of Fear" in Nancy Rosenblum, editor, *Liberalism and the Moral Life* (Cambridge, MA: Harvard University Press, 1989.

102. Arendt, *OT*, p. vii.

103. Arendt, *NT*, p. 344.

104. Judith Shklar, *Ordinary Vices* (Cambridge, MA: Harvard University Press, 1984), pp. 5–9.

105. Arendt, *MT*, p. 302.

106. Of course, Arendt discusses both constitutionalism and civil rights at some length in *On Revolution*, but she is remarkably dismissive of both. It is interesting to note Arendt's own shift in her discussion of the nature of totalitarian evil, namely, from the Kantian idea of radical evil to her celebrated (and widely misunderstood) notion of the "banality of evil" (in *Eichmann in Jerusalem*). For a good analysis of the issues involved in this shift, see Richard Bernstein's essay "Did Hannah Arendt Change Her Mind?" in *Hannah Arendt—Twenty Years Later*, edited by Jerome Kohn and Larry May (Cambridge, MA: MIT Press, 1996). See also my discussion in chaps. 1 and 2 of this book.

107. This is clear from her analysis of the "right to have rights," to membership in a political community, as more fundamental than the "rights of man" and as the precondition for their effectivity. See Arendt, *OT*, pp. 290–302.

CHAPTER NINE
ARENDT AND SOCRATES

1. Arendt, *HC*, p. 21.

2. See Arendt's essay, "Tradition and the Modern Age," in Arendt, *BPF*.

3. Arendt's discussion of the three similes is found in Arendt, *LM*, vol. 1, pp. 172–73, and in Arendt, *TMC*, 7–37 (originally published in *Social Research* [autumn 1971]).

4. Hannah Arendt, *PP*, p. 81.

5. Ibid., pp. 84–85. Arendt argues this point by drawing out the implications of Socrates' interpretation of the Delphic oracle's pronouncement,

as found in the *Apology*. To know that one does not know, that one is not truly wise, is to accept "the limitations of truth for mortals," to recognize that *human* truth is never absolute, but limited by its mode of appearance, *doxa*.

6. Ibid., p. 80.

7. Ibid., p. 81.

8. Ibid.

9. Ibid. (my emphasis).

10. Ibid., p. 82.

11. Ibid., pp. 82, 83.

12. Hannah Arendt, "Civil Disobedience" in Arendt, *Crises of the Republic* (New York: Harcourt Brace Jovanovich, 1972), p. 64.

13. Arendt, *TMC*, p. 8.

14. See Hannah Arendt, "Organized Guilt and Universal Responsibility" in Arendt, *EU*, p. 130, where she stresses how the privatized mass man, "the exact opposite of the *citoyen*," was ready to perform any function in order to avoid the personal and familial disaster brought on by unemployment. (The "great criminal of the twentieth century" statement also derives from this essay.)

15. Arendt, *TMC*, pp. 17–18.

16. Ibid., p. 23.

17. Ibid.

18. Ibid., p. 25.

19. Ibid., p. 24.

20. Ibid., p. 26.

21. In a radio address from 1964, titled "Personal Responsibility Under Dictatorship," Arendt says strikingly similar things, and gives a surprisingly positive account of how conscience as the demand for self-agreement or self-harmony works: "The total moral collapse of respectable society during the Hitler regime may teach us that those who are reliable in such circumstances are not those who cherish values and hold fast to moral norms and standards. . . . Much more reliable will be the doubters and sceptics, *not because scepticism is good or doubting wholesome*, but because [such people] are used to [examining things and making up their own minds]. Best of all will be those who know that, whatever else happens, as long as we live we are condemned to live together with ourselves."

22. Arendt, "The Crisis in Culture" in *BPF*, p. 214. As Philippe Lacoue-Labarthe points out, with this rendition of Thucydides' Greek, Arendt takes a "very great risk." See Philippe Lacoue-Labarthe, *Heidegger, Art, and Politics* (Oxford: Basil Blackwell, 1990), p. 97. Lacoue-Labarthe proposes "We love the beautiful with frugality and knowledge without softness." Rex Warner's English translation runs "Our love of what is

beautiful does not lead to extravagance; our love of the things of the mind does not make us soft." (Thucydides, *The Peloponnesian War*, trans. Warner [New York: Penguin Books, 1979] p. 147.)

23. Arendt, *BPF*, p. 214.
24. Thucydides, *The Peloponnesian War*, p. 147.
25. Ibid., p. 149.
26. Ibid., p. 148.
27. See George Kateb's essay, "Arendt and Individualism," *Social Research* 61, no. 4 (winter 1994): 765–94.
28. Arendt, *PP*, p. 78.
29. Nietzsche, *GM*, III, 7 (p. 107).

Index

Printed in the United States
18203LVS00001B/1-52